THE POLITICAL
ECONOMY
OF IVORY COAST

THE POLITICAL ECONOMY OF IVORY COAST

Edited by
I. William Zartman
and Christopher Delgado

A SAIS Study on Africa

PRAEGER SPECIAL STUDIES • PRAEGER SCIENTIFIC

New York • Philadelphia • Eastbourne, UK
Toronto • Hong Kong • Tokyo • Sydney

Library of Congress Cataloging in Publication Data

Main entry under title:

The political economy of Ivory Coast.

(A SAIS study on Africa)
Bibliography: p.
Includes index.
1. Ivory Coast—Economic conditions—1960s—   —Addresses, essays, lectures. 2. Ivory Coast—economic policy—Addresses, essays, lectures. I. Zartman, I. William. II. Delgado, Christopher L. III. Series.
HC1025. P64 1984   330.9666'805   84-1998
ISBN 0-03-064097-0

Published in 1984 by Praeger Publishers
CBS Educational and Professional Publishing
A Division of CBS, Inc.
521 Fifth Avenue, New York, New York 10175 U.S.A.

© 1984 by Praeger Publishers

56789 052 98765432
Printed in the United States of America

to
Robert Lystad and Charles Steedman,
for their long commitment to Africa

Contents

THE POLITICAL
ECONOMY
OF IVORY COAST

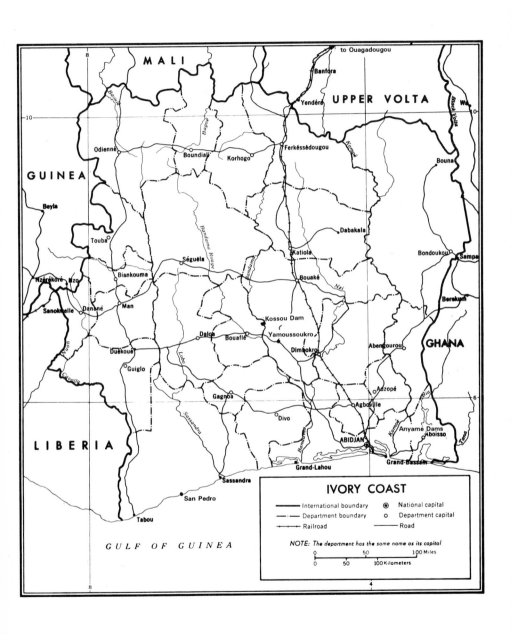

IVORY COAST

International boundary — National capital ⊛
Department boundary —·—·— Department capital ○
Railroad ┼┼┼┼ Road ——

NOTE: The department has the same name as its capital

0   50   100 Miles
0   50   100 Kilometers

1

INTRODUCTION
Stability, Growth, and Challenge
I. William Zartman and Christopher L. Delgado

A quarter of a century ago, in the midst of the mounting euphoria of impending independence, West Africa was startled by a serious wager between two of the most important African leaders. The subject concerned one of the broad dichotomies of human relations, the contrasting values of gradual versus sudden change. Felix Houphouet-Boigny of Ivory Coast bet Kwame Nkrumah of Ghana that an evolutionary and cooperative future in collaboration with the French colonial ruler would in ten years yield a better life for the Ivorians than the total rupture and independent option of Nkrumah would provide for the Ghanaians.[1] It was a subject which had captivated theorists from Aristotle to Lenin to Margaret Mead, but had never been the topic of a direct competition between two neighboring states. It was the closest thing to an experiment that practical politics and real-life economics could provide.

In the short run, Houphouet-Boigny soon lost. The pressures for independence that Nkrumah and Ghanaian decolonization spearheaded swept across the region, compelling even opposing leaders to adopt its forms. On August 7, 1960, Ivory Coast became an independent state, compelled by competition with other territories of former French West Africa (AOF) to reject even the French offer of cooperation agreements prior to independence (Foltz 1965; Zartman 1966; Zolberg 1969). By the end of the decade covered by the wager, the tables had turned. Nkrumah was removed by a coup of his own officers, and the Ghanaian economy was beginning a long slide downhill. In neighboring Ivory Coast, on the contrary, politics were held tightly within the benign but firm grasp of the chieftan–president; and the economic fortunes of the country were on the rise, absorbing the productive energies of Ivorians and immigrant neighbors alike.

The 1957 wager was about the most beneficial path toward independence. Twenty-five years later, it has conferred an important heritage on Ivory Coast and confronted the country with a new challenge. The heritage is one of stability, a rare condition shared by less than a dozen African countries and not all with (or because of) the same conditions of growth that underlay stability in Ivory Coast. Stability—the absence of sudden or extra-institutional shifts in leadership and policy directions, and the presence of established institutionalized processes—is important because it contributes to basic patterns of responsive government at a formative period in a new nation. There is, of course, no guarantee that initial stability will be perpetuated, for guarantees and perpetuation are not standard political phenomena. An initial period of stability does appear to increase chances for continued stability, as the political body learns to seek and find responses to problems *within* the framework of established political processes, rather than outside. If a polity learns that it must create processes for problem solving each time it has a problem to solve, it wastes its energies in reinventing political wheels rather than being able to expend those energies on more productive movement. To be sure, it is not just reinforcement of institutions per se that has value, but the public knowledge that those institutions are the repository of expectations, providing the public with confirmable standards for handling change, and then performing in such a way as to reinforce (or reduce) citizens' confidence in both institutions and incumbents' abilities.

The key to stability is its handling of change. In a world of change stability must be flexible and dynamic. The longer basic components of stability in a given country resist change, the more destabilizing the change becomes when or if it finally occurs. The heritage of stability of nearly a quarter century under a single leader leaves Ivory Coast confronted with a new challenge of maintaining the same degree of stability as it changes leadership, a challenge compounded by a simultaneous need for new policy directions in a number of important areas. Maintaining reliable performance by the established institutions under new management is the new Ivorian wager. Unless the hand of God moves earlier, that wager begins to come due in 1985, when the current presidential term runs out, although the regime may be called to accountability even before then, by rising and restive generations or falling economic fortunes or contagious coups next door.

THEORIES OF STABILITY

To understand the dimensions of the new challenge, it is important first to comprehend the components of the past quarter century of stability. Ivorian stability can be related to a number of concepts, some prominent in the early days of African independence, some seemingly outmoded. The value of the Ivorian experience in social science terms, however, lies not in its belated support for past explanations but in the way the terms of these explanations can be used in new situations that they had not foreseen. These five explanations focus on legitimacy, mobilization, institutionalization, resources, and dependency. Elements of stability in Ivory Coast include a transitional charismatic leader, a single party that absorbs rather than mobilizes politics, an institutionalized state structure, and a growing political, economic and social elite in the political realm; an economy of both growth and distribution that provides the payoffs for participants in the political system; and a combination of regional economic organizations which support the national system and reduce the possibility of opposition from some of the surrounding states.

Weberian theory holds that the shift from religious and customary sources of legitimacy to sources of routinized performance within task–appropriate organizations is accomplished by a powerful individual whose personal magnetism and leadership provides the vehicle for change from one mode of legitimacy to the other (LeVine 1980). As the agent of transition, the charismatic leader must not only be legitimized by his own charisma but must also draw on rather than break with traditional sources in order to create the new, modern sources. Charismatic legitimacy is a passing moment, and unlike the other two modes it is judged on its ability to provide for the sources of its replacement as well as its ability to perform on its own terms. Traditional leaders succeed each other, as does rational-bureaucratic leadership, but charismatic leaders do not. The effective charisma of one leader is an obstacle to his successor's amassing impressive charisma of his own.

No leader better embodies the qualities of charismatic legitimacy than Houphouet-Boigny (Asso 1976). Baoule chief and son of a chief, coffee planter and son of a coffee planter, probably born about 1900 rather than the 1905 officially claimed, he was also a public health official (or African doctor in the colonial system), minister delegate, minister counselor, minister of state, and a minister of public health and population in various French governments. He founded and was president of both the African Democratic Rally (RDA) and its territorial section, the Democratic Party of Ivory Coast (PDCI), before becoming president of the Republic of Ivory Coast. At various times he held twelve different ministerial portfolios in his own governments. Thus, from chief of the Baoule nation Houphouet worked his way into the position of paramount chief of the Ivorian nation, using both the modern mobilizing nationalist party and the colonial and state institutions of government as a vehicle. Rather than abolishing or combatting the tribal chiefship, Houphouet has eliminated it by coopting and transforming it, leaving it in the space of a short generation only as ceremonial as an English lordship without a House of Lords. By stepping into the newly created presidency upon independence he made it the active center of government, a politician acting above politics, creating the central institution of government around which other new institutions gravitate.

Houphouet has a particularly identifiable style in his operations as the modern chief and the founding president. Known with respectful familiarity as "le Vieux" ("the Old Man"), he is the Great Patron, the Great Manipulator. Houphouet's national speeches are paternal admonitions to his people on subjects of state policy and public morality. At times of crisis he gathers his flock around the radio and explains causes and remedies, just as he gathers his cadres around him in his home-village-turned-Versailles at Yamoussoukro. Houphouet-Boigny's approach to politics is dialogue, a combination of palaver and chiefly audiences under a tree, to the point where dialogue has been institutionalized at home and proposed as a policy abroad. The dialogue was instituted in 1969 and has been used regularly since then, gathering together some thousands of people from different professional categories in a national retreat (Cohen 1974, pp. 115–144). Dialogue can also be personal as well as collective: Whenever political disaffection is suspected, Houphouet keeps the individual under scrutiny, gives him enough leeway to prove or hang himself, and then calls him to Yamoussoukro for a long and intimate father-and-son session. Few political leaders have resisted this treatment and few have not returned to the family fold after having repented their exposed prodigality.

Houphouet's charisma has never flagged. Unlike Tunisia's Bourguiba, who has outlived his charisma, but more like the other "historic chiefs" of French Africa such as Cameroun's Ahidjo and Senegal's Senghor (both retired after some twenty years in power), Houphouet's right to continued authority has not been seriously questioned nor his leadership and decisions seriously challenged. There have, of course, been ups and downs of various kinds, the downs almost running in regular decennial cycles. In 1963–65, both the discovery and the questionable nature of the plots against the regime cast a malaise over the political system; it is still not clear whether the plot was real or a fabrication of Ivorian politics. A decade later, a military coup attempt in June 1973 was followed in January 1974 by the first in a series of leadership conferences (*conférences de cadres*) on administrative mis-management. In 1981 and thereafter the sources of uneasiness were again several: the prolonged absence of a vice-president as the Old Man became older; the succession of bad decisions on the northern sugar refineries and on the withholding of Ivorian cocoa from the world market (two decisions which cost the country several hundred thousand dollars); an assassination arrest in April 1980 and an attempt in October; growing economic indebtedness and successive years of austerity budgets as the supposed oil boom only trickled in. Spiralling stories of corruption culminating in the May 1983 speech of the President portraying his foreign bank accounts as frugality. Yet, through all of these problems, the authority of the president has remained strong.

It is harder to cite the ups, which stand as plateaux of continuing leadership and respect rather than peaks of specific triumph and victory. Through renewed dialogue, revised decisions, continuing activity and prosperity, and repeated lectures and critiques of his own followers' performance, Houphouet remains the focus of stable leadership and direction.

Father of the Country is a tough act to follow. Its very success makes succession all the more difficult. Charismatic leaders overshadow their successors, as Anthony Eden, Harry Truman, and Daniel arap Moi well knew. The tendency is frequently to rely on a heavy—sometimes even repressive—state machinery to retain control in the absence of the predecessor's legitimacy, as Anwar Sadat, Georges Pompidou, P.K. Botha, and Josef Stalin knew, although sometimes such control is also paralleled by an apparent liberalization to let many competing oppositions fight it out among themselves. The patterns are several but not infinite, and it is certain that the test of legitimization is never really made until the charismatic leader has passed and left his successor to his own devices (which almost never include the same charisma). Yet, charisma makes devices palatable, so that the more successful the charismatic leader the more difficult the task of his successor.

One of the misleading fixations of African studies in the early years of America's African discovery was a belief in the nationalist single party as an effective agent of mobilization that would turn protest into institutionalized participation. In fact, instead of creating a political takeoff into sustained participatory development, African single parties in general have acted only as the first stage rocket that lifts new elites into the orbits of powers but then drops away, spent and burnt out by the effort of the nationalist struggle. Furthermore, a closer look has shown that even that struggle did not involve majority mobilization (Zolberg 1966; Collier 1982). In its formative years, the PDCI—a better performer than most in West Africa—received only about an eighth of the adult male population's votes in 1946, a tenth in 1952, and even less than half of the adult registration in 1957. Yet, those performances turned the state into a single party system and placed all politics within the one party, where it was soon to be reduced to a bare minimum under the skillful control of the Great Patron and Manipulator. Furthermore, just to make sure that it remained controlled, the electoral system was reduced from 19 constituencies in 1957 to four in 1959 and then to a single nationwide consistency in the year of independence, with all national assembly candidates running at large, without opposition, after personal selection by the President and party secretary general.

Despite these characteristics, the PDCI did not wither away like many other nationalist movements turned single party (Faure and Medard 1982a; Semi Bi 1973). It has remained very much alive as a channel of recruitment and control, a two-way pipeline that pumps up grievances and people and carries down information and rewards. The PDCI has been a club of the people in power and a civic congregational meeting and intercessor for local constituencies. It works as a troubleshooter in relations between people and administrators, sending delegations to towns and villages where some problem has arisen, to carry the authority of the national organization to operate as delegated ombudsmen. There is an active rivalry and competition between prefects native to their districts and younger active party secretaries from outside, and also between more conservative national party leaders and local party secretaries eager for development, improvement, and activity.[2]

Yet underneath an appearance of continuity and even static stability has been a more dynamic role for the party. The chronology can be marked by PDCI congresses, which have been regularly held at about five year intervals. The party approached independence by expanding into a Grand Coalition of all major social groups. At the III Party Congress in 1959, an increase in the size of party organs opened the scramble for positions among the various groups. New members of the party leadership were elected, adding youth, party auxiliary and local committee members who were more militantly anticolonial than the original party leaders from the planters' reform group. The new secretary–general, Jean-Baptiste Mockey, supported by the new members, was eased out within the year. Soon afterward the regime reversed its policies on the same issue by demanding independence, while maintaining its position in favor of private enterprise and integration within the French economic zone. However, rivalry among the factions continued within the enlarged party leadership. A widespread plot involving younger, distributive–oriented, more anticolonial and antiBaoule leaders coopted into the party was discovered in mid–1962 and it members tried the next year; a second round of allegations and trials continued through 1964 as the preindependence rivalries were worked out of the political system.

A new dual thrust of government policy aimed at increasing popular benefits of independence (salaries, educational opportunities, production, freedom of expression) and tightening political control (military reform, party renovation, control over auxiliaries). There was particular difficulty in reorganizing and controlling the student auxiliaries. When all this was accomplished in 1965, the IV Party Congress met and ratified the coopted elite, after which a governmental change provided the new ministers with authority formerly concentrated in the President's hands.

The rest of the decade was spent in working out the two consequences of the previous period—the reintegration of the authoritative elite and the integration of the younger generation of educated manpower—as other (particularly economic) policies remained relatively unchanged. The alleged plotters of 1962–63 were released in 1967 and amnestied, and many were put into economic directorships or coopted back into the authoritative elite by the time of the V Party Congress of 1970. The "student problem" has been harder to handle. The government in 1967 expanded secondary and higher education, and in 1969, 1971 and 1978, reorganized the student auxillary. But student unrest intensified, putting pressure on the government for Africanization of management positions. The revival of a thriving export trade in the early 1970s (after poorer years in 1964–67), the formation of a new generation of technically better trained aspirants for government jobs, and the growth of a new commercial bourgeoisie began to put pressure on official policies and elites for the first time since the plantation economy created new elites in the colonial period. On a record of economic growth and political stability, the VI Party Congress of 1975 was a congress of satisfaction, marking the beginning of a new expansive five year plan (1976– 80) and featuring industrial development and economic diversification.[3]

By the end of the decade, the focus of politics had turned squarely to the succession issue and at the same time to economic austerity (Plan 1981– 83). A number of "barons" were apparently eliminated from the contest: Mohammed Diawara, Konan Bedie and Usher Assouan were dropped from their leading ministries in wake of presidential castigation of economic mismanagement of the country in a speech before the party National Council in 1977. Philippe Yacé, who had so maladroitly administered the local elections of 1978 in an attempt to place his own supporters that the elections were cancelled by the President, had his position as party secretary general abolished and lost his Assembly presidency in 1980. Mockey was removed by accidental death in 1981. Then, in the VII party congress of 1980, Houphouet announced an opening up of the political system to competition for the first time in Ivorian history, and pointing at corruption as a major cause of mismanagement, he invited the voters to use the opportunity for housecleaning. The lame duck Assembly passed a constitutional amendment conferring the succession on the newly created post of vice-president, which had no occupant. The national elections of 1980 and the municipal elections of 1981 (the first in 25 years) shuffled the order of precedence among lieutenants in the party; retired some to positions in the appointive or the private economic sector; and restored others, notably the new Assembly President, Konan Bedie.

Throughout all of these phases of change, the party has remained the constant framework for politics. During the 15 years from the mid-1960s to the late 1970s, it was the arena for restrained maneuvering to stay within the good graces of the president. During the subsequent years, to that constant goal has been added the need to appear as an effective politician with constituency creditials. The nature of party activity has obviously changed some as this focus has changed, but the party has remained alive and flexible enough to meet the needs of the time. As the country moved from the VII to the VIII Party Congress and the presidential and vice-presidential elections scheduled for 1985, the overriding concern became the selection of a new leadership out of the old elite, for which the party provides the institutional framework. Bakary investigates this process in the following chapter, examining both the pool of party leadership and the potential emerging candidates and sowing the characteristic stability within the political elite.

Another theory of stability in developing countries points to the need for institutionalization, usually as a standard against which Third World polities are judged wanting (Huntington 1969). Indeed, institutionalization is often seen as synonomous with stability, since it refers to recognized and reliable organizations and routines for handling government's business. There are at least three aspects of this task, although other conceptualizers of the state–building process have seen more facets or rearranged the material into different categories. First, there is the need to invent, establish, maintain and defend the proper state structures that combine to make the whole—the state itself—a legitimate, functioning entity, larger than the sum of its parts. Second, these component bodies need to establish relations among themselves, leaving each an appropriate area of operations but making each partially dependent on others for its place and performance in the system. Third, each unit needs to review and reform its operations periodically to ensure that it is performing its functions effectively, and not just defending its corporate interests. Obviously, these are asymtotes, counsels of perfection that are never attained in the real world but which social creations are obliged to seek if they are to do their job and, ultimately, to stay alive.

The tragedy of African states is that the primary, pressing need is to build the base essentials of the state and then to defend its corporate existence against all demands, attacks and criticisms. For it is so new, fragile, weak, and poor that any attempt to reform, improve or, even simply, impose demands on its operations is seen as more of a burden than the new system can handle. The implications are many: Politics is wrung out of the system and reduced to bureaucratic and autocratic maneuvering. Accountability is eliminated along with constituency politics, until the only control of the governors by the consumers of government is revolt. Institutions cannot be reformed, only maintained or abrogated.

Some of these signs of fragility are visible in the Ivorian experience, as elsewhere in Africa. Critics of the regime become famous in Ivory Coast, and although they are never very radical, they soon find it more prudent to live in Paris than in Abidjan. In 1979, it was Noel Ebony writing in *Demain l'Afrique* who opened a debate on the manifestations of social tensions in housing, speculation, prices, unemployment, decline of services, and inefficiencies, which was answered in turn by the Foreign Minister in the same magazine and then by the President in his annual National Day address. In 1982, it was Laurent Gbagbo, a university lecturer, who circulated a speech he was prevented from delivering on democracy and the values of multiparty competition. Some accountability has been restored within the single party system in the 1980 elections, but mostly the voiced criticism comes only from the top, in the regular castigations and analyses which the President makes of his lieutenants and their performance.

But other aspects of institutionalization in Ivory Coast are quite different from the African norm. Stability and reform have characterized state building. From the beginning, the country adopted the colonial institutions and converted them to its own use. A purely presidential regime was installed, more American than Gaullist, for there was no prime minister to stand in the way between the president and his technical lieutenants. The National Assembly, a "branch" of the party, has served as a useful sounding box for government policy, but essentially government is an executive exercise, a hierarchial organization reaching down into the country through the regional administration.

As the occasion demands, this line organization is supplemented by various specialized staff bodies to handle specific problems or sectors. Although other bodies are involved, the largest number of these organizations are parastatal companies, which grew from five in 1960 to 31 at the beginning of the next decade to 84 at the end of the 1970s (Johns 1982). At the beginning of the 1970s, first the World Bank and then the President criticized the parastatals for empire building, proliferation, lack of coordination, and poor financial management; new executive regulations in 1972 imposed stricter controls on operations and administrative practices. The parastatals fought back within the bureaucratic arena to defend their corporate interests, and the decrees were never applied. The following year, a French expert called in to study management practices wrote a critical report calling for greater performance incentives, which was then the subject of a conference of officials in Yamoussoukro, but without effect. The parastatals were also impervious to new attempts at state control and standardization in a series of decrees in 1975. However, when the World Bank report the following year continued to criticize the administrative and fiscal impunity of the bodies (den Tuinder 1978), the president decided on direct action against the parastatals, bypassing the previously ineffective attempt at controls. Mathieu Ekra, one of the President's closest lieutenants, was charged with the reform of the state sector in mid-1977, at the same time as the government underwent its most serious reshuffle since independence, with 9 ministers removed, including the four major architects of the economic system. Three years later, the reforms were announced. Of the 36 financially autonomous state corporations, only nine were retained, but the total number of parastatals only dropped from 84 to 72 because some state corporations as well as other bodies were constituted or maintained as public agencies (*établissements publics*), with administrative autonomy but financial dependence on the state budget.

The methods and results of parastatal reform are illustrative of the patterns of Ivorian institutionalization. Initiative for reform came from within the top executive, under pressure from abroad, but neither party nor parliament nor any other agent of accountability was involved in any aspect of the reform except in limiting its ultimate impact on urban employment. A series of attempts at control was resisted by the bodies defending their corporate interests even at the cost of their effective performance; as a result a frontal attack on the agencies themselves was required. In the reorganization, functions were redistributed and individuals were reassigned, many to the competition provided by the newly enlarged political process in the 1980 elections or by the private economic sector. There was no public or personal retribution. While an attempt to reduce personnel in inefficient sectors was abandoned in 1981 because of labor and management pressure, the reform measures did bring the agencies under central administrative control and standardization. The reform was consistent with the state ideology of cooperation between public and private enterprise. In sum, the course of the parastatals was corrected in such a way as to preserve the institutional values of corporateness, interrelatedness, and effectiveness, although it is normal to the process of institutionalization that later review and reform will also be necessary.

Theories relating stability to resources tend to be less direct than those involving legitimacy, mobilization, and institutionalization. Furthermore, it is often assumed that the direction of the causal relation runs from stability to economic growth, with little investigation of the reverse. To be sure, the first wager was between two relatively well endowed territories, and one of them—probably the better endowed—has shown no stability and has lost the wager. In addition, much writing has underlined the correlation between domestic unrest and development, showing that poor societies tend to be unmobilized and low enough in their horizons of expectation to be unable to sustain rebellion, whereas, disorder comes with a rise in expectations, an uprooting from an established social system, and the appearance of ideological differences over the resources.

Paradoxically, none of these notions is necessarily in conflict with a reverse interpretation that growing resources allow for successful cooptation of aspirant elites, for satisfaction of otherwise disruptive demands, for cushioning the transitions from tradition to modern systems and values, and for softening the competition among social groups for not-so-scarce resources. By the same token, nothing in these latter relations is inevitable; expending resources can be used to "purchase" stability, but only when skillfully wielded and only when those at the other end of the process accept cooptation. Cooptation and purchase are habit-forming and must be sustained, since they may indeed be training grounds for accentuated instability if expectations do not continue to be met. But as long as expectations can be kept in line with rewards, and rewards with expectations, expanding resources can turn zero-sum political conflict into positive-sum competition and cooptation.

While the Ivorian experience does not permit disproof of some of these notions over others, it does illustrate the stabilizing effects of economic growth under proper conditions for a given period of time. Subsequent chapters investigate aspects of economic policy and income distribution, and raise some questions with respect to the sustainability of earlier growth strategies. For the time being, it is helpful to recall the political uses of economic growth in contributing to stability. There is no doubt that Ivorian economic growth was fostered and used to coopt and absorb sources of dissatisfaction in the country, and to focus energies on economic and material goals instead of on political competition for power. More interesting, conceptually, is the fact that this strategy operates at four levels: individual, ethnic–regional, class, and international regional (the latter to be explained in the next section). In the often-dichotomous context of class and ethnie, Ivory Coast uses its economic growth to pursue integration and stability on both levels, using one to combat the other but not one at the expense of the other. As a paradoxical result and contrary to all theoretical predictions about the way these perceptions operate on each other during development, the sense of nation, ethnie, class, and materialism have *all* been heightened in Ivory Coast.

Economic incentives are used first to coopt individuals, either to curb potential sources of instability or to reintegrate them when they consider challenging the system. All former opposition leaders have found a place in the Ivorian polity or economy, and there are no opposition leaders either in jail or in exile (an unusual situation for an African country). Second, economic benefits are subjects of competition among regional political and administrative leaders, and are distributed with an eye toward regional and ethnic balance as well as reward. Ministers, National Assemblymen, and regional and departmental administrators are encouraged to bring home the bacon to their local constituencies. Assemblymen who did so won in the 1980 elections; administrators who did so were promoted in the party. In the process, pork barrel politics has stimulated regional and ethnic awareness on the squeaky wheel principle but it has also meant that better regional distribution of economic benefits comes not from simply moral notions of equality but as a result of pressure and competition within state bureaucratic channels.

At the same time, economic benefits have been used to create or at least expand a middle class or bourgeoisie, long touted as the condition and motor of development (Faure and Medard 1982). By all appearances, this middle-class—which combines education, money, and urban dwelling—bridges ethnic divisions and reinforces national identification. Brokers for ethnic and regional distribution are usually beneficiaries of class distribution (and of individual benefits) tying the whole system together. Not only is the class dimension growing in wealth, but it is also growing in size, continually drawing in more people; part of this growth includes its own offspring but part includes new members and families coopted in from outside the bourgeoisie. No more eloquent testimony to the effectiveness of growth in producing stability can be found than the words of Samir Amin (in 1967, p 280): "The political stability, the popularity of the regime, . . . stems without doubt from the great prosperity which accompanies the remarkable development of foreign capitalism in Ivory Coast. For up to now, everyone has something to gain from this development." While Amin goes on to enumerate potential tensions and antagonisms, they remain accurate but not noticeably stronger in the period since he wrote, twenty years ago.

Economic growth has not only produced stability but also an unusual reorientation of values not found elsewhere in most of Africa (Toure 1982; Clignet and Foster 1966). In few other countries is materialism as open and avowed an ideology to the exclusion of other contemporary value attractions. Not only are opponents bought off, but their value structures are revised. Political radicalism has little attraction, even among students, and material motivations dominate. Such orientations underlie stability as long as material benefits are available, but they also leave society ill-prepared to vent its frustrations in times of belt-tightening. At worse, that leaves society with another characteristic Ivorian feeling as its only safety value: xenophobia. Ivory Coast has lashed out at the African foreigners in its midst at earlier times, notably 1959 but also less violently at other later times, and it could also strike out at the French and Levantines. But in a backhanded way, these feelings of both materialism and a search for national scapegoats in times of trouble are related to the longlasting stability as well.

A final explanation of stability combines many of the previous elements but comes from a very different direction than the developmentalist theories used to this point. The dependency explanation of stability, already alluded to in Amin's quotation, assigns the cause to Ivory Coast's well integrated position in the Northern or world capitalist economy, operating through both the cooptation of Ivorian elites into Western economic values and circuits, and through the actual stationing of Western capital expatriates and soldiers in Ivory Coast itself (Zartman 1983). The structural analysis can be extended by recognition of Ivory Coast as a subcenter in the periphery, serving as a source of capital and trade for the French-speaking West African region through its port, roads and railroad, and through the various regional organizations of which it is a key member—the Council of the Entente, the

West African Economic Community (CEAO), the West African Monetary Union (UMOA), and the Economic Community of West African States (ECOWAS), as explored by Atsain below.

The predominance of Frenchmen, in numbers more than four times as large as the French population in colonial times, of French products and tastes, and of French capital in all the leading sectors of the Ivorian economy except the plantations is an important element in the original wager and in the ongoing economic stability of the country. Ivorians in the public and private sector are trained, employed, and advised by Frenchmen. If an alternative is sought, it is found in Americans' and other Westerners' will to fill in the gaps.

Ivory Coast's favored position in the active African zone of French interests—the arc of countries from Mauritania to Zaire—is expressed in an impressive number of firsts that contribute to stability in various ways (Traxler 1982; *Jeune Afrique* 1082: 16–20; Zartman 1983). Its 50,000 Frenchmen comprise the largest French population in any country outside of the metropole, on the same level as Morocco and Algeria, and nearly four of every five have lived in Ivory Coast more than five years. Although its per capita ratio of one Frenchman to every 160 Ivorians is high, it is not the highest in Africa. Ivory Coast also has the highest number of teaching and nonteaching French technical assistants (*cooperants*) in Africa, the highest number of students in French universities, and the highest number of large French firms in any African country (examined in Mytelka's chapter below). It has the largest percentage of French imports and exports of any African state (still only about 1 percent in either direction) and has been paired with Senegal for the highest bilateral aid from France since independence (although not the highest per capita aid). Politically, Ivory Coast has had the highest average number of heads of state visit per year since independence and the highest number of nonroutine diplomatic visits between any African country and France. All of these indicators show the importance of Ivory Coast's close relation with its former metropole, contributing both to its penetration and its stability.

Not only is Ivory Coast highly penetrated by and oriented toward the former metropole, but it also serves an intermediate position as a subcontractor of dependency with its intermediation serving to lock it even more firmly and stably into its current relationship. Thus, the 400 French troops in Port Bouet have had no role to play directly in Ivorian politics or security. Their presence and, above all, the demonstration effect of French interventions in the periphery of the Ivory Coast—in Chad, Zaire, Mauritania, and the CAR in the 1970s—protected the Ivorian core area and assured its stability. Similarly, economic growth was used as the basis for the Entente, by which some of Ivory Coast's wealth was shared with its least developed neighbors to keep their own penury-fueled dissatisfaction within manageable limits and to prevent it from contaminating Ivorian domestic tranquility and civic order; acceptance of a million African foreigners from many of the same countries to find employment in the Ivorian economy also served the same purpose. The other West African economic communities also allowed French capital and goods to seek a wider market in the region, providing capital returns for the investors and growth and employment for Ivory Coast. Thus both the center–periphery relations between France and Ivory Coast, and the mediatory (relay) relation of Ivory Coast between the metropole and the further periphery contribute to the maintenance of stability (Vellas 1981; Ikonicoff and Sigal 1978; Gabriel 1974).

Dimensions of Challenge

These five theories of stability are alternative but not necessarily competing explanations. They all point to important aspects of the Ivorian situation, setting off the country from its neighbors and competitors and contributing to its stability (and also to our understanding of the mechanisms of stability). Furthermore, they all either assume or are facilitated by a high rate of economic growth, a constantly expanding pie. As Ivory Coast approaches a new turning point, each element of stability faces a new challenge in this respect. The post-oil–shock world is a considerably more difficult place to expand into for small, energy-importing, nations. The future of the Ivorian experiment will depend largely upon creative responses to a number of policy challenges in the economic sphere.

In the two decades prior to 1973, world trade grew twice as fast as ever before, at about 8 percent per annum. Developing economies as a whole were able to grow at an average annual rate of 6 percent (Lewis, 1980). Ivory Coast did better than most, with the real value of exports expanding at 9 percent and output at 8 percent over the same period. (World Bank, 1981). Income distribution, while not without problems, was not obviously worse than in other African countries. The forty percent of the population living in the poorest administrative districts, based on average per capita income within the districts, received 20 percent of total income in 1973–74. The 20 percent of the population living in Abidjan, the richest area, received 52 percent of total income (den Tuinder 1978). These figures do suggest the urban–rural dichotomy so prevalent in Africa, but do not elucidate the size distribution of personal incomes. However the chapter by Gbetibouo and Delgado shows that farm income during this period, in the cocoa zone at least, was both high and remarkably evenly distributed.

Following the first oil shock in 1974, sluggish growth in the industrial economies led to a halving of the growth rate of world trade. The implication for developing countries was, as Sir Arthur Lewis has pointed out, "the slowing down of the engine of growth" (1980). The consequences are particularly serious for the relatively small, open economies of Africa, which are now forced to adjust to the new order at precisely the time that they are just beginning to be able to reap full national advantage from world trade opportunities. In the case of Ivory Coast, the net barter terms of trade (what a unit of Ivorian exports will buy in terms of Ivorian imports) declined by roughly 40 percent from 1978 to 1982, after fluctuating around a fairly level trend during the 1970's. This was due both to higher oil prices and, more importantly perhaps, to a precipitous decline in cocoa and coffee prices following the boom in the late 1970's. Faced with the need to finance both imports and investment to diversify away from overreliance on commodity exports, external long-term borrowing increased rapidly after 1973, growing four times larger in nominal terms by 1981 (IMF, 1982). Of even greater concern, the ratio of debt service to exports grew steadily from 10.6 percent in 1977 to 29.1 percent in 1981 (*Marchés Tropicaux et Méditerranéens*, 21 Jan. 1983).

Thus, the implications for continued political stability in Ivory Coast must be assessed in the context of a number of fundamental changes in the external economic environment. However, the internal changes in the structure of the Ivorian economy have also been radical, and may have significant impact on future trends in both growth and equity, and thus on stability. Cohen's chapter shows that urbanization, occurring at an average annual rate of 8 percent over the last twenty years, has led to much greater relative importance being attributed to strictly urban issues in both the political and the policy agenda. If the 1970s witnessed considerable experimentation on the part of the government as to how to integrate urban needs and interests, the 1980s will be a period where policy innovation in the urban sector will be essential to maintain political stability. At the same time, heavy demand for state resources devoted to this end will intensify competition with rural areas, particularly in the context of difficult overall economic growth.

Various effects of a structural shift in Ivorian economic policies in favor of urban interests are investigated in the chapters by Michel and Noel with respect to growth and the balance of payments, by Gbetibouo and Delgado with respect to the sustainability of export crop-led growth, and by Mytelka with respect to the clash of interests arising from a move of Ivorian capital out of its traditional place in agriculture into the manufacturing sector, heretofore controlled by foreign capital.

In effect, there was a major shift in Ivorian economic strategy in the mid-1970s. Whereas earlier growth might be characterized as export crop–led growth of the "vent-for-surplus" type where expanded demand releases previously idle factors of production, policy in the 1971–75, 1976–80, and 1981–83 plan periods put increasing emphasis on diversification and industrialization. The chapter by Michel and Noel shows that the 1973 tariff reform bill, and the subsequent proliferation of rent–generating industrial import quotas thereafter, marked a new departure in industrial policy. From a position of relatively free trade in the 1960s, a policy of import-substituting industrialization behind tariff barriers was implemented in the 1970s. The effective production coefficient for the industrial sector as a whole went from 1.23 to 1.76 in the seven years following 1971, while a value of 1.00 would be consistent with free trade.

Michel and Noel find that the growth potential of Ivory Coast has severely deteriorated since the policy changes. While much of this is attributable to increased difficulties of the external environment, internal factors such as low returns on public investment, distorted domestic incentives that discriminate against agriculture, and economic losses due to rent-seeking (and obtaining) activity of those interests affected by import quotas have contributed to this situation. They employ a comparative static computable general equilibrium model to investigate the effects of returning to earlier formulas of freer trade. The model is used to stimulate the effects of changes in the trade regime—the constellation of exchange rate convertibility, tariff, subsidy and quota policies that govern foreign trade—on growth and internal structure of the economy. Their results suggest the need to consider a realignment of domestic incentives *vis-à-vis* world markets. One way to accomplish this would be a devaluation or change of parties within the franc zone. Another would be the "second best" strategy of tariff and subsidy reform to achieve the same objective.

Putting the industrial policy changes of the mid-1970s into a longer–term perspective, Ivory Coast presents a curious, and fairly unique paradox on the African economic scene. It is one of the few countries within Africa to have based its growth strategy so heavily upon agriculture, and export agriculture at that. Yet, it is also one of the countries that has been most successful at industrializing, in part through reinvestment of agricultural surplus and the linkage effects of higher agricultural incomes, but also through a massive inflow of private foreign investment. Thus, Ivory Coast has diversified its export earnings more rapidly than virtually any other country in the continent. Whereas the three principal commodity exports accounted for 81.2 percent of export earnings in 1961, they accounted for an average of 68.1 percent in 1976–78. Merchandise exports, totalling 1 percent of exports in 1962, accounted for 7 percent in 1978. The share of agriculture in Ivorian GDP declined from 43 to 26 percent from 1900 to 1929, compared to significant increases in this share over the same time period for Ghana, Senegal, and Zambia, countries that have traditionally given priority to nonagricultural development.

The chapter by Gbetibouo and Delgado examines the record of export–crop contributions to Ivorian growth in the case of cocoa, the crop most intimately associated with the political and economic development of the country. From the earliest days, cocoa planters were the most important power base for the current leadership. Many fortunes have been made in this commodity, which accounted for an average of 30 percent of total Ivorian exports from 1977 to 1979. Production expanded rapidly in the 1970s, nearly doubling between 1972 and 1982. Ivory Coast's share of the world market reached 27 percent in the latter year; the country has been the world's largest producer since 1980. Transfers from cocoa and coffee producers to the state via direct and implicit taxation provided well over one-third of all government revenue during the 1977–78 boom in world prices.

A curious aspect of successful Ivorian cocoa development is that government policy towards producers appears to have many of the structural elements diagnosed as being responsible for stagnation in other countries: exhorbitant price taxation of production, parastatal intervention in input distribution and marketing, overvalued exchange rates and so forth. Gbetibouo and Delgado argue that in fact, the similarities between Ivorian strategies and those elsewhere are more apparent than real. Perhaps because the interests of the Ivorian power structure since independence has been so bound up with those of the planters, the country has consistently implemented a series of nonprice policies on the supply side favorable to the expansion of production. However, the future success of these policies is put in jeopardy by both the internal structural shift of the economy and by developments in the world market. Distortions of incentives in favor of urban-based manufacturing and uneconomic import substitution in the agricultural sector are causing agricultural production costs to rise faster than productivity. Furthermore, a stagnant world market and increased competition from non-African producers suggest that there are also significant external constraints to export crop-led growth strategies of the 1960s and 1970s type in the foreseeable future.

The shift in emphasis from export agriculture to import-industrialization during the 1970s was accomplished largely with public funds borrowed from abroad. Thus, publicly guaranteed but privately held foreign debt grew from a negligible $112 million in 1970 to just under $3 billion in 1979 (World Bank, 1981). Drawing inspiration from dependency theory, Lynn Mytelka diagnoses changes in industrial policy and structure during the 1970s as an inevitable consequence of contradictions in the Ivorian economy, arising from changing roles of foreign and domestic capital in the economy and the response of the state to competition between them.

Mytelka views the economic growth of Ivory Coast in the 1960s as the result of a mutually profitable division of labor, mediated by the state, between domestic capital in agriculture and foreign capital in manufacturing. However, this inevitably led, it is claimed, to overly capital intensive patterns of industrialization and growing urban unemployment. In an effort to deal with the situation, the state sought to regain control of industry through direct intervention and participation, leading to the rapid rise in publicly guaranteed borrowing abroad. Thus, deterioration in Ivory Coast's balance of payments, and the ensuing stagnation, is seen primarily as the reflection of increased capital outflow through foreign ownership of capital, although the composition and source of this outflow has yet to be quantified.

Therefore, the 1970s saw a major structural shift in the Ivorian economy, whether seen through the theoretical lenses of the neoclassical macroeconomist, the structural agricultural economist, or the dependency theorist. Yet, the shift might not make much difference for growth prospects of the country, and thus, for stability, were not the external environment so unfavorable. If world trade were likely to continue expanding at its earlier rate of 8 percent per annum, it is also likely that Ivory Coast would be able to increase its export receipts from both agriculture and nonagriculture to the point at which foreign exchange constraints, the need for balanced growth between agriculture and industry, and dependency concerns based on capital outflow would not be very relevant. As Sir Arthur Lewis has pointed out, foreign-exchange constrained models, balanced growth models, dependency theories and schemes for regional economic integration were largely developed in the 1940s and 1950s by persons reflecting upon the stagnation of the world economy between 1913 and 1939 (1980).

Echoing a pessimistic view of world trade opportunities, the chapter by Atsain extends this tradition of economic theorizing in a stagnant world by examining the potential gain for Ivory Coast from regional economic integration. Although such schemes have typically had a sad history in Africa, they may have a greater role to play now than ever before. Atsain reviews past attempts at integration in West Africa and explores the reasons for failure. He contrasts the current experience of CEAO, a relatively small Francophone grouping, and the newer ECOWAS treaty, covering all of West Africa. Advantages are found in the more concrete step-by-step approach of CEAO than in the more ambitious, but ill-implemented, proposals of ECOWAS. He explores the current applicability of traditional barriers to economic integration, specifically: unequal development among partners, trade diversion costs, absence of complementary economies among members, transport difficulties and political competition. He concludes that the time is ripe for increased policy attention to this area.

As Ivory Coast enters the mid-1980s, a new generation prepares to take over. They face seven critical choices in the realm of politics and economics. With one exception, they all involve complex tradeoffs in both spheres. Without exception, the choices made in the mid-1980s will determine both the rate of economic expansion and the degree of political stability Ivory Coast will enjoy in the forseeable future.

The first choice concerns the means and results of succession. A choice that is merely "a shadow of the Old Man" rather than a heir and leader in his own right (an arap Moi rather than an Abdou Diouf, to draw parallels from Kenya and Senegal) can allow generational, ethnic and policy disputes now submerged in consensus to rise boiling to the surface. A choice that occurs only after Houphouet Boigny's death would be operating under the handicap of having to maintain its own stability during the transition, whereas the nomination either of a new president in 1985 or of a vice-president as a running mate for the aging Houphouet would allow him to cover the transition with his own respect. In any case, favorable world economic conditions that spill over onto the Ivorian economy would be a welcome blessing to the new president.

Second, the rate and manner of reducing the European presence will doubtless be an issue of the 1980s. Whether or not this choice has an economic cost will depend upon the ability of education and incentive policies to produce national replacements. It is clear that countries that had largely dispensed with expatriate input early on, such as Ghana and Mali, have paid a heavy price, especially in the context of skilled manpower-intensive growth strategies of the type increasingly espoused by Ivory Coast.

The third choice involves adopting a clear position with respect to the status of resident Africans from non-Ivorian origins. As economic pressures trigger outbreaks of xenophobia, so will they create a disaffected migrant proletariat in the large cities. To an increasing extent, the migration south has become permanent, leading to an increasingly large indigenous class of northerners living in Southern areas. On the other hand, authorities may be tempted to divert attention from other problems by blaming misfortunes on "the foreigners".

The fourth choice for the mid-1980s concerns policies that alter the balance of incentives between rural and urban areas. This includes, but goes beyond concerns experienced by the World Bank and the IMF concerning trade and budgeting policies. As universities turn out potential members of the new elite with increasingly urban allegiances, the ability of planter interests to secure policies favorable to agricultural development will surely be diluted. Yet past growth and stability in Ivory Coast depended in an important way upon these policies.

The fifth critical choice facing Ivory Cost involves finding means of reducing the level of publicly guaranteed foreign debt. This will necessarily involve reducing the role of government in financing public and mixed enterprises. On the other hand, means must be found to increase the level and stability of domestic savings available for developmental purposes.

The sixth critical choice concerns regional equity. In the past, distributive projects targeted at the poorer North have been financed out of export taxes and price stabilization surpluses. While the strong comparative advantage of Ivory Coast in cocoa and coffee, combined with high world prices, permitted this in the past without undue harm to export proceeds, this is not likely to be the case in the future. A choice in favor of higher farm incomes in the North will necessarily mean income redistribution from towns, a political bridge that has not been crossed in the past due to the existence of an exploitable set of crops in the south.

The seventh critical choice involves a decision vis-a-vis the terms on which to stay in the franc zone. Without doubt, adherance brings many benefits, both political and economic. On the other hand, the Ivorian economy has become important enough on the world scale to necessitate some degree of autonomous monetary policy. If the decision is to remain within the zone, as it is fairly clear that it will be, it may be necessary to seek means to adjust the parity of Ivorian currency versus that of the country's trade partners.

No single book can encompass the host of considerations pertinent to evaluating these seven choices. However, we hope that the papers that follow are a useful contribution to that end, as well as a contribution to understanding the underlying political and economic mechanisms of a fascinating, innovative and dynamic country.

NOTES

1. The famous wager is the subject of two books, Foster and Zolberg 1971, and Woronoff 1972. References to the wager itself are not as explicit as one might wish; Zolberg 1969, p. 221, refers to Afrique Nouvelle, 9 & 30 April 1957; Woronoff 1972, pp. 10–13, 313, refers to Le Monde, 17 April 1957, Marches Tropicaux du Monde, 13 April 1957, and later sources, also including an affirmative interview with Houphouet-Boigny, pp. 328–29. Houphouet did talk explicitly of a "wager" in his address to François Mitterand at the time of Ghanaian independence text in the *Bulletin of the Association pour l'Etude des Problemes de l'Union Française* 110, pp. iv–v (March 1957). However, much later, in an interview with Sennen Andriamirado, Houphouet denied there ever was such a wager; *Jeune Afrique* 1043:221–222 (31 December 1980) and 1048:30 (4 February 1981).

2. The party's local activities are also paralleled by the administration, well described by West Africa (4 April 1977) as "judge, agricultural extension worker, civil servant, and fundraiser at one and the same time."

3. For the new directions of 1966 (Plan 1967–70), see Lawson, 1975, pp. 226–30; for the new directions of 1975 (Plan 1976–80), see den Tuinder 1978, and PDCI 1975.

2
ELITE TRANSFORMATION AND POLITICAL SUCCESSION
Tessilimi Bakary

Succession in black Africa is an issue surrounded by well accepted preconceptions. The first of these is that political instability in newly independent nations is inevitable. The second is that frequent leadership turnover is common. According to these notions, African states are monocracies, tempered only by the possibility of change through coups. Constitutional provisions regarding succession are formalistic and without effect because the government is so strongly personalized. Because they did not give up power in time, numerous heads of state are thrown out by force without benefit of constitutional provisions. Exceptionally, if the president dies in his bed, less constraining rules of the game than the constitution organize the transition.

A brief look at different cases of succession or permanence in power among African heads of state (which is not the central purpose of this study) would allow us to examine the reality of the often discussed—even in Africa—"succession apocalypse." This examination would have shown that the problem of the transmission of power at the top of the political hierarchy has not, in most cases, been resolved in as troubled and violent a manner as is often suggested (Decraene 1982).

The most recent and edifying examples of this are undoubtedly those of Leopold Sedar Senghor in Senegal and Ahmadou Ahidjo in Cameroon, who resigned on December 31, 1980 and November 4, 1982, respectively, both after more than 20 years in power. In both cases the transfer of power followed constitutional stipulations. Prime Ministers Abdou Diouf and Paul Biya, respectively, legally succeeded the resigning presidents. Diouf received

Translation by Jerome Savage.

an electoral consecration in February 1983, and Biya awaits it in April of 1985 or later.

The situation in Ivory Coast is obviously presuccessoral. The President of the Republic Felix Houphouet-Boigny will be 80 years old in November 1985 and at the end of his fifth successive mandate since 1960—a venerable age for a chief of state.

The Ivory Coast case is interesting for several reasons. It is a pillar of economic success, a "showcase of the West," a "model" which the Reagan administration's experts on African policy would want to see multiplied throughout the Third World. (*Newsweek* 26 October, 1981). Important western economic interests (mostly French, but increasingly American, British and German) reinforce the attention of these countries on the issue of political succession in Ivory Coast. It is also a pillar of political moderation and stability in a general environment of coups and military regimes.

Another reason for interest in the Ivorian case is the "traditional" and "fraternal" rivalry existing between the Ivory Coast and Senegal since the 1950s. This rivalry is symbolized by their respective leaders, Houphouet-Boigny and Senghor, who represent Franco–African community versus federalism; liberalism versus African socialism; single-party system versus multipartism, etc. In this context, the surprise resignation of the Senegalese leader is a last episode in this "fraternal" conflict. Senghor made his point by leaving. He wanted to be remembered as the African president who effected a smooth succession while still alive. The Ivorian president also thought of resigning but decided against it, preferring to set up a team from which his successor would emerge (*Jeune Afrique* 1048: 30, 4 February 1981).

The much more surprising resignation of Ahidjo in November 1982 poses much more acutely the problem of transmitting power the Ivorian way, especially since three years after the creation of the position of vice-president in Ivory Coast no one has been elected or nominated to fill it.

The subject of this chapter is not to forecast about Houphouet-Boigny's successor nor to reveal the stategy that will be used. In fact, these questions matter little. More interesting and instructive is to approach the succession issue (certainly the major political event of the decade in Ivory Coast) through an analysis of the team which has grown up around and under the tutelage of Houphouet-Boigny, the group from which his successor will emerge.

What does the concept of political elite cover in the context of today's Ivory Coast? Of whom is it composed? Have its characteristics and mode of recruitment evolved since its emergence as an indigenous leadership group in the aftermath of the Second World War through 1980? Why and how? What influence might these characteristics have upon the transmission of power at the highest state level and upon the policies of the new president?

The political elite, as we shall define it, is very small in size and of rather recent origin (I). The characteristics of the leaders and the mode of their recruitment, despite appearances, seem hardly to have changed (II). Whatever the means of transmitting power—and granted its importance—and despite the fears and worries of Ivorians and non-Ivorians regarding Houphouet-Boigny's succession, the game has already been played out and probably has been since 1949–1950. The next president will emerge out of the same mold as that of the present leadership and will have no alternative but to pursue his predecessor's policies. Thus, despite its spectacular nature and despite its importance, the succession will probably take place more quietly than is anticipated (III).

THE IVORIAN POLITICAL ELITE

There is no consensus on the definition of the word "elite" (Aron 1950, 1960; Bottomore 1967; Lasswell, Lerner and Rothwell 1952; Mosca 1939; Nadel 1956; Pareto 1966; Putnam 1976; Zartman 1974). There is even less agreement on the usage of "elite" in the study of African societies (Berrady et al 1973; Blanchet 1977; LeVine 1970; Lloyd 1966; Miller 1974; Sklar 1967, 1969; Wallerstein 1965; Bakary 1980, 1983; Campbell 1978; Bocoum 1972, 1973; Cohen 1974; Clignet and Foster 1964, 1966; Faure and Medard 1982; Keita 1966; Loucou 1976a/b, 1977; Sylla 1977; Toure 1982; Wodie 1969; Zolberg 1964, 1971). Hence, we need here to clarify what is understood as "elite" in the Ivory Coast before identifying its dimensions in reality.

The Elite: Concept and Usage in the Ivory Coast

In order to avoid useless debate about its definition or a vain search for an "ultimate concept," (Zartman 1974, p. 470) the word "elite" in the Ivorian context refers to a division common to all societies between those who govern and those who are governed, between those whom the Ivorian calls "the top of the tops" ("les en-haut de en-haut") and "the bottom of the bottoms" ("les en-bas de en-bas").

Because of the current relatively simple power structure in Ivory Coast, it is fairly easy to identify the members of the political elite. This can be done on the basis of their reputation, their position, or their participation in the decision-making process. Indeed, in the socio–political context of this country the three criteria for identification of elites coincide in an almost perfect manner. The best known and the most active Ivorians are also the ones who occupy official posts and who, as a result, constitute the political elite.

The "300 Families" of the Ivory Coast

We shall define the political elite as the 320 women and men who occupied a position since 1957 in either the assemblies, the government, or the top organs of the political parties (LeVine 1970, p. 373): the government from May 1957 to January 1981; the National Assembly from April 1959 to November 1980; the Economic and Social Council from January 1961 to January 1981 and the Political Bureau of the PDCI-RCA from March 1959 to September 1980.

One of the immediate consequences of the 1956 *loi cadre* was, on May 15, 1957, the establishment of a government council which was presided over by the governor of the then–colony, Ernest de Nattes. From this date to February 1, 1981—the eve of the new government's constitution—73 Ivorian personages have had ministerial functions. These ranged from President of the Council and Prime Minister to State Secretaries.[1]

Officially, the assembly elected on April 12, 1959 constitutes the first legislature of the Ivorian National Assembly, with extensive powers at its disposal over all domestic policy issues, including an ability to censure the government. However, it is really the third step in the evolution of deliberative assemblies in former French colonies: General Council (1946–1952), Territorial Assembly (1952–1957), Legislative Assembly (1957–1959), and the National Assembly at independence in 1960. From 1959 to 1980, 200 persons belonged to one or the other of the five legislatures in Ivorian National Assembly.[2]

The first 25 members of the Economic and Social Council were nominated in January 1961. This consultative organ was established by virtue of Title X of the November 3, 1960 constitution. From 1961 to 1981, 39 persons in this assembly have contributed to the efficient economic and social development of the country.

The leading organ of the PDCI, called the Executive Commission from 1946 to 1953, was named the Political Bureau after the III Party Congress in March 1959. Seventy-eight persons were coopted to the top ranks of leadership in Ivory Coast's sole political party from March 1959 to the VIII Congress in September–October 1980.

All considered, from 1957 when the Council of Government was formed to September 1980 on the eve of the VIII Party Congress of the PDCI, 1,040 leadership positions were available in these four main institutions. Since officials simultaneously occupy at least two positions (e.g. Political Bureau and government institutions) and some persons have moved from one institution to another, only 320 persons actually occupied these offices. These 19 women and 301 men who filled the positions were for a quarter of a century the most well-known and, in principle, the most politically active personalities in Ivory Coast. They constitute the political elite, the enlarged team to which probably belongs Houphouet-Boigny's successor.

What characterizes these men and women today? What distinguishes them from other Ivorians? What is their social background? How did they attain their privileged status in the society?

These questions represent a classical approach to elites, applicable to all social and political systems. Although a detailed justification of the approach would be instructive, we will attempt more particularly to describe the evolution in the characteristics of the members of the political elite (social origin, education, profession, age, sex, etc.) and the modes of selection and, if possible, the causes and implications of these characteristics.

A "REVOLUTION" OF SOCIO–POLITICAL STATUS

From its colonial past Ivorian society inherited two characteristics common to numerous African countries. The first is its artificial nature. Nothing (or almost nothing) in the political entities which now comprise Ivorian society, would seem to resemble the precolonial socio–cultural structure. The second characteristic is that, although these groups are familiar with the division between those who govern and those who are governed, the emergence of the political elite as studied here was something new. This elite appeared in the wake of colonial aggression in a political, socio–economic and cultural context that was broader, more complex and more diverse than that in which the precolonial political entities and socio–cultural groups functioned. It is not possible here to specify all the effects of colonization on different systems of socio–political stratification or on relations between precolonial leadership groups. Without wishing to ignore references to the more distant past, however, this analysis will start from the system of socio–political stratification as it appeared after the Second World War.

The changes which occurred in the modes of selection and recruitment between 1960 and the 1980s are only perceptible if compared to practices between 1945 and independence. The earlier period bears the mark of the colonial context, in which a system was established and then improved on and applied with little change over the following 20 years.

The Pattern of the French Colonial Past

The many–centuried history of each of the traditional societies within the current borders of Ivory Coast has been marked by the great shock of colonial intrusion, bringing many brutal and radical changes which one might classify as a secondary modernization process in the economic, social, cultural and political realms. In this context, the short political history of the "Ivory Coast" colony has been mainly influenced by a series of French legislative acts following the Second World War in 1945 (right to representation in France), 1946 (universal citizenship, creation of the General Council), 1956 (self-government), and 1958 (Republic). Indeed, colonization was the source of a new system of social stratification (the creation of new social status or new social elite positions) through the introduction of new activities (primarily plantation agriculture and the use of civil servants). The legislation introduced important structural changes in the French colonial administration starting a process of political stratification different from the traditional system. These changes had two important effects. First, new social institutions (such as trade unions) and, even more, political institutions (such as political parties, deliberative bodies becoming legislative assemblies, and the territorial executive) provided the first elite positions in the political field and a new type of political leadership, the emergence of a new territorial political elite. The second change was the establishment of a territorial political life that through a process of gradual autonomy led to independence in 1960.

The managing group which was formed in 1945 bears the mark of a dual process of new social and political stratifications. Its social composition (1) and its means of recruitment (2) make it a creation—and initially a prolongation—of the colonial system.

The Social Composition of the Elites: The Product of the French Colonial System

The new elite is the product of the colonization and not a continuation of the traditional predecessors (Table 1). It is marked not only by a new stratification but also by a new relation between social and political strata, and is both multiethnic and drawn from various social levels.

A Multiethnic elite. The first striking characteristic of the elite is that for the first time power was exercised by people from many different political and socio–cultural groups (N'gatta 1970). Previously, whether in proto–states (Akan, Manding, Voltaic) or stateless societies (Kru, Mande), whether in large or small units (empires, kingdoms, clans, lineages, villages), power was never shared with members of another unit. It was the colonization which broke the power of these units and created of them a new

TABLE 1 Characteristics of the Ivory Coast Officeholders 1947–1959

	Assemblies			*Territorial Executive*
	1947–1950	*1952–1957*	*1957–1959*	*1957–1959*
Ethnic Origin:				
Akan	8	9	20	8
Kru	5	3	10	1
Voltaic	3	4	5	—
Manding	4	6	10	—
Mande	1	1	2	1
Others	6	4	1	—
Social Status:				
Chief's Family	8	7	8	—
Commoners	19	22	40	10
Education:				
University	—	—	4	5
W. Ponty	21	14	23	3
E.P.S.	3	7	13	2
Primary	3	2	8	—
Other	—	5	—	—
Profession:				
Public Sector:	22	17	31	8
Teacher	7	6	13	1
Clerk	8	6	15	4
Doctor	6	5	3	2
Pharmacist	1	—	—	1
Private Sector:	5	10	17	2
Lawyer	—	—	1	—
Business Clerk	1	1	5	2
Planter-Trader	2	7	8	—
Other salaried	2	2	2	—
Chief	—	—	1	—

"confraternity of power." Nonetheless, some groups had better access to power than others. The Akan was preponderant, the Kru underrepresented. This condition might be interpreted as a survival of traditional power relation of vassalage, flattering some minds and posing succession problems for the country, but it is of dubious validity. Most groups portray themselves as the strongest in their national histories, but in fact there is little to support the notion of proto–states' dominance over stateless tribes (for example, of Akan vassalage over the Voltaics or Manding), even with the conquest of the Senoufo by Samory Toure. Within ethnic groups, however, domination did exist. Subgroups and individual names testify to the place occupied in the collective history and in the social stratification of the larger group.

The better explanation for Akan dominance is that it was made possible by the colonization, emphasizing new inequalities stemming from social stratification brought about by the colonizer. This explanation is common to many African countries. The coastal regions which first had contact with colonization had a considerable advantage, a "jump" on the others elsewhere in the country. From south to north and east to west, regional disparity seems to have followed the path of colonization and of the modernization it represented. This "jump" is not only material or economic. Psychologically, the groups which first came in contact with Europeans changed their views of themselves. The accident of colonization either added to or detracted from the value of the groups' various conceptions of the world. This sometimes went too far. For example, in France, leaders of the Right find it incongruous that the Left is in power and not themselves (who are "naturally" called to govern); in Ivory Coast, some Ivorians (and probably not the least of them) have doubts as to the capability of some ethnic group members to govern after Houphouet-Boigny.

Social Pluralism—A New Deal. The social origins of the Ivorian leaders are difficult to trace, particularly before independence. Official biographies are vague, if not silent, on the subject, and the leaders themselves are very discreet as to their origins. They seem to care much more about their present or professional future than about their parents' past, especially if that past is modest.

Nevertheless, is it possible to say that, on the whole, Ivorian politicians come from very modest milieux, with some small admixture of former chiefly members. It is this social pluralism which must be kept in mind. Power is shared between those who were once predestined to it by their social status and those who were excluded from power on the same basis. If the presence of decendants of chiefs (with all ambiguities of that position after the arrival of the colonist) symbolizes the precolonial past, a larger group represents the new order. Indeed, if a division between the leaders and the led characterized precolonial societies, it is an important event—for some, a sacrilege—that "slaves" and "sons of slaves" can now be called to govern.

This second point of divergence from precolonial leadership models also finds its origin in colonial rule. Colonization was an opportunity for a new deal, a new distribution of opportunities where the have-nots of yesterday got revenge on the privileged. To be sure, the latter are not absent: many were successful in adapting, converting, conserving, even reinforcing their social status. They did so thanks to colonization (creation of schools for sons of chiefs, utilization of tribal or ethnic lands and collective property for personal purposes) and in spite of some people's misgivings. But the have-nots could and knew how to use faster, better, and without scruples the new means of social mobility: the French school system and new economic activities. The result was not so much the replacement of the haves by the have-nots in the political elite as a change in the nature of social status itself, a revolution in the criteria and the paths of recruitment of the political elite as a consequence of colonial rule.

Acquired social status and electoral competition: The new means of access to power

Even more than their social composition, the means of access to power for the political elite are a determinant breaking point with the pre-colonial models. The changes occurred at two levels: new sources of social status, and then new modes of selection in a competition with increasingly numerous candidates for leadership.

New Social Status. The figures in Table 1 show education and professions that were nearly unknown before. The French school system is a necessary step, the first and most important on the social ladder. The diploma itself, rather than any particular branch of education, is the first new social status. The second lies in new economic activities. Among the leaders there is no farmer, hunter, fisherman, cattleman, artisan; in other words, no representative of the most common precolonial occupations. All belong to new professions (the term "farmer" here must not be confused with that of planter).

The professional structure of the elite appears to show the disproportional size of the public compared with the private sector. Since a diploma is necessary for a job in the administration, this shows the error of the thesis of a "planter bourgeoisie" in the Ivory Coast. The small representation of planters may be explained by the fact that plantation owners and state agents are often the same persons. Most politicians were civil servants before turning to the plantation economy; others managed both activities—as the Ivorian Chief of State did himself at the beginning of his political and professional career.

The coincidence between the elite of education and the elite of economic success confirms the crucial role of the school. Education allows students to know better the new economic norms and market mechanisms, as well as the new means of access to power. Thus, new professional activities are the second step on the road to power. Not only do they provide social prestige, but also the material means to compete with other applicants.

Competitive elections. Within the extreme diversity of African precolonial political systems, and most particularly those in the Ivory Coast, the means of leadership selection are various, ranging from natural cooptation or biological selection (gerontocratic, age classes in the societies with diffused or segmented power) to heredity (in societies with a structured and hierarchical state). Where there is some form of competition, through the presence of several candidates for leadership, in the age strata system, or in the rivalry between branches of the royal family, it is not especially close to modern means of selection and designation of political leaders (Memel-Fote 1980, Paulme 1971). In the first case, collective exercises of power and multiple functions made competition for access to leadership irrelevant. In the second, solutions range from unanimity or consensus on one candidate to the physical elimination of the rival(s) (through murder, poisoning), war between partisans, or finally exile of the defeated faction.

Thus, the means of selection and designation of Ivorian political leaders after 1945 are new only in their forms (Loucou 1976a). The end remains the same: to choose those who will lead. But the means represent a dramatic change from the past and were previously unknown: associations, political parties, voters' sanction, through a mass of men and women whose ethnic and social composition goes beyond the family clan or common origin.

The competitive feature of the elections which took place in Ivory Coast from 1945 to 1959 is shown by the number of political organizations, candidates, and results.

(i) The political organizations: from electoral committees to political parties. The history of Ivorian political organizations remains to be written. However, its broad lines are available, showing that the period 1945–1959 is indeed crucial to understand the Ivorian party system (Zolberg 1969, Loucou 1977). The first political or parapolitical organizations appear with the first elections in the wake of World War II and are renamed electoral committees. They were based on the earlier "native" or voluntary associations which brought together members of broad ethnic groups in the urban centers. These associations supported candidates in the first Constituent Assembly election of October 21 and November 18, 1945. The electoral committees, native associations (U.F.O.C.I., A.D.I.A.C.I., U.O.C.O.C.I., etc.) and professional organizations (S.A.A., S.E.P.A.) joined to form real political parties.[3] The new parties—Ivory Coast Democratic Party (P.D.C.I.), Ivory Coast Progressive Party (P.P.C.I.)—faced each other during the second Constituent Assembly election of June 2, 1946.

This period shows a relative political pluralism, best defined as a particular form of multipartism, resulting from the ethnic origins of the associations and committees (Sylla 1977). Organizations merged and split according to colonial, electoral, and local concerns, leading to as many ethnic or tribal lists as the district had important ethnic groups.

Together with multipartism, and probably because of it, this period is also marked by the strong unification movement within the party system. The first attempt took place during the municipal elections of August 1945 in Abidjan, with the formation of an antisettler united front, the "African bloc", which won the elections (Zolberg 1969, p. 69). Several efforts followed this victorious consensus around a single candidate. They were unsuccessful in the constituent election of October and November 1945 and June 1946, but in the November 1946 election to the French National Assembly another "united front" was successful, and was partially so in December 1946 and May 1948. In each case the unification nucleus was the PDCI. But the front could not hold up against the centrifugal pressure of contradictory interests. In June 1951, seven political organizations participated in the election. In the March 1952 territorial assembly elections, the PDCI which had enjoyed a monopoly over political life from 1945 to 1949 and then lost it, temporarily regained its ground by forming a new coalition, the Union for the Defense of Ivory Coast Economic Interests (UDECI). Yet, in January 1956, the PDCI slate of candidates was in competition with twelve others. By the March 1957 territorial assembly elections, the strategy of gathering all political organizations into the PDCI had nearly reached its goal and in April 1959, for the first time, the 100 candidates to the Legislative Assembly were all on the PDCI ticket. The party became a de facto single party with a little help from the electoral system. A single national slate with no preferencial or cross-slate voting was used from April 1959 to 1975. The legislative and presidential elections in November 1960 sanctioned the institutionalization of the PDCI as a single party. The trend toward union and unanimity proved stronger than the trend toward pluralism and a multiparty system.

(ii) Number of candidates and number of seats: from competition to monopoly. More than the number of parties, the relationship between number of seats and candidates is the critical test of competitiveness in elections. Except in November 1946, candidates always outnumbered seats until April 1959. The election to the first Constituent Assembly was a bitter contest; there were 14 candidates for one seat in the first round in October 1945, 8 during the second round, and 3 in the June 1946 elections for the second Constituent Assembly. This sharp drop shows the effects of the different coalitions' efforts to monopolize the selection of candidates. In November 1946, for the first time, the number of seats (three) equalled the number of candidates. This, however, proved to be but an interlude. One month later, in elections to the General Council, 39 candidates ran for 15 seats, despite a coalition of the principal parties (PDCI, PPCI, SFIO). The same occurred during the partial reelections for the General Council in May 1948, after the representative of Upper Volta departed.

The PDCI reached the height of its power in the multiparty system during these last elections, when the candidate of the dominant party was sure to be elected. PDCI hegemony temporarily ended in 1948, with the association of the PDCI–RDA with the French Communist Party and its ensuing repression (Cherif 1978). The four following elections were very close and bitter, and the candidates always outnumbered the seats, up to 26 for the two seats in the French National Assembly in January 1956. However, the PDCI remained the dominant party. Houphouet-Boigny was reelected to the Assembly in 1951, even though his running mate, Ouezzin Coulibaly, lost to Sekou Sanogo. The PDCI reaction to this relative loss of influence started to bear fruit in 1959. In the interim the PDCI had created the UDECI, disengaged itself from the French Communist Party (PCF), and started to collaborate even more closely with the colonial administration. During the period 1946–1959 there were always dissident electoral slates or candidates.

(iii) The Results: The PDCI's political representation monopoly. The PDCI only lost its monopoly of political representation once, in 1951. The PDCI's "hegemonic trend" goes back to the "African Bloc" municipal elections of August 1945, and then the Constitutional Assembly elections in October when Houphouet-Boigny obtained 79 percent of the votes in the Ivory Coast and 38.8 percent in Upper Volta (totalling 49.8 percent) against his leading rival with 5.2 percent and 52.5 percent (totalling 38.2 percent). Supported by the future PDCI, Houphouet-Boigny received 83.5 percent and 24 percent in the second round (totally 50.7 percent) against 7.9 percent and 73 percent for his opponent (totalling 45 percent). Supported by the newly created PDCI, Houphouet-Boigny was reelected to the second Constituent Assembly with 98 percent of the votes.

The 1946 elections confirmed the trend towards a monopoly of political representation. In November, the PDCI-dominated coalition, "The African Rally," won 100 percent of the votes for its three candidates to the French National Assembly. In December, 95 percent of the votes for the 15 seats available for the Ivory Coast General Council again went to the PDCI.

In May 1948, the PDCI monopoly came under strong attack. The opposition gained two seats out of 27, with the rest going to the PDCI with 90 percent of the votes. In June 1951, after the peak of colonial repression, the PDCI was able to keep one seat at the French National Assembly with 61 percent of the vote while the second seat was taken by the opposition candidate with 32 percent of the votes. However, the elections to the Territorial Assembly in March 1952 allowed the PDCI to win 72 percent of the votes and 28 of the 32 seats. The PDCI regained monopoly at the French Assembly seats in January 1956, with 87 percent of the votes. However, its 58 representatives with 89 percent of the votes still faced a two man opposition in the Territorial Assembly.

With the reform of the electoral system, the PDCI managed to recover the monopoly of both selection and representation. With nearly all the votes and all 100 seats in the Legislative Assembly, Houphouet-Boigny's party could envision its institutionalization as a single party.

What are the lessons of 15 years of competitive elections? First, the means of access to power were absolutely new, even if the competition tended to be along tribal or ethnic rivalry lines rather than on the basis of a more modern clash of ideas. The tribal or ethnic parties did not carry on sharply differentiated political convictions. But this lack of ideological competition is not particular to Ivory Coast; it occurs in many American cities as well.

The second lesson is the emergence of a trend contrary to social pluralism and multipartism, aimed at ensuring unanimity in the selection of leaders from diverse socio–political and ethnic backgrounds. The principal means of this unanimism are a single party and an adequate electoral system—a national slate without cross-balloting or choice and a majority one round vote. The negotiating and coalition building talents of the PDCI founder and his associates would do the rest.

One can explain this unanimous stream with a sort of atavism or continuity of precolonial leadership. Another objective cause might be Houphouet-Boigny's personal strategy of domination, since he was the first to benefit from the system. Finally, the system itself was justified by the complexity of the population's ethnic structure and by the fact that the competition was more ethnically than ideologically identified. The nature of Ivory Coast's political and economic future will largely depend upon the strength of the unanimous trend.

The Ivorian political elite emerging in 1945 was a colonial creation. Since it was difficult to create *ex nihilo*, it borrowed features particular to the milieux which engendered it. Victor LeVine (1970, p. 337) wrote in his analysis of the recruitment of French speaking Africa's political elite: "What is at once striking but not unexpected is the fact that well over 50 percent of the total recruited to the 1946-1952 Assemblies were products of the colonial system itself... " He follows the same line of reason of R.S. Morgenthau (1964, p. 13) who writes; "Indeed, had they been disqualified, it is difficult to see where alternative educated candidates might have been found to fill political offices."

However accurate these comments may be, they run the risk of reinforcing an elitist vision of the leadership of political societies, or "government by the best." Was this political elite really socially representing the societies it claimed to lead? If not, could not the system have allowed leadership by lower social status, minority groups? Obviously, the modernized elite, the social group which got to power in 1945 in Ivory Coast as well as in other ex-French colonies, is very much of a minority social group which does not at all represent the whole population (Seurin 1958). Its members, who have new professions, are relatively old (between 40 and 50 on the average) in 1960 and are all men, when *women* constitute about half the population and had participated very actively in the fight for emancipation. In fact, the political elite only represents the electoral group of the time, itself sharply reduced by restrictions on suffrage in the colonies between 1945 and 1958.

In these conditions and in the context of its assimilation policy, France had no choice but to give power to the social group it had formed. To be sure, the exercise of power by more representative groups was conceivable, if utopian: Ivory Coast experienced such systems of government prior to colonization. However, this would have required imagination, autonomy and trust in the capabilities of the colonized people. The solution chosen by the colonizing power was consistent with its "civilizing mission" and with its own interests.

The Ivorian political elite knew better than others how to take advantage of the historical circumstances in the aftermath of World War II, and of the opportunity offered by France to establish a system of leadership selection. The elite would control the system that, in turn, would allow them to consolidate the bases of their power in every domain.

The Houphouet-Boigny System

The domination Houphouet-Boigny exercised upon his country, his political system, and more directly upon the elite reached a point where the members of the elite are perceived and perceive themselves as his men and the access to power as his.

The President's Men

Who are these Men? What is their social milieux? Are they different from the men who were in power in the previous period? There seems, at first sight, to be very little change. At the ethnic level, the ruling group still claims to represent the whole population; socially it shows the results of strong social mobility for some Ivorians; and in some ways, these Ivorians are the symbols of the economic and social success of the years 1960-1980.

Ethnic structure of the population and elite representativity. The original ethnic plurality of the elite appeared as a consequence of French colonialism. In a colonial society with a complex ethnic structure, the weight of primary loyalties was soon felt in political life through electoral committees and ethnic parties. Inevitably the elite would be a multiethnic microcosm of society. However, this raises the question of the leaders' representativity born within their own regions (which are far from being ethnically homogenous) and at the national level. In fact, the most important groups are likely to be overrepresented, and the regions which had earlier contact with the colonizer tended to use their advance exposure to monopolize political representation. From 1945 to 1959, when the means of access to power were competitive, some correction might have been expected. The excesses stemming from the numerical importance of each group and from its cultural level might be corrected by the law of supply and demand in the political market of the time, with its particular features of colonial repression and interethnic tensions.

The issue of ethnic plurality arises when one dominant party is made up of essentially the most important ethnic group and attempts to federate the other groups, to acquire the double monopoly of candidates' selection and political representation.

Ethnic leadership as a form of leadership with official use of a tribe as a political base ended with the formation of the PDCI-RDA as a dominant and then single party. But, in fact, what disappeared were the most striking and exacerbated signs of this type of leadership. Since then, another form of ethnic leadership has appeared in its place. Still based on regional or tribal identity rather than pretenses of representativity, it is now linked to the new form of leadership selection, which is no longer influenced by the supply and demand of the political market but rather by a monopoly of supply and monopoly of the evaluation of demand. Thus, ethnicity is still the basis of the answer to the problem of representativity, measured by both the numerical importance of the ethnic group and its degree of acculturation (Table 2). A skillful system of ethnic "quotas" allows a certain balance between the groups. The Akan, the most numerous group (about two fifths of the population in 1975) were represented by half of the leaders in 1980 (50.9 percent). Two groups have a representation that is about half of their numerical importance in society: the Voltaics and the South Mande. The Kru and the Malinke have representation roughly equal to their size. Roughly, the same relationship holds for each leadership body.

Unless one says that the Ivorian political elite is "the Akan's business," one cannot deduce from the figures that any institution is reserved for a precise ethnic group. But Akan overrepresentation must be tempered by the fact that this group is subdivided in 17 major subgroups, and that in each ethnic group (Akan included) one major subgroup dominates: Baoules are 39.25 percent of the Akan, just ahead of the Agni and their related five subgroups (36.58 percent); Bétés are 53.9 percent of the Kru; the Senoufo are 48.25 percent of the Voltaics; and only the Mande group is relatively homogenous.

Acculturation is a second aspect of regional and national imbalance, referring to those who enjoy modern social attributes brought by education and the plantation economy. The subgroups located at the southeast of the country thus, are the most advantaged, since they were the first to meet the colonizer. The overrepresentation of the Agni and related subgroups in the political elite is a case in point. This group does not exceed 6 percent of the total population, and yet, 18.75 percent of the elite is Agni, including 20.5

TABLE 2 Elite by Ethnic Group 1959–1980

Ethnic Group	Total Elite		Minister		Deputy		Economic & Social Councillers		PDCI Politburo		Total Population in 1975
	No.	%	No.	%	No.	%	No.	%	No.	%	%
Akan including Lagunes	163	50.90	39	53.4	100	50.0	50	56.1	43	55.10	41.4
Kru	63	19.60	15	20.5	41	20.5	13	14.6	10	12.80	16.7
Malinke	33	10.30	7	9.5	19	9.0	10	11.2	8	10.25	14.8
South Mande	17	5.30	2	2.7	13	6.5	4	4.4	4	5.1	10.2
Voltaic	29	9.06	6	8.2	9	4.5	4	4.4	7	8.9	15.7
Others	13	4.06	4	5.4	6	3.0	7	7.8	5	6.4	1.2
Unknown	1	0.30	—	—	1	0.5	—	—	—	—	—

percent of the ministers, 36 percent of the members of parliament, and 25.6 percent of the members of the PDCI Political Bureau. As one moves further from the point of impact of colonization, underrepresentation of the groups increases. The Baoulé are underrepresented, although they make up 20 percent of the population. The Krumen and Neyo to the south, the Voltaics to the north, the Foula and Bambara to the northwest and the Lobi, Koulango, and Abron to the northeast—all these groups are underrepresented when measured by their numerical importance. In sum, representativity is based on objective realities: size of ethnic groups and the degree of acculturation to the new norms of political leadership.

Furthermore, both ethnic pluralism and some slight imbalance in proportions are natural in a society with such a complex ethnic structure. The leaders want the elite to reflect an indispensable national unity, but also some groups and regions will profit from economic and social advantages closely linked to power positions (Faure and Medard 1982; 1983). Continuity is the main feature regarding the political elite's representativity despite the arrival of independence. It applies also to the leaders' social origins.

Access to political elite and social mobility.   The political functions are still far from being hereditary after independence. One cannot yet say "like father, like son" but at best, "like son, like father." Indeed, the leaders' social origins are as modest as they were in the past. Table 3 shows the strong social mobility of one generation of Ivorians who managed to escape their fathers' condition, thanks to politics.

The social restratification process induced by colonization is continuing today, a quarter of a century after independence, but the social reproduction processes are not yet fully at work on the level of political elites. The vast majority of Ivorians are made of people with modest backgrounds, most of the elite share these same origins, and were chosen as socially representative

TABLE 3 Father's Profession of Ivorian Elite 1959–1980

Father's Profession	Ministers	Deputies	Economic & Social Councillers	PDCI Politburo Members
Farmers	71.25%	77.0%	75.25%	64.1%
Artisans & Traders	19.10	19.0	17.90	24.3
Traditional Chiefs	1.30	1.5	2.25	5.1
Clerks	1.30	—	1.10	1.2
Civil Servants	6.80	2.5	3.30	3.80

during the competitive period of selection. With the end of that period these men really became *the president's men* because they know who knighted them.

None of the leaders were ever representative of any region or ethnic group. Inspired by General deGaulle's policy to never name a party leader as prime minister, Houphouet-Boigny always made sure that those who entered the political elite were not well known—and sometimes totally unknown— within their own region. (Houphouet-Boigny in *Jeune Afrique* 1048:29; *Paris Match* 1629). These men had then to become recognized by their home districts, just as the Fifth Republic Prime Ministers had to work to become leaders of the majority. However, they often did not succeed, as the November 1980 elections demonstrated when only 80 of the 120 incumbents ran again and only 28 were reelected. Thus, these men of modest origins, unknown in their regions, owed everything to the one who gave them power. The return to semicompetitive elections in 1980 means for them the loss of prestige and power to which they had grown accustomed. However, if the independence elite were not the ethnic leaders of the colonial period, they did have similar professional activities to the pre-1960 elite.

The Symbols of Economic and Social Success

The post-1960 Ivorian political elite is numerically larger than the pre-1960 elite. 236 people shared power from 1960 to 1980, compared to 84 in the previous period. This new elite of "good students" is divisible into two generations but, is primarily an elite of civil servants closed to women.

"The best and the brightest"

Post-1960 Ivory Coast could be called "the Republic of good students." (Table 4). Among 320 leaders, half went to a University and another 40 percent have high school diplomas, while only one seems to never have gotten beyond primary school. In the government, the percentage of university graduates is higher (68.4 percent), and in the National Assembly, the proportion is lower (40 percent); the Politburo and the Social and Economic Council have about the same proportions as the total elite 49.4 percent university and 38.2 percent high school graduates). The updating from the previous period is quite clear. The old elite was composed of the best of William Ponty School's graduates. Today, with university education available, its graduates are the core of the elite. Even the changes of 1980 changed little in this regard, since 64.5 percent of the new elite were university graduates. The differences between two generations of leaders representing two different levels of education created conflicts and complexes, largely unjustified, and eventually, a crisis in 1963–1966, as we shall see below (Baulin 1980; Zolberg 1975).

TABLE 4 Education of Ivorian Elite 1959–1980

	Total (%)	Ministers	Deputies	Economic & Social Councillers	PDCI Politburo Members
Primary	1	—	—	1	—
	(0.3)			(1.1)	
Secondary	134	22	96	34	31
	(41.8)	(30.1)	(48.0)	(38.2)	(40.25)
Higher	157	50	81	44	47
	(49.0)	(68.4)	(40.5)	(49.4)	(54.50)

Unlike France or the United States, the scientists—not the lawyers—govern the country. They are 36.8 percent of the total elite (43.8 percent of the Cabinet and the Economic and Social Council, 34 percent of the Assembly, and 32.4 percent of the Politburo), compared with 15 percent lawyers (21.9 percent, 14.3 percent, 10.5 percent and 27.2 percent, respectively); students in humanities are third with 4.6 percent of the total (13.6 percent, 2.2 percent, 3.5 percent and 6.4 percent, respectively), and the economists are last with 3.1 percent of the total (5.4 percent, 2.3 percent, 1.5 percent and 3.8 percent, respectively). In the previous period, doctors and pharmacists were predominant, whereas today the needs of development call for scientists and technicians (and perhaps also there is a general suspicion of lawyers and literary types with a penchant for discourse and debate, if not dispute).

Political Generations and the Exercise of Power

Since the number of incumbents in 1960 was so small (a quarter of the total by 1980), and waves of new university graduates entered the elite thereafter, a generational analysis is called for (Table 5). Six age groups can be identified on the basis of birth date between 1895 and 1949:

The children of precolonial societies, born before 1905.
The children of colonial conquest, born in 1905 to 1919.
The children of colonial peace, born in 1920-1934.
The children of World War II, born in 1934 to 1940.
The children of the independence struggle, born in 1940 to 1956.
The children of Independence, born after the 1956 *loi-cadre.*

Uncontested Domination of the 1920-1934 Generation. Half of the elite were Children of the Colonial Peace, between 26 and 40 years old on

TABLE 5 Elite Generations—1945–1980

Year of Birth	Number of Elite	Percent
Before 1905	7	2.10
1905–1919	79	24.75
1920–1934	158	49.50
1934–1940	37	17.90
After 1940	18	5.60

Independence Day. Another quarter (including Houphouet-Boigny) were Children of the Colonial Conquest, between 41 and 55. By 1980, the leaders born before 1905 had disappeared, and the Children of Conquest dropped to 7 percent. Children of the Colonial Peace now constitute 63 percent of the elite, Children of the Struggle for Independence 30 percent, and a Child of Independence has entered the government.

Clarifying the Relation of Forces within the Elite. At the end of the activist period of the PDCI in the early 1950s, the first university graduates began to enter in number. Expecting to replace their elders, they based their claim to govern on their higher level of education, and they accused their elders of treason through collaboration with the French. The elders instead looked to cooperation under their leadership and without ideological dispute. The issue of their integration into the political elite quickly turned into a generational conflict, which ended with the brutal crisis of 1963. By "discovering subversive actions" the "elders" managed to arrest and emprison many "youngsters." The former, better entrenched in the politics and economics of the country and ready to collaborate with the "moderns," decided the ideological issue of collaboration that surrounded this conflict. Thereafter, the "moderns" or the "youngsters" could gradually return to the elite, in the later half of the 1960s.

Unequal Access to Power. The first decade after independence was marked by the presence of older men to the most important bodies—the government and the political bureau (Table 6a). Between 1960 and 1970, the Political Bureau was an assembly of "senators", partly as a normal reward to the elders who had struggled and suffered for their country's liberation, and partly because of an absence of politically "safe" young leaders and because of the distrust the young graduates provoked among their elders.

The regime opened up with the arrival in January 1966 of five new leaders: Konan Bedie, Mohammed Diawara, Abdoulaye Sawadogo, Bissouma Tape, and Assouan Usher. In the 1970s, the number of younger

TABLE 6a Elite Generations 1960–1970

Institutions									
Year of Birth	*Government*		*National Assembly*		*Economic & Social Council*		*Political Bureau*		*Total*
	No.	*%*	*No.*	*%*	*No.*	*%*	*No.*	*%*	
Before 1905	—	—	2	4.0	—	—	1	3.25	3
1905–1919	13	44.8	14	28.0	16	35.50	20	64.50	63
1920–1934	16	55.1	30	60.0	27	60.00	10	32.25	83
1934–1940	—	—	4	8.0	2	4.40	—	—	6
Total	29	100.0	50	100.0	45	100.00	31	100.00	155

people grew in every institution (Table 6b). In the government and the Assembly, nearly all members were born after 1920 (compared with 55 percent and 60 percent the previous decade); one minister and 11 deputies were born after 1940. In the Economic and Social Council and the Politburo, the pre-1920 generation was larger—a fifth and an eighth—and the post-1934 generation represents 15 percent and 22 percent. Thus, the Children of the Conquest, dominant among the pre-independence elite, gave way to the Children of Colonial Peace in the 1960s and to the Children of World War II and the Independence Struggle after 1970, a rather rapid generational shift occasioned by the sudden access to elite positions opened by independence.

An Average Age Rather High.   Yet, throughout these periods, the average age remains about the same. The youngest Ivorian to find access to a ruling post is Martin Kouakou N'guessan, who was elected a member of Parliament at age 23. The eldest are Mamadou Kone and Moustapha Soumahoro, elected to Parliament in 1965 at the age of 67. Although the political discourse (especially in the IV Party Congress of 1965) has tended to present Ivorian leaders as young, the reality is quite different. The average age of the ministers is 42; the age of the consellors is 43; the members of Parliament are 44 on the average; and the members of the Political Bureau are 47. In comparison, the 1975 general census showed the Ivorian population to be very young; over half is under eighteen, 40 percent are 15 to 39 and people in their forties make up only 0.075 percent of the population.

Ministerial careers start at 39 and in the National Assembly at 40. It takes two to three more years to enter the Economic and Social Council or the Political Bureau. The renewal of the political elite in 1980-1981 did not bring any change; 67 percent of the new members were between 35 and 50 upon entry into the elite, despite official claims in the VII Party Congress of a massive arrival of young blood. To the contrary, the average age increased. Among the 14 new members of government only three are less than 40 (two state secretaries Ehui and Laubouet, and one minister Lohourignon Zagote). The two state secretaries are alone among the six new members of the Politburo to be under 40. Eighteen of the 112 new deputies are under 40, including three under 30; the youngest is Djah Koffi, 24, from Yamoussoukro. In general, the new generation does not enter the elite any earlier in life than did those whom they call "the old men."

This distortion between official discourse and reality may be explained by the Ivorian or African perception of the "young" and the "old," the latter always considering the former as "a child," according to a "young" leader. But this discourse also tends to calm the zeal of a number and active part of the population who might otherwise make claims on elite membership. Because political careers are long in Ivory Coast and some members quite

TABLE 6b Elite Generations 1970–1980

Institutions

Year of Birth	*Government* No.	%	*National Assembly* No.	%	*Economic & Social Council* No.	%	*Political Bureau* No.	%	Total
Before 1905	—	—	—	—	—	—	1	2.1	1
1905–1919	1	2.9	3	4.4	9	20.4	6	12.8	19
1920–1934	13	38.2	31	45.5	20	45.5	29	61.8	93
1934–1940	19	56.0	23	34.0	15	15.0	10	21.0	80
After 1940	1	2.9	11	16.1	—	—	1	2.1	13
Total	34	100.0	68	100.0	44	100.0	47	100.0	206

venerable—Houphouet-Boigny is 78 or more, Auguste Denise 77—elites circulate only slowly.

An Exceptional Political Longevity. Already in 1945-1959, it was clear that Ivorian leaders had a tendency to stay in office for a long time. Fifty of the 84 persons who made up the elite during this period reappeared after 1960. Very often only death would end their careers (like American Supreme Court Justices, it was not always true that they "rarely died and never resigned").

Since 1945, Houphouet-Boigny has occupied all political positions, from municipal counselor to President of the Republic. Auguste Denise, another example of political permanence, has occupied a ministerial post since May 1957. There two cases are not unusual. A governments' duration is, on average, one year 11 months and 16 days, for the thirteen governments that have been formed between 1957 and 1981. But ministers stay in office, on average, for seven years and six months (compared to the French average, between 1958 and 1974, of 3 years and 6 months). More than a quarter of ministers have stayed in power for over 10 years and a twelfth for over 16 years. Denise is the longest, and Amadou Thiam, Information Minister for six months and 26 days in1963 (but then again since February 16, 1978) the shortest.

A member of Parliament is elected for a five year term (with some shorter exceptions between 1957 and 1959 as Ivory Coast moved toward independence). But the average deputy has served for eleven years, more than a fifth (21.5 percent) for 15 years, and 27 (13.5 percent) more than 20 years. The record—over a quarter century—is held by Sounkalo Djibo (29 years), Vame Doumouya, Lamine Fadiga and Philippe Yacé. The Economic and Social Councillors, chosen for five year terms, average seven years but 22.4 percent served for 15 to 20 years and eight have been members since the Council's creation in 1961. On the Politburo, terms are also five years but memberships average twice that figure, a quarter of the members serving two to three terms, another quarter three to four terms, and seven members more than 20 years. The records of longevity are held by Houphouet-Boigny, Auguste Denise, First Secretary from 1946 to 1959, Mamadou Coulibaly, Treasurer from 1959 to 1980, and Mathieu Ekra.

The stability of the ruling elite is a reflection of the general political stability of the country. This political stability allows this country to create the necessary conditions for its development, as Ivorian economic performance shows (Amin 1967, den Tuinder 1978). But there is also a link between leaders' stability and their own economic and social advantages. These men are veritable notables, whose economic base is above all the state that they control. Catapulted by a university diploma from regional anonymity and modest social origins to the controlling posts of the country, the elite are a model of social and economic success.

TABLE 7 Professions of the Political Elite 1957–1980

Professional Categories	Numbers	Percent
Public Sector	241	75.3
Higher civil servants	116	36.2
Middle civil servants (professors, teachers, doctors, nurses, midwives, agents, etc.)	125	39.0
Private Sector	79	24.6
Planters	14	4.3
Traders	8	2.5
Businessmen	5	1.5
Management	15	4.6
Liberal Professions (lawyers, pharmacists, doctors)	23	7.1
Clerks, wage earners	13	4.3
Unknown	1	0.3
Total	320	100.0

A Civil Servant Republic

Ivory Coast between 1945 and 1960 was not led by a bourgeoisie of plantation owners as most descriptions indicate (Gastellu and Affou Yapi in Faure and Medard 1978). It was rather a republic of civil servants.

Table 7 shows the heavily represented socio-professional categories: middle (39 percent) and high ranking (36 percent) civil servants, liberal profession (7 percent), and plantation owners and shopowners (7 percent) and private businesses (6 percent). Over three-quarters of private sector employees were civil servants before entering private life. The disproportion between the public and private sector is enormous: 83.5 percent compared to 13.6 percent, in the government; 65.4 percent versus 34 percent in the National Assembly; 57.6 percent versus 41.9 percent in the Economic Council, and 75.5 percent versus 24.3 percent in the Political Bureau. As in France, civil servants have always dominated Ivory Coast's political, economic and social life, even though they were only 2.2 percent of the total population in 1975.

From 1945 to 1959, restrictions on universal suffrage narrowed the electorate, essentially to those with education and economic success. Their representatives reflected these characteristics, and the introduction of universal suffrage in 1958 coincided with the end of electoral competition and the PDCI control of the selection of the candidates and of representation. The Ivorians never really expressed their electoral choice between 1959 and 1980. Once elected, the new strata of elites created under the colonization imposed their leadership on society. The continuity is clear: the ruling group has always been made up of the symbols of economic success and education. In 1945–1959, the public health official, teacher, civil servant, and clerk were the top positions open to Ivorians, who then became elected officials; after 1960, it was the doctor, professor, ministerial official, and businessman but also the engineer and lawyer.

The semicompetitive elections of 1980 did not break this mold. Among the 601 candidates, 99 percent came from the same socio-economic stratum. Among the elected members of Parliament, 67 percent come from the public sector and 32 percent the private sector, but the latter began their lives in government service. The new elite maintained its monopoly of leadership and representation.

Houphouet-Boigny also placed the members of the same social strata in the appointed positions. When the VII Congress of the PDCI ended on October 1, 1980, there were 29 members (88 percent) from the public sector in the Political Bureau and four from the private sector. There are 35 civil servants (95 percent) and two from the private sector in the government. Three-quarters of the 85 members of the Economic & Social Council come from the public sector.

This continuity reflects the preindependence principle of "government by the best." Without an organization of their own, without any leader in whom they could recognize themselves, those excluded from power between 1945 and 1960 came to convince themselves that they were really incapable of leading the country. To be sure, the situation is more complex and there are multiple relations between leaders and the led. Yet, the 1980 elections, above all, meant the legitimization of the present elite in power.

One new group has nonetheless begun to appear within the elite. Military officials were appointed to government in July 1974—a naval officer as State Secretary for the Navy and a gendarmery officer as State Secretary for Domestic Security, both promoted to ministerial rank in March 1976. These appointments occurred after what was incorrectly called "a military coup attempt" in June 1973 (*Fraternite Matin*, 13 June 1980), and were accompanied by the integration of many military personnel into the Administration. The government decided to avoid the contagion of surrounding military regimes by integrating the military more closely into the state rather than by isolating them.

A Male Chauvinist Republic

There are 19 women (5.9 percent) among the 320 elite members in a population that is 48 percent female, many of whom were active in the struggle for independence (Piat 1981, Diabate 1975a; Monnet 1976). There were no women in the elite prior to 1960 and their appearance thereafter has been seen as a major political event. In September 1965, 10 women first entered the PDCI Executive Committee, an organ with no real political role but the only body with any significant feminine membership. Their number rose to 41 (20 percent) in 1975 and dropped back to 10 (10 percent) in 1980.

Two months after the first postindependence PDCI Congress, three women (3.5 percent) were elected to the National Assembly: Mrs. Gladys Anoma, daughter-in-law of one of the earliest political leaders, Joseph Anoma; Mrs. Hortense Aka Anghui, wife of a politician and daughter of a founding member of the S.A.A., Gabriel B. Dadie; and Mrs. Jeanne Gervais, then Vice President of the Ivorian Women's Association (AFI). The number of women in Parliament increased only in 1975, when eight more women joined (9.1 percent). Gladys Anoma and Jeanne Gervais entered the Political Bureau in the same year and were reappointed in 1980. Mrs. Gervais became the first and only woman minister, not surprisingly, for Women's Affairs, in March 1976 at the age of 54. The Economic and Social Council accepted women in 1965; the three women members (8.3 percent) increased in 1970 to four (9 percent), 1975 to eight (11 percent) and in 1982 to nine (10.5 percent).

Like most of the men, Ivorian political women are of modest origins and come from the south. There are 14 Akan, three Kru, one South Mande, and one Voltaic. Outside of a few militants in their own right, like Mrs. Gneba, Raggi, and Sacoum, most of them are wives, daughters or otherwise relatives of well-known political men.

Compared to their men, their level of education is lower: only eight are university graduates, the rest from secondary school or lower. Another difference is their relatively higher age. The youngest elite member, Mrs. Marthe Achy Brou, entered Parliament at the age of 26 in 1975 and the eldest, Mrs. Anne-Marie Raggi, entered the Economic and Social Council at 57 the same year. Curiously, it is in the latter body, known as the fief of the technocrats and the elders, that the women with the lowest levels of education are found and that the two members under 40 were both women (Mrs. Alexise Gogoua, 37, and Mrs. Marguerite David N'guessan, 38, in 1965).

The 1980 reshuffling did not prove better for women. There are still only two women in the Political Bureau and one in government, but only eight (5.4 percent) in the Assembly, and 9 (10.5 percent) in the Economic and Social Council, a setback compared to previous bodies with 11 (7.1 percent) and eight (11.4 percent), respectively.

Sociological factors not limited to Ivory Coast or developing countries explain this underrepresentation. Oddly enough, the Muslim north (Dabakala–Bassawa), where social barriers are heavier, elected a woman,

Mrs. Assana Sangare nee Ouattara, in 1975 and reelected her in the first round of 1980.

A Generalized System of Cooptation

The January 2, 1956 elections for the French National Assembly were the last fully competitive elections Ivory Coast held (Vignaud 1956). The March 1957 elections for the Territorial Assembly and the April 1959 elections for the Ivorian Legislative Assembly marked a partially competitive transition to 20 years without choice, beginning with the November 1960 election for the Presidency and the National Assembly.

"Elections unlike the Others". In April 1959, the electoral system of a national and a complete slate of candidates with no cross-balloting and no stating of preferences was established (Hermet, Rouquie and Linz 1978). One needed only to be a candidate on the PDCI's slate to be elected. Election was a mere formality. From 1960 to 1975 the number of candidates equalled the number of seats available. Primaries held were within the party subsections to choose three candidates, ranked by votes received, but the final decision was always Abidjan's. Even candidates rejected by their subsections were put back on the lists. Elections became a system of cooptation. Perhaps studies in political sociology will find some meaning to these elections, where the turnout was always nearly 100 percent in a part of the world where abstention is a tradition, as the 1980 elections showed. The selection process thus became a matter of relations between the candidate and the top political leaders, not between candidate and electorate, on the basis of new criteria.

New Loyalties. During previous periods, when the PDCI was building its monopolistic position, its leaders negotiated with the opposition for their support. In turn, the leaders of different parties and associations obtained political posts, breaking the bargain when their interests were not served. As the PDCI grew in power, solidified its position, and lost its position of supplicant, the few remaining "opponents" or "dissenters" had no other choice but to join the PDCI or retire early.

Today, ethnic or regional representativity, college degrees, or even past political activities are not enough to land a political post. What matters today is fidelity, loyalty, and attachment to PDCI ideals and to its principal and prestigious leader, Houphouet-Boigny. He and his team make and unmake the leaders according to unwritten rules. These criteria apply to the nominations for election, and appointments to the Economic and Social Council and the Government of the President, or to the party Political Bureau and Executive Committee by Philippe Yace, Party General

Secretary until 1980. Today, Houphouet-Boigny himself controls all the lists.

The new criteria, at least, lessened other competing loyalties, such as ethnic or tribal ties. There was a new feeling around Houphouet-Boigny; a feeling of belonging to a new community which transcended old groups. But this feeling went too far. The elite members would feel so indebted to the one who had knighted them that many forgot their real source of authority, the voters.

To be sure, this practice of promising rewards to faithful supporters is not new, even in Ivory Coast. It started in 1946–1947 with the promise to some opponents of seats on the Grand Council of French West Africa and at the Council of the Republic in exchange for their support of the PDCI–RDA. There was also an attempt to have noncompetitive elections as far back as the first elections of 1945 with the "African Bloc".

The real change came in 1980 with the replacement of the single national slate with semicompetitive elections within the single party system. Yet, this procedural change still leaves the substantial characteristics of Ivorian political elite unaltered. The politicians have the same origins and come from the same socioprofessional milieux (the civil servants) as their predecessors. As always, some regions are overrepresented and others are under-represented. The average age has not changed, nor do the newcomers have earlier access to political careers. To be sure, they are better educated; most have college degrees. However, the elite has always been also an elite of education, and they have kept up with the expanded education system. The entrance of women and the military to the elite is a novelty but rather limited in number. All in all, the elite's social composition is an essential fact. The ruling group has become "petrified" and reproduced, consolidated rather than transformed, confirmed in the form it had before independence. The PDCI's strategy has been to extend itself to rival socio-political organizations and coopt them, as it does to the university, then the women, then the military. The Ivorian political elite shaped itself from 1945 to 1960, and transformed itself into a ruling class from 1960 to 1980. In 1980 it undertook a large scale process of social reproduction already noticeable in the educational system (Clignet & Foster 1966). These elections are only the beginning, although already they mark the political entry of children of the elite, such as Marie-Christine Bocoum and Gilles Laubhouet.

The elections came at the right moment. The 1960–1980 period was one of economic expansion and graduates' full-employment. But by the end of the seventies, the effects of the world economic crisis and of some managerial mistakes began to be felt. The full employment of the new college graduates could no longer be assured. "Free and democratic" elections appeared to be the best method to choose among the overproduction of aspirants to power. The ruling social groups have had twenty years to establish themselves and become veritable notables. They passed the test of the elections successfully, with a margin of security the first time since the elections were only semicompetitive, but the elections allowed them to legitimate democratically their domination.

The same year, 1980, the head of state announced that he would officially start the process of succession to the Presidency of the Republic.

AFTER HOUPHOUET-BOIGNY, WHO?

The question of Houphouet-Boigny's succession rightly preoccupies Ivorians, neighboring African countries, and the West. More important than the means of succession or even than the man himself, is the impact of this succession on Ivory Coast politics.

The Ivorian Solution: Article 11 of the Constitution

As in Senegal and Cameroun, the procedure of Ivorian succession seems rather well established. Article 11 of the Constitution, as revised in 1975, states that in case of death or resignation of the President of the Republic, he will be replaced by the President of the National Assembly.

The dumping of the *dauphin*, Philippe Yacé, General Secretary of the PDCI and President of the National Assembly since 1959, took place during the reshuffling of the political class in 1980, and the order was brutally changed by a new version of Article 11, on November 25, 1980. The new provisions create an American-type Vice Presidency. In case of death, the President is to be replaced by a vice-president elected at the same time on the same ticket. But this change took place a month and a half after Houphouet-Boigny had been elected for his fifth five–year mandate. The President probably did not want to appoint anyone as he had just put aside his political heir. Yet, three years later the position remains open.

Unlike the American system, the President during his term is not allowed to choose a Vice President in case of vacancy. He will thus have to wait for the presidential elections of October 1985.

However, some of his countrymen and some western countries want Houphouet-Boigny to nominate a Vice President before 1985. An early resignation and elections seems improbable, especially since the Senegalese and Cameroonian presidents already chose part of that path. There would be nothing wrong with his acting like George Washington, whom Houphouet-Boigny admires, but in today's economic and social conditions, he views early retirement as an abdication of responsibility (*Jeune Afrique* 1048:30). Should he name a Vice President as Yace has suggested (*Fraternité Matin*,

27 November 1980), citing the case of Nixon, Agnew and Ford? This would mean a rather too liberal interpretation of Article 11.

If it were to be made, a vice-presidential appointment would be made as a political, not a juridical, act, some kind of dramatic gesture, similar to the transfer of the capital to Yamoussoukro voted by the Assembly in 1983. After many meetings of the Politburo, the name of a candidate could be announced. Or a respected national leader would publicly suggest the name of a candidate for Vice President, with Houphouet-Boigny's prior agreement. The most likely solution would be that Houphouet-Boigny would not stand again for election in 1985, leaving the place to a candidate nominated by the VIII Party Congress. The leadership shuffles of 1980 would be well in the past and the work of the Congress would allow a consensus to form about a single candidate.

Houphouet-Boigny's Heirs

Houphouet-Boigny has said that he will appoint no one, but that his successor should emerge from a team he is presently setting up. What team? The Executive Committee of 9 created in 1980 to assist the President is too small. The Political Bureau of 33 is more likely, but certainly the successor is among the 320 members of the present elite.

Many Ivorians stress the need to make a "good ethnic choice," saying that a "bad choice" could bring tribal war. Since political power means access to economic resources, the ethnic group which will obtain supreme responsibility will also obtain the means to enrich itself. Some think that a "compromise" candidate should be chosen, between the historically "dominating" groups and the "dominated." Neither Baoule of the Akan, Bete of the Kru, nor Senoufo of the Voltaics nor Manding; the successor should be Aboure or Alladian, for example, although they too belong to the Akan group.

The ethnic factor is not the only one in the choice of a successor. The age and education factors will also be important. How many generations and cohorts of "children" will be jumped to find a successor? For some analysts, an elder politician must be chosen in order to avoid the inevitable crisis of confidence stemming from the succession process, such as arap Moi as in Kenya. For others, a younger "technocrat" will be needed to face the economic crisis, as Abdou Diouf in Senegal. The ideal leader would be one with both these qualities: a "politician–technocrat." Since 1980, the country rumbles with rumors as it chews over the latest news and mulls over the proper mix of criteria.

The Favorites

Three Politicians. Auguste Denise, Baoule, 77 years old and in poor health, has been acting President whenever Houphouet-Boigny is absent. His credentials are the best after the president's.

Vangah Mathieu Ekra, Dan, 66, has an excellent background of service and a reputation for decisiveness. He would be a strong candidate.

Mamadou Coulibaly, Malinke, 73, never was minister but was everywhere else, from Political Bureau to the Economic and Social Council. He is the northerner who might arbitrate quarrels of the southerners.

Five Technocrats. Henri Konan Bedie, Baoule, 49, is President of the National Assembly, and was for 11 years the Minister of Economy and Finance. His name is linked with Ivory Coast's economic performance. He is the leading favorite but a Baoule like Houphouet-Boigny.

Jean Konan Banny, Baoule, 54, is Minister of Defense and one of the strong men of the nine member Executive Committee (not necessarily an advantage in the race). Another disadvantage is his Baoule origin and the fact that he is the nephew of the President.

Camille Alliali, Baoule, 57, was Minister of Foreign Affairs from 1963 to 1966 and has been Justice Minister since 1966. He is the other strong man of the Executive Committee.

Charles Banza Donwahi, Bété, 57 years old. He is the three term deputy from Soubre–Buyo after having been a Minister of Agriculture from 1959 to 1963. He is the nephew of one of the first nationalist leaders, with the further advantage of being from the southwest.

Gaston Ouassenan Kone, Tagouana, 44, has been Brigadier General since 1977, and entered government as a symbol of the integration process of the military. As a Minister of Domestic Security, he showed his tough conception of public order against striking students. He might be a transitory solution, if the succession process encounters problems.

The Outsiders

Three Politicians. Phillippe Yacé, Alladian, 63, has impressive credentials as Party and National Assembly leader, although he was never a Minister. Despite his removal in 1980 he is not a "has been." He still appears as an authoritarian politician, sometimes brutal and often feared, characteristics that may act as a positive factor. But his succession to the presidency might be an opportunity for revenge against his rival and successor as Assembly president, Konan Bedie.

Germain Coffi Gadeau, Baoule, 68, was several times Minister between 1961 and 1976. He is Grand Chancellor de l'Ordre National and might be a good compromise candidate because of high contacts with second generation members despite his Baoule origin.

Alphonse Boni, Agni, 74, is former candidate to the 1945 constituent Assembly, former Justice Minister and present Supreme Court president. He might also be a candidate of compromise and transition who could arbitrate ethnic conflict in the elite.

Five Technocrats. Paul Akoto-Yao, Baoulé, 45, was the Minister of National Education for more than 10 years. With his rapid promotions he is a model university graduate. His major handicap is his Baoule origin and some solid opposition, particularly from teachers and professors.

Maurice Sery Gnoleba, Bété, 48, Minister of Industry and Planning, is another case of a rapidly promoted civil servant. He is a member of the Executive Committee and is one of the leaders of the Kru–Bété group, which may be a strong advantage.

Denis Bra Kanon, Bété, 47, has been Minister of Agriculture since July 1977 and mayor of Daloa since 1980. His civil servant career is quite exemplary. His political role will be important in the coming negotiations as a spokesman for the Bété.

Lamine Fadika, Malinke, 41, is the youngest of all potential candidates. As a Navy officer, he was nominated Navy Minister in 1974. His advantages are his northern origins, his technical competence, and above all, his military position, if things turn difficult.

This catalogue of names is of course not authoritative. Like all politics, it is based on reputations and subjective appreciations. But less important than the name of the successor is that this man will be a representative of Ivory Coast's present elite, of this group which has been ruling the country since the mid-1940s.

Change in Continuity

Unless a military coup like Samuel K. Doe's or Jerry J. Rawlings' occurs, there should not be any sudden changes in policy.

Failure of Military and Socialist Regimes. Ivorian elites and masses are certain that military regimes have never worked and will not work. They only have to look around them to realize this. The same is true with socialist regimes, beginning with the oldest, Sekou Toure's Guinea next door. The only prosperous countries are the countries which did not have coups and which chose a liberal and cooperative economy, such as Gabon and Cameroon.

The sudden appearance of the military on the political scene is rather improbable. The military has been the object of a concerted integrative process within the state. Although this process only involves the superior officers, the material life of a sergeant or corporal is comfortable enough not to lead him to adventures. Ideological true believers also seem absent from the ranks. If a coup ever took place, Ivorians would quickly end support for a regime that led to queues in front of stores, as in neighboring Ghana. The Ivorians' attachment to a certain lifestyle, and quality of life is probably the best guarantee against any Marxist–socialist temptation, as in the sad experience of neighboring countries on all sides of Ivory Coast, and this judgement is shared by governors and governed alike.

Elite Unity and Political Consensus

The bases of elite unity are numerous: Social origin, socialization process and recruiting patterns, single power pattern under a single party, and the presence of the same chief executive for 25 years. All of these elements draw them closer. They studied together in Ivory Coast or abroad; they have the same lifestyle. They live together, relax together, visit each other, intermarry, and join the same professional associations. They also share the economic advantages which are a result of prolonged tenure in political positions.

There will be no succession war in Ivory Coast. There will be maneuvers and skirmishes, certainly: quarrels are unavoidable when ambitions are inflated. If the succession process takes place when Houphouet-Boigny is still alive, quarrels will not degenerate into wars, out of respect for him.

There is additionally a consensus around economic policy, since it provides the elite with advantages. The elite members will be quick to unite around the Chief of State if the group is threatened. Such reactions seem to not only be dictated by short term interests. An example is the April 1983 secondary teachers' strike. It was a difficult social conflict, two ministers left the government, and strong means (suspension of salaries, expulsion from government housing) were used to break the strike. The strikers expected these measures and were prepared for them, since they are customary. The amazing thing was the show of support for the President coming from all over the country. Marches and huge demonstrations in Abidjan took place (on April 28, 1983), reminiscent of the famous "meeting of fidelity" of September 28, 1963, and showing the seriousness of the situation.

Do the authors of these shows of support feel obliged to organize them? Are they afraid to lose their jobs? The short-term constraints are not sufficient explanation. There is a custom in Ivory Coast, dating back to the 1960s, of showing support for the president and condemning striking students or civil servants. Beyond or beneath this, there is the desire to show solidarity with the group, around its leader. The group will survive its leader. It will go on preserving its members' interests. The absence of an alternative organization prevents would-be dissidents from excluding themselves from the group that assures their interests.

> Ivory Coast, under the leadership of President Houphouet-Boigny, has an independent policy, providing it with stability and credit abroad. But after he is gone, will young people follow this policy . . . Will they feel the need to change for the simple pleasure of change? Will it be worth it to change a policy which has provided the population of this country with a standard of living which many African nations envy? A standard of living which gives Ivory Coast great respect and great prestige abroad?
>
> No, No, the young people in the PDCI who in turn will be the elders will not feel the need to change our practice of stability and continuity.

With these words, Ivorian Head of State wondered about the impact of his succession on policy. And with these words was he answered by Henri Konan Bedie, one of the favorites for the succession. It was in 1965, during the IV PDCI–RDA Congress.

NOTES

1. In fact 76 people have been ministers in that period. The number 73 as indicated does not take into account three French members of the Ivorian government: Jean Miller (1957–1959), Georges Monnet (1959–1961), Raphael Saller (1959–1965).

2. The number does not take into account the 19 Frenchmen who were members of the "Assemblee legislative" from 1959 to 1960. Since 1960 there were no French elected at the "Assemblee nationale."

3. "Union fraternelle des originaires de la Cote d'Ivoire" (U.F.O.C.I.), "Association pour la defense des interet des autochtones de la Cote d'Ivoire" (A.D.I.A.C.I.), "Union des originaires des six cercles de l'ouest" (U.O.C.O.C.I.), "Syndicat agricole africain" (S.A.A.); "Syndicat des Planteurs et Eleveurs africains" (S.P.E.A.).

3

URBAN POLICY
AND DEVELOPMENT STRATEGY*
Michael A. Cohen

Town Planning is total planning in this sense. Not only does it treat the community as a whole, but it affects and must take into account all social activities, customs, and interests. It aims at creating new physical environments which will actively foster the growth of new human societies. It must decide what these societies are to be like, and try to provide for all the major diversities which they ought to contain.

(Marshall, 1965, pp. 116–17)

INTRODUCTION

The role of cities and towns in the economic development and political life of Ivory Coast has been an interesting feature of the country's postindependence history (Cohen, 1974). The evolution of the colonial economy and administration from the immediate post-World War II period to the economic turbulence of the late 1970s and 1980s can be divided into several different stages characterized by important economic and political events and pressures. The growing importance of the urban sector in national development, particularly the role of the Abidjan metropolitan region, has resulted in increased attention to urban policy issues by the national government and in a number of major policy and institutional reforms. Many of these reforms represent significant changes in policy from earlier government positions during the 1960s and demonstrate the pragmatic,

*The views expressed in this article are solely those of the author and may not be quoted as representing the views of the World Bank or its affiliated organizations.

flexible approach to development policy that has been the hallmark of Ivory Coast since independence. This chapter will review this process of evolution and change within an historical framework and suggest that institutional change by itself will not necessarily resolve many of the economic, financial, and social problems facing the urban population. This perspective is supported by the urban experience of other African countries (Stren, 1978) and the growing recognition that national development strategy and the international economy can interact to create difficult obstacles to efficient and equitable development.

The historical evolution of urban Ivory Coast can be divided into the following major historical periods:

1. The Colonial Administration and Urban Policy: 1890s to 1960
2. Post-Independence Consolidation, 1960–1968
3. Dialogue and Experimentation, 1969–1980
4. Policy Reform and National Development Strategy, 1980–

Each of these periods is examined in this chapter, concluding with general observations about the likely direction of the urban sector in national development.

Colonial Administration and Urban Policy: 1890–1960

In contrast to other West African countries such as Nigeria or Mali, Ivory Coast did not have a settlement pattern with significant indigenous concentrations. The arrival of colonial explorers and later administrators in the 1890s involved the establishment of administrative outposts on the eastern coast, first in Grand Bassam and Bingerville, the latter named for the first colonial governor, to serve as communications centers to the metropole. The decision to build a rail link to the interior from the coast in 1903 led to the concentration of population in Abidjan, initially a small Ebrie village, and upcountry settlements along the railroad which later became Agboville, Dimbokro, Bouake, Katiola and Ferkessedougou. The process of colonial penetration through infrastructure, including roads, heavily influenced subsequent settlement patterns. As the agricultural potential of the territory was recognized from 1890 to the outbreak of World War II, large coffee, cocoa, and banana plantations were established in fertile areas in the southern, eastern, and central regions of the country. Cashcrop agricultural activity in turn led to the creation of new settlements of both Europeans and Africans to provide needed services. The country remained largely rural until independence when the establishment of African administrative and political authority provided new stimulus to urban growth.

At the city level, the colonial administration was concerned with the policies and principles implied in the patterns of spatial development. Urban planning was considered a strategic instrument for determining how European and African political, economic, and social relationships should evolve. This is demonstrated in the first plan for the town of Abidjan which was developed by the *Direction des Travaux Publics* in 1925. This plan was based on five principles which established a framework for urban policy which in many respects has endured since it was approved. These principles were:

1. the functional division of Abidjan for economic, administrative, residential purposes;
2. the separation of European and African residential districts;
3. the absence of bridges connecting European and African *quartiers*;
4. the movement of existing Ebrie villages to other locations;
5. dramatic differences in projected population densities and land use patterns in the respective neighborhoods.

These principles reflected the perceived permanence, discrimination, and economic purposes of colonial rule. The use of circular boulevards, squares with multiple exits, and other geometric patterns illustrate the influence of pre-World War II French urban planning practice.

The 1925 plan also had a number of important implications for social and economic life. Its projected densities and land use provisions suggested large differences in income, access to land, and relationships between residence and work place for Europeans and Africans, and later between income groups. The enduring physical character of the plan was reflected in the fact that Africans were not permitted to cross the bridge after dark between Treichville, the first African neighborhood, and the Plateau, the administrative center, up to 1960. The dramatic present differences in residential densities between Treichville and Cocody find their origins in this colonial conception of urban life, even though detailed planning of Cocody occurred in 1960.

Having established a framework for the growth of Abidjan, colonial authorities moved their capital to Abidjan from Bingerville in 1934. The city's locational advantages at the terminus of the railroad, the *Regie Abidjan-Niger,* the Ebrie Lagoon that provided an excellent site for a future port, and its natural beauty all justified this decision. Increasing attention to urban questions by the colonial administration, including Paris, occurred during the 1930s, leading in 1937 to the observation in one brochure issued by the *Commissariat du Gouvernment General* that the West African colony has "without doubt reached an urban stage" (*Urbanisme* 1969, p. 10). This was somewhat overstating the reality because the institutional framework for urban concentrations had not evolved since 1914 when Grand Bassam had been named a *commune mixte* by the Governor. Within the French municipal code, this meant that an appointed Mayor–Administrator was responsible for the administrative affairs of the jurisdiction, supported by an elected municipal council consisting at the time of Europeans. Further development of Abidjan and other centers during the 1930s had in any case slowed down during the Great Depression and the associated lack of public funds to finance further development exploitation of the territory. The fall of France in World War II and creation of the Vichy government also reduced the pace of colonial penetration and economic development.

One major result of the war was to expand contacts between Africans and Europe. Colonial education and later military service multiplied manyfold the number of Africans who had some appreciation of the political and economic opportunities that colonial rule denied them. Political mobilization in Ivory Coast occurred during the war years, with the creation of the *Syndicat Agricole Africain,* led by Felix Houphouet-Boigny, which was an association of African planters that sought to influence colonial agricultural policy in their favor. This essentially rural-based organization was complemented by the creation of the urban *Union Fraternelle des Originaires de la Cote d'Ivoire* that nominated a *Bloc Africain,* an electoral list of 18 Africans in the Abidjan municipal elections of 1945 (d'Aby 1951, pp. 47–50). This activity later became integrated into the political *Parti Democratique de la Cote D'Ivoire* (PDCI), which became the Ivory Coast branch of the *Rassemblement Democratique Africain.* The links that were established between rural and urban political groups at that time provided an important basis for understanding subsequent national policy affecting urban settlements, and Abidjan in particular.

Increased economic activity in the early 1950s was stimulated by the opening of the Vridi Canal in 1950, which permitted maritime freight to enter the protected inland Ebrie Lagoon and the port of Abidjan. Agricultural exports grew rapidly after the opening of the Canal and led to many new employment opportunities in Abidjan. The city's population grew from about 50,000 in 1945 to 127,000 by 1955. Renewed economic growth led to a plan for the development of Abidjan, which was approved in 1952. The Badani plan was based on the following principles:

1. the development of portuary and industrial zones;
2. specialization of the Plateau into commercial and administrative zones;
3. highways linked to the airport at Port Bouet;
4. extension of residential areas in Cocody, Treichville, Marcory, and Adjame.

Development of a planning framework was accompanied by the establishment of organizations intended to provide necessary urban services, including the creation of the *Societe Immobiliere et d'Habitat de la Cote d'Ivoire* (SIHCI) in 1952, which was financed largely by the French *Caisse*

Centrale de la France Outre-Mer, the predecessor of the *Caisse Centrale de Cooperation Economique* (CCCE). A second corporation, *Societé Urbanisme et de Construction de Cote d'Ivoire* (SUCCI) was created in 1959 and financed by the *Caisse de Depots.* Housing legislation in the post-World War II period evolved from occupancy permits (*permis d'habiter*), which had been established in 1909, into a system for provisional and permanent concession of urban land to individuals. The system was intended to provide incentives to investment in housing by improving the security of land tenure.

One of the most important parts of the institutional framework for urban development was the Municipal Reform Law, approved in November 1955, which made Grand Bassam, Abidjan, and Bouake all *communes de plein exercice,* municipalities which elected mayors and municipal councils, with the rights of tax assessment and collection, based on the French Municipal Law of 1884. This upgrading of the major towns had been preceded in 1953 by the designation of six upcountry towns as *communes mixtes,* with appointed 18 member municipal councils. These towns were Abengourou, Agboville, Daloa, Dimbokro, Gagnoa, and Man. Administrative reform was followed by political reform in June 1956 with the passage of the *Loi Cadre,* which permitted municipal elections in all *communes de plein exercice* and *communes mixtes,* the latter being renamed *communes de moyen exercice.* These elections were not, however, dominated by Africans; their purpose was to include Europeans on electoral lists for the position of municipal councilors. These municipal elections were the last local elections before 1980, a span of some 24 years in which local questions of urban development had been politically transformed into national issues to be resolved by national ministries. Urban issues, particularly those involving resource allocation, were important and included housing, infrastructure, land, and related services, and the policy and spatial frameworks for development.

Urban employment was another important area of colonial urban policy. Although most of the economic product of the colonial Ivory Coast was generated in agriculture, the creation of the port and the nascent industrial zone in Abidjan led to growing requirements for an urban labor force. Given the relatively lesser emphasis accorded to education by the French in Ivory Coast, compared to countries such as Dahomey and Togo, the colonial administration promoted the recruitment of foreign Africans into the country to perform skilled jobs, including the administrative sector. At the lower end of the employment ladder the colonial authorities established, with French businessmen, a system for the importation of labor from Upper Volta for construction and manual labor. The resulting patterns of employment, along with growing French presence in the colony, led to a situation where most urban jobs by the end of the 1950s were occupied by non-Ivorians. This led to xenophobic rioting in 1958 and the expulsion and repatriation of some

20,000 Africans. Violence in Abidjan led to similar events in upcountry towns such as Agboville, where local ethnic groups asserted their economic privileges on the urban scene. This pattern was repeated after independence and has resulted in a set of particularly difficult policy problems affecting urban services in the 1980s.

In summary, the colonial period as described above reflected a growing convergence of colonial administrative and economic policy as it affected urban centers. The emergence of municipal government first as an instrument of administrative control and later as a political arena created an institutional framework for urban development. Subsequent decisions to centralize the provision of urban services created significant financial and organizational dilemmas in the postindependence period. Tools such as zoning, taxation, and even the provision of specific services were all used to establish urban centers capable of supporting economic development that depended heavily on productive agricultural exports. In this context urban development investments were subsidized by public revenues in order to facilitate exports and to encourage continued foreign investment. In the financially constrained 1980s, urban centers have also become a locus for change.

Postindependence Consolidation: 1960–1969

The 1960s in Ivory Coast have often been referred to as *le miracle ivoirien.* The 1960s were a period of rapid economic growth in which agricultural production generated large revenues which were used to establish the physical and educational infrastructure for future development. The country deliberately did not sever its ties with France, but rather encouraged greater French involvement in the economy, both through direct private investment and through technical assistance that managed most public sector institutions. Skilled management was coupled with unskilled imported African labor to provide needed inputs to the economy. Sustained high growth rates during the 1960s attracted foreigners from all parts of West Africa and rural migrants to metropolitan Abidjan. By 1963 more than 160 different ethnic groups were represented in Abidjan, four times more than in Dakar and eight times more than in Freetown (Gibbal, 1968 pp. 65, 75).

The male–female ratio in the city in 1963 was 1.22, in contrast to Dakar 1.04, Brazzaville 1.06, or Accra 1.14. This balance suggests the attraction of job opportunities perceived throughout the region and the ability of Ivory Coast economy to generate incomes several times higher than those found in poorer neighboring states. During this period, the dynamism of Abidjan was consistently underestimated by demographers who projected that the city would reach 400,000 by 1980; a threshold that was attained by 1967. The city grew at roughly 10 percent growth compounded annually for 5 years, a 61 percent increase through the 1960s, more than doubling every five years.

Institutional Framework

Rapid growth generated problems that, in turn, emphasized the need for a framework for urban development. During the 1960s, many new specialized institutions were created to develop land, finance and construct housing, prepare technical studies, and formulate urban policy and planning regulations. In some cases they grew out of colonial institutions; in other cases they reflected recent French thinking about the delivery of urban services. Establishing new institutions, however, turned out to be easier than making them work effectively.

The Ministry of Construction and Town Planning was created in 1961 to regulate urban development through the preparation of urban plans, the formulation of zoning and other regulations, and through undertaking specific development schemes. A National Council for Town-Planning, Regional Development, and Architecture was created nine months later, with representation from all government ministries, to coordinate urban development policy and investments for the country as a whole, as well as for individual towns. This process of centralization was furthered by the establishment of the National Bureau for Technical Development Studies (BNETD) in 1964 and its urban department, the Urban Planning Office for the Abidjan Region (AURA) in 1968. The Bureau later became the leading technical agency in the government and the Office became responsible for the technical preparation of all studies. The centralization of technical expertise in urban development soon transformed local level issues into national level decisions. By the early 1970s, this process resulted in the creation of a single Ministry of Public Works, Transport, Construction, and Town-Planning, all under a single minister.

This trend was also extended to urban investments with the creation of the Housing Finance and Management Corporation (SOGEFIHA) to construct housing. This agency was intended to supplement the efforts of SIHCI and SUCCI that were to be combined in Ivorian Housing Construction and Management Corporation (SICOGI) in 1964. These agencies were to receive public revenues through the Office for the Support of Low Cost Housing (OSHE) which received tax revenues earmarked for low cost housing. All of these institutions operated at least in part under the supervision of the Ministry of Construction and Town-Planning and were the instruments of national policy. A subsequent addition to the institutional framework was the Land Development Corporation (SETU), which was an agency primarily responsible for providing urban infrastructure.

The centralization of urban institutions was coupled with the progressive weakening of municipal government during the 1960s. While the municipal reform and elections of 1956 had suggested that the urban arena would be a lively political stage, this perception was quickly squashed by the independent government and the PDCI that insisted on centralized single party government. Several indicators of weakening of urban government were: the refusal to hold elections to fill empty positions on municipal councils; the transfer of specific sources of municipal revenue from the municipal to national government; increasing control over municipal decisions by the Ministry of Interior; and establishment of a system of prefectures and sous-prefectures that placed centrally appointed administrative officials in charge of most local jurisdictions. The resulting weakening of municipal government is reflected by a statement by a municipal councilor in 1969 that "the Mayor (of Abidjan) is not free enough to do anything. He is like a child of 21 or 22 who is under the skirt of his mother" (Personal interview, December 10, 1969). When Felix Houphouet-Boigny was mayor in 1956 he had six assistant mayors. They increased to ten by 1960, but diminished to two by 1969. Expenditures, which would have increased municipal capacity to undertake new activities, were curtailed while police and security expenditures increased. One consequence of this process was the contracting of municipal services such as garbage collection and street cleaning to private enterprises in the city.

While the reasons for the weakening of local government in Ivory Coast are to be found in the politics of the period (Cohen, 1974) described below, it is important to note that this process was also occurring in other francophone African states (Cohen, 1980, pp. 415–424). The process of political and administrative consolidation immediately after independence led to growing concentration of power in national capitals and a reluctance to delegate authority to the municipal level. The francophone system of urban government, closely tied to the national Ministry of Interior, offered a convenient vehicle to control political activity at the local level and to assure that decisions concerning resource allocation were dominated by central political forces rather than local groups. This process, however, proved to be unresponsive to many urban problems that became evident by the mid-1970s.

During the 1960s the driving force behind centralization of urban government in Ivory Coast was political. A series of incidents during 1962–1963 led to Government allegations that a plot had been uncovered to overthrow the PDCI dominated government. These allegations led to the imprisonment of several major political leaders, many of whom had important power bases in urban centers, including Grand Bassam and Agboville. Threats to political control at the national level led to the tightening of party discipline and the perception that local political activity would be a destabilizing force in a new nation. The decision to "nationalize" the selection of political leaders through the five yearly PDCI Congress was ratified in 1965 and maintained until 1980.

Urban Policy

A second important aspect of urban development during the 1960s was the formulation and articulation of policy by the National PDCI government. In 1961, the Minister of Construction and Town-Planning, Kacou Aoulou, articulated the bridge in urban policy between the colonial and post-independence period:

> The Government is now concerned about building Treichville and Adjame in order to erase the memory of the so-called African quarters of Abidjan, as opposed to the European sectors. Equally, in the interior of the country, the Government sees to it that the sites are no longer divided into European and African districts. In fact, when one considers today the the composition of the population which lives on the "plateau" is a white district, nor to say that Treichville is a black district. This is why the Government concerns itself to see to it that, henceforth, in this independent republic, there is one same city for all. (Town-Planning and Rural Housing Modernization, p. 39).

The view of "one same city for all" proved to be more difficult in concrete terms, particularly as policy was developed on the standards of urban development. In 1962, Aoulou declared:

> This will be housing of quality. We do not wish to construct towns which must be "destroyed" in 5 or 6 years, from the point of view of volume, form, or materials; the effort of the government will try to obtain definite results (Kacou Aoulou 1962, p. 6, 2).

These views were epitomized in a slogan coined in May 1963, "Construct beautiful, big, and forever." (*Fraternite Hebdomadaire*, May 24, 1963). This perspective was based on the striking differences in neighborhoods in Abidjan, inspired by the 1925 plan, and the official perception that "modern" urban development meant that anything less than the most recent architecture, regardless of cost, was unacceptable. It was reinforced in a 1960 plan for Abidjan developed by a French consulting firm, SETAP, which included a proposal for a "Voie Triomphale" or grand boulevard crossing the city. This approach was termed "double or nothing" at the time by a skeptical French observer (Haeringer, 1969). Its physical manifestations were to be found in the construction of Hotel Ivoire, the Presidential Palace, a new bridge across the Ebrie Lagoon, and the design of many housing projects. Modern urban development was also a conscious effort to inspire foreign investors with spectacular achievements at their first port of call.

While the economic and financial objectives of this approach were important, the government was not oblivious to its social dimensions. President Houphouet-Boigny declared in 1965, at the PDCI Congress: "Our goal . . . is the elimination of all slums in Ivory Coast within a decade" (Cohen, 1974). In fact, that statement was taken at face value, resulting in an extensive use of the bulldozer in demolishing substandard housing. Between 1969 and 1973, about one-third of the housing stock of Abidjan was leveled by bulldozers in an effort to "eliminate slums." This approach did not address the question of generating new housing to replace the old. In a city that was adding about 100,000 persons per year for the decade of the 1965–1975, it was evident that removal of slums within the city limits could result in only one solution: extensive illegal housing outside those limits. This occurred in the northern suburb of Abobo-Gare, which grew from 20,000 to 200,000 from 1969 to 1980. Other areas such as illegal settlements in the Gonzagueville and Koumassi areas to the east of the city also grew rapidly, as refugees from the bulldozer were forced to seek shelter wherever they were not disturbed.

Another dimension of urban policy concerned the growing expatriate urban population. By 1970, half of the Abidjan population consisted of foreign Africans. Many landlords in neighborhoods such as Treichville and Adjame were Malians and Senegalese who had migrated to Ivory Coast in the late 1950s and early 1960s. Later migrations to secondary towns such as Bouake or Daloa also produced a pattern whereby most small enterprises were controlled by foreign Africans. This process was reflected in the allocation of business licenses during the first decade of independence. Desiring to attract foreign investment, including Lebanese, the Ivory Coast government encouraged commercial and industrial activity at all levels. By the late 1960s, however, many of the markets for services and small consumer durables had been taken over by non-Ivorian firms. This was also reflected in employment patterns, with few Ivorians being hired by foreign Africans. The consequences of these trends were seen dramatically with outbreaks of xenophobic violence in some towns and a tightening up of opportunities for foreign African employment. In some cases, foreigners were deliberately harassed by police to send the signal to foreign Africans that they had to leave to open opportunities for Ivorian nationals.

One important aspect of the multinational character of the urban population concerned the ownership of land. As the spatial area of cities and towns expanded, the Government became increasingly involved in the allocation of land for residential, commercial, and industrial purposes. This was a major source of political patronage, (Cohen, 1974 p. 44) but also an opportunity to limit foreign access to and ownership of urban land. By 1970, it was virtually impossible for foreigners, including Europeans, to own urban land. This presented a difficult policy problem in the 1970s when new housing involved the allocation of land to potential owners, many of whom were foreigners. The problem was also evident when it was proposed by the World Bank that tenure arrangements in squatter areas be regularized through the granting of property rights. Since many of the squatters were non-Ivorians, this approach would have allocated extensive amounts of land to foreigners, which was in conflict with official policy. As a result, the provision of infrastructure such as water supply, drainage, and improved roads in areas such as Abobo-Gare was delayed for more than five years.

Resource Allocation

A third feature of urban development during the 1960s was the heavily skewed pattern of resource allocation. Within the urban sector as a whole, Abidjan was heavily favored in relation to other towns. The standard and costs of infrastructure in the capital were comparable to those found in cities in developed countries. Public investment in the city was heavily subsidized, since the level of urban taxation was minimal. In contrast, upcountry towns were dependent on the political decision to grant them special allocations, usually as part of the rotating national Independence Day celebrations, when towns would receive major infrastructure and hotel investments. The only exception to this pattern were the home towns of the President and a few major political figures. Yamoussoukro, the President's birth place and official residence, received more than one-third of total urban investment outside the capital during the 1960s and 1970s. In March 1983 it was proclaimed the new national capital, a subject that is discussed later in this chapter.

In addition to the total level of subsidy devoted to urban investment, it is important to also identify major areas that benefitted (den Tuinder, 1978). The most obvious was housing, particularly the operations of SICOGI and SOGEFIHA. The SICOGI had received subsidized credit from the *Caisse Centrale de Cooperation Economique* since its refurbishing as SIHCI in the late 1950s. As a result it built modern apartment units and single family houses without the obligation of recovering costs. After these French credits disappeared in the mid-1970s, it continued to build the same type of units, although some effort was made to reduce costs. SOGEFIHA, on the other hand, received major public subsidies to amortize its debt from the time of its creation and was permitted to borrow extensively on external capital markets. Its costs and debts grew, while its rents remained stable during the 1960s and into the 1970s. Monthly rents were subsidized by up to 50 percent by the mid-1970s. This proved to be an important political instrument in building support among the Ivorian middle class, particularly civil servants, although its financial consequences for the economy became increasingly serious. Given the scarcity of funds available for the housing sector, public housing conformed to the "double or nothing" approach of the government.

A minority of households were fortunate to receive public housing, while the majority were obliged to live in housing lacking essential services.

Dialogue and Experimentation: 1969–1980

Despite the economic successes of Ivory Coast during the 1960s, many political pressures grew up within the single-party state. These were permitted to be articulated over several months starting in September 1969 and extending into January 1970, when a new government was formed by President Houphouet-Boigny. Public meetings were held at the Presidential Palace at which the President listened to the opinions of various groups such as public servants, unions, teachers, parents of school children, and other interest groups (Cohen, 1974). Many of the grievances expressed during this process focused on the quality of urban life, including its high cost, the scarcity of urban amenities, (particularly housing) and the lack of popular participation in decisions affecting urban development. While some of the demands reflected regional groups who felt excluded from modern development in Abidjan, it was noteworthy that in a largely rural country—with only a quarter of the population living in urban areas—most of the demands were expressed by urban interest groups. The urban policies of the 1960s had stimulated the creation of urban interest groups, in part because of their double or nothing character. One of the most unpopular targets of discontent was the then Minister of Construction and Town-Planning, who represented the urban policies of the Government.

In many respects the Dialogue was a watershed in Ivorian political life because it articulated a set of issues which dominated the next ten years. From an urban perspective, the 1970s were a period of discussion and experimentation, much of it unsuccessful, in addressing issues such as housing, urban services, and opportunities for employment. Despite the widespread perception that severe shortages of housing and services existed, the Government was unwilling to overcome many of its initial policy positions concerning standards. As a result, the gap between those receiving urban subsidies and those who did not grew significantly. Similarly, the dominance of Abidjan in the national economy became more pronounced as its economy and quality of life reached levels that other centers, not only in the country but in West Africa more generally, could never hope to reach. This section describes some of these issues and efforts at experimentation during the 1970s.

One of the issues that reflected many of the policy questions mentioned earlier concerned the possibility of public housing corporations financing service schemes as an alternative to complete housing. Such schemes involve the public provision of infrastructure such as water supply, drainage, roads, electricity, and social services; house construction becoming the responsibility of individual households. In the Ivorian context, a proposal was developed in the early 1970s for *lotissement d'équipement minimum* (LEM) that would have been essentially sites and services, with some construction of a sanitary core unit (water pipe, shower, and toilet). This program was discussed at length before it was finally accepted by the Government. SICOGI initiated such schemes in the late 1970s, with financial support from the CCCE. They represented a significant alternative in housing policy, given the prior order to "construct big, beautiful, and forever"; the program permitted some degree of architectural flexibility according to the preferences and financial capacity of individual households. Unfortunately, the LEMs have not yet become a major part of shelter policy, but they do represent an important experiment and option for the future.

A second related experiment concerned the improvement of neighborhoods lacking infrastructure. The rapid spatial extension of Abidjan and other towns outpaced the growth of infrastructure networks, particularly water and drainage. By the early 1970s the political costs of using the bulldozer in these neighborhoods had increased. In addition, there was some interest in increasing the density of existing older neighborhoods, such as Adjame, through filling in vacant land, in order to slow down the spatial extension of towns, particularly Abidjan. Spatial growth was accurately perceived as increasing transport and infrastructure costs. Proposals were made within this context for the improvement of neighborhoods in the capital, such as Abobo-Gare and Adjame, an older, centrally located neighborhood. A similar proposal was developed for the squatter area on the periphery of the new town of San Pedro, the Bardo. San Pedro is both a port town and a growth pole for the southwest region of the country. These proposals involved the introduction of infrastructure into deprived areas and the legalization of land tenure arrangements, with the expectation that these would serve as incentives to households to invest in improving the quality of their housing. The costs of infrastructure improvements would be recovered both directly from households in the areas, as well as from a city-wide urban development tax. These programs were finally accepted by the Government in October 1980 after earlier opposition and received financial support from the World Bank and USAID's Housing Guarantee Program. Works were completed by the end of 1983.

While the neighborhood improvement proposals seemed to respond to existing problems they nevertheless posed problems for the Government that either delayed their execution or rejected them totally, as was initially the case for Bardo. One of the first problems was the fact that households occupying land would be given secure tenure arrangements, regardless of nationality. This was initially unacceptable, given problems discussed earlier, because tenure was understood to mean freehold. This provision was subsequently modified to a long-term lease which did not imply ownership of urban land, but rather granted usage rights. A second issue was skepticism that infrastructure improvements would lead to housing investment. Earlier policy emphasized the modern quality of "acceptable" housing. The view of housing improvement as a progressive process over time differs sharply from official Ivorian views on the subject. Government officials feared that improving infrastructure would be legitimizing slums. This led to delays in approval of final engineering designs and construction contracts until 1980, after which infrastructure improvements were made in both Abobo-Gare, Port Bouet II and Adjame. Happily, these improvements have in fact been followed by housing investment, resulting in visible amelioration of the neighborhoods.

A related area of experimentation was in housing finance. Until 1975, very few Ivorian households benefitted from public mortgage financing for housing construction or improvements. At that time, the Government sanctioned the establishment of a "savings and loan" bank. This bank received technical assistance from USAID and was able to attract significant savings during its first two years of operation. In 1976, OSHE became the *Banque Nationale pour l'Epargne et le Credit (BNEC)*, which was to act as the major housing finance institution in the country. Its purpose was to attract savings in the U.S. model of savings and loan associations, receive government equity, and manage the Social Housing Fund of the Government. Potential borrowers who had previously tried to seek loans at the *Credit de la Cote d'Ivoire* were likely to receive more favorable treatment across the street on Rue des Banques in Abidjan. Despite growing financial pressure on the Ivorian economy from 1977 to 1980, BNEC was managed by an Ivorian banker who sought to expand his share of the mortgage market. As a state-owned institution, however, BNEC was to suffer the same fate as many other public enterprises in June 1980, when President Houphouet-Boigny abolished several dozen public enterprises, either absorbing them within the Government administration or selling them off to private shareholders, as was done with BNEC. BNEC's record had not been examined carefully and was unfortunately not considered on its own merits. A promising experiment to channel public housing finance was prematurely halted. Its future depends on the mobilization of long-term financial resources.

A fourth area of experimentation concerned the installation and application of an effective land registry system or cadastre and its implications for the assessment and collection of property taxes in Abidjan. As noted earlier, the population of the capital was undertaxed during the 1960s. Most services were provided on a highly subsidized basis. As financial pressures grew during the 1970s, the Ministries of Finance and Interior supported the development of a computerized numerical cadastre, which was installed by French technical assistance. This system permitted the registration of all plots of land in the city and was to be updated as part of the scale of all urban land. Important information such as the location, dimensions, value, and ownership of land was registered in easily retrievable form. This permitted a more systematic assessment of property taxes than existed or presently exists in any other African city. During the first year of operation, property tax revenues increased by about $2 million, well justifying the expense in installing the system. It also marked a significant improvement in the financial management of the city. Not to be lost, however, was an important political lesson that, with proper technical support, the Government did have the intention and ability to collect taxes, even from civil servants. This point was emphasized in 1979, when President Houphouet-Boigny declared that all civil servants who did not pay their back taxes would lose their jobs.

Another interesting experiment in urban management was the completion of a ten year development study for the Abidjan metropolitan region. In contrast to most urban planning studies the Government with financial and technical assistance from the World Bank carried out a study of investment priorities for the region which was based on the dynamics of growth. Given the rapid spatial growth of settlements and the demand for housing and infrastructure, a strategic investment plan was formulated for the 1980s. This contrasted sharply with classic urban plans because it included both economic and financial considerations in its formulation of development options. It also provided the first realistic planning framework for a city that had reached some 1.8 million persons by 1980.

While the experiments of the 1970s cannot be said to have dramatically changed the development path of Abidjan and secondary cities, they did demonstrate to the Government that alternatives existed to the policies of the 1960s. Rapid urban growth required policy adjustment and financially affordable technical solutions. Given inevitable conflicts between old and new ideas, between national decision-makers and expatriate technical assistants, and the dynamic political environment of the period the adjustment process was not straightforward. Major economic problems began to impinge on the "Ivorian miracle," as energy prices and world economic recession reduced the Government's margin for maneuver in macroeconomic policy and sectoral investments. While these pressures might suggest that decision-makers should seek cheaper, more modest solutions to the problems of urban growth, this was not evident in a country whose political stability had been based on ever increasing personal income and material goods. Even when continued rent subsidies were becoming impossible to justify financially, as in 1975, the Government refused to increase rents significantly, knowing that the political costs would be high.

This deferral of political costs proved to be an error because in the austerity conditions of the 1980s, the pressures have proven to be even more severe.

Policy Reform and National Development Strategy: 1980–

In many respects, the first two decades of independence were a period of growth and expansion in the Ivory Coast with few constraints. The combination of political stability and economic growth permitted a rapid transformation of an agricultural colony to a diversified national economy within a generation. Throughout this period the country was not forced to face hard choices like most other developing countries. The Government believed that the opportunity cost of its decisions was rather low because agricultural exports continued to fuel investment in other sectors. Even as the prices of coffee and cocoa dropped by the end of the 1970s, there was still the expectation that newly found petroleum would provide necessary funds to meet development expenditures. Indeed, "black gold" would usher the country into the 21st century richer than anyone imagined. By 1980, many new ideas for development expenditures were under consideration against a backdrop of expected future national wealth. This hope for the future tended to obscure difficulties in sectors such as housing, where foreign borrowing had placed strains on the national treasury. This contradiction had, in fact, been a continuing theme since independence: difficulties in a given period tended to be minimized by the expectation of future wealth. This expectation had been confirmed in many cases, with freezes of the coffee crop in Brazil, increasing the return on Ivorian coffee exports on numerous occasions. In the 1980s, however, several factors have come together to create what the Ivorians call *la conjoncture*, or outlook, which has dramatically revised their expectations for the future. This concluding section will review the likely consequences of these factors for the urban sector.

The major factors of *la conjoncture* are the following for the short term: decline in prices of agricultural exports, stability or even decline in petroleum prices, relatively high interest rates for external borrowing, and the coming due of earlier medium and long-term debt. Financially, these factors have placed great pressures on the foreign exchange reserves of the country, as its traditional sources of finance and particularly foreign exchange are not presently sufficient to meet short-term liquidity needs. This crisis has resulted in requests to the International Monetary Fund, the *Caisse Centrale de Cooperation Economique*, and the World Bank for urgent financial assistance. In addition, it has necessarily meant a slowdown if not prohibition on new investment projects in all sectors. The earlier promise of oil wealth has diminished both in terms of oil prices and likely production for export in the near future. The country, therefore, has finally faced its decade of development choices, where the opportunity costs of strategic decisions will be felt throughout the economy and polity, between sectors and constituencies, between town and countryside, and between the generations that have already materially benefitted from two decades of growth and those that have been educated at great cost but who now see few future opportunities for employment and income.

The impact of austerity policies in Ivory Coast will fall most heavily on urban areas. First, in order to sustain agriculture at a time of falling international prices, Government is seeking to reduce subsidies to urban consumers. This will mean rising urban food prices. Secondly, in order to reduce enormous subsidies in existing stock in the housing sector, Government will once again attempt to increase rents in SOGEFIHA and SICOGI units, mostly in Abidjan. Earlier increases in energy prices led to increased public bus fares in 1980. These moves towards higher consumer prices have been justified for more than a decade, but have not been considered as necessary as they now appear. Better financial and economic management of existing resource allocation will be a first step towards meeting short and medium term macrofinancial needs. New investments in these areas are likely to either be deferred or to result in shifts in approach towards less costly solutions in housing, infrastructure, and other services. While, as suggested earlier, these measures have been discussed and even subject to experimentation during the 1970s, their adoption on a larger scale has become essential in the constrained 1980s.

The combination of increased costs and dwindling resources for new investment will result in growing urban unemployment in Ivory Coast. Scarce employment opportunities will be heavily felt by young Ivorians, many of whom have graduated from the University of Abidjan, which has an enrollment of approximately 10,000 students. The Government has fully subsidized university education for almost two decades. It may now find that economic difficulties will be felt most sharply by the beneficiaries of past subsidies. As in earlier periods of unemployment, the Government may be forced to limit the entry of foreign Africans and even send some home, as Ghana and Nigeria have done on earlier occasions. Xenophobic violence, a frequent occurrence in Ivorian political life, is also likely, as national frustrations are taken out on available scapegoats. In the 1980s this will be particularly problematic because Ivory Coast has supported increasing West African regional cooperation, particularly among the francophone countries.

Tightening resources for investment will also affect the housing sector. It is likely that fewer publicly financed housing units will be constructed during the 1980s, thereby requiring a revised approach towards housing, such as the provision of serviced land rather than construction of completed housing units. A less likely alternative would be the complete withdrawal of the public sector from housing, providing only mortgage finance on unsubsidized terms. It is nonetheless evident that some of the policy and project experiments of the 1970s will have to be institutionalized during the 1980s. This would significantly change the position of Abidjan and of the urban sector in public finances, reducing massive subsidies and moving the sector towards a more financially self-sufficient basis.

All of the above is likely to occur in spite of shift of the national capital from Abidjan to Yamoussoukro, as adopted by the National Assembly in March 1983. Unlike such decisions elsewhere, Ivory Coast has implicitly prepared for this shift for almost two decades with the extensive public investments made in the President's home town. As a result, the country has already borne the heavy overhead cost of the new capital, which have without exception proven to be a serious financial burden in other countries. Since most of Yamoussoukro's investments took place in prosperous times, they are perhaps less likely to incur popular disaffection than was the case in Nigeria or Tanzania. Their long-term economic consequences, however, may be similar when considered from a thirty or forty year perspective.

The national political significance of this decision also deserves some attention. As in earlier periods, decisions about the location of population and the allocation of public resources have been at the heart of the political process in Ivory Coast. Having established Abidjan firmly as the commercial and financial capital of the country, it is quite reasonable to believe that the President sees the shift in the administrative capital to the locus of political power as a stabilizing long-term force. Such a decision may help to bridge the gap between ultramodern Abidjan and the rest of the country, bringing the political elite closer to its rural roots and thereby insuring that some measure of African culture will be retained in the development process. Its symbolism, inextricably bound to the President himself, may help to facilitate the succession of political power, a problem that had not resolved itself when the transfer decision was made.

Finally, perhaps the most significant decision affecting the urban sector in the future is the municipal reform of 1980. Responding to local political pressure and the need for greater local participation in local affairs, the President agreed to hold municipal elections in 1980. These elections, coupled with the first primary elections at the national level, were the first local elections since 1956. At the same time, it was decided to divide the Municipality of Abidjan into ten *communes*, each with local municipal councils. This decentralization was a major step towards a recognition of local control over certain local issues. Municipal decentralization also included local authority to assess and collect taxes. Given the relatively weak municipal finance situation of the city as a whole, it was not a surprise that the neighborhood-level *communes* were ill-prepared either to institute revenue-generation measures or to embark on a program of expenditures.

This situation resulted in a slowdown of the implementation of the municipal reform, which took several years to become operational.

The significance of this process is also political at several different levels. Not only does the reform permit local political activity, indeed require it, but it also led to a succession process in the office of the Mayor of Abidjan. The nomination of a politically important new mayor, one of the contenders for political leadership in the country, was an important indicator of the much improved status of that job. While the effective power of the mayor may have diminished a bit, given the financial difficulties facing the country, it is nonetheless correct that urban resource allocation decisions have been an important part of the strategy of Ivory Coast's political leadership. The reemergence of the city as a formal political arena also suggests that the social and economic significance of urbanization is recognized by the country's leaders. This recognition itself is an indicator of the evolution of development strategy. In Ivory Coast, it is also a promise of interesting responses to the challenges that lie ahead.

4

THE IVORIAN ECONOMY
AND ALTERNATIVE TRADE REGIMES*

Gilles Michel
Michel Noel

After two decades of continuous growth, the economy of Ivory Coast experienced a series of external shocks over the last six years: the coffee and cocoa boom in 1976 and 1977; a 40 percent decline in the terms of trade between 1978 and 1982; and sharp increases in international interest rates. These shocks have led to a rapid deterioration of the country's financial position and to two consecutive years of recession in 1981 and 1982.

These dramatic changes have affected Ivory Coast at a critical phase of its development. Since the mid-seventies, the growth potential of the country progressively weakened primarily because of low returns on public investment, inefficiencies in the management of public enterprises, and inadequate support for agricultural development. At the same time, the ability of the economy to adjust was hampered by rigidities and distortions in the system of macroeconomic and sectoral incentives, particularly with respect to the exchange rate, tariffs, quantitative restrictions, and export incentives.

In order to remedy this situation, the government has embarked on a stringent financial recovery and structural adjustment program that calls for substantial policy reforms, in particular in the system of incentives for industry and agriculture.

The purpose of this chapter is to analyze in a general equilibrium framework the short-term effects of various trade and related policies that

*This paper draws heavily upon a larger paper by the authors for the World Bank entitled "Short-Term Responses to Trade and Incentive Policies in the Ivory Coast," (1983b). We are indebted to Sherman Robinson for his continuous support and advice throughout this study. Valuable research assistance from B. Deloy and T. Condon is gratefully acknowledged. The views expressed in this paper are those of the authors and they should not be interpreted as reflecting those of the World Bank.

could be adopted within the framework of these programs. This is done through a series of comparative static simulations carried out with a computable general equilibrium (CGE) model of the Ivorian economy, which has been built along lines already followed in other developing countries (Dervis and Robinson 1982, World Bank, *Yugoslavia* 1982).

In Section 1, we present an overview of 'the Ivorian economy and discuss the most salient economic developments over the last six years. Section 2 is devoted to a general discussion of CGE models, and to a presentation of the specific features of the Ivory Coast model. Turning to policy simulations, an analysis of the flexible exchange rate experiments is presented in Section 3. Section 4 contains an analysis of the experiment on tariff and subsidy reforms. This policy issue is directly related to the reforms envisioned by the government in the framework of the structural adjustment program. In Section 5, we examine the impact of the removal of quantitative import restrictions on the economy, first under the flexible exchange rate regime, and then in conjunction with the implementation of a tariff-cum-subsidy scheme.

OVERVIEW OF THE IVORIAN ECONOMY

Structure of the Economy

In the first two decades following independence, Ivory Coast's GDP grew 7.5 percent annually, which is one of the fastest rates in Africa and among the top fifteen countries in the world. This record has been based on a rapidly growing agricultural sector (primarily coffee and cocoa), which generated surpluses for investment, and on liberal and pragmatic economic policies that combined domestic and foreign factors in productive uses. Out of a total population of 8.3 million, 1.5 million are immigrants who responded to employment opportunities in Ivory Coast and to the growing income differentials with its neighbors. With an annual growth of 4 percent per year (including 1.5 percent due to migration) per capita income increased 3.5 percent annually until the end of the 1970s. Although a severe slowdown has since occurred, Ivory Coast had a per capita GDP of $1,150 in 1980, ranking second among sub-Saharan developing countries (World Bank, 1982a). This compares with $1,010 for Nigeria, $670 for Cameroon and $650 for Senegal, and $4,400 for Gabon.

This impressive record has been achieved in a multifaceted economic system. The country has the features of a mixed economy, in which the public sector played a leading role in key areas (particularly in agriculture), and where private initiative has always been encouraged, especially in industry and commercial activities. The economy is also semi-industrialized.

It is still strongly based on agriculture but increasingly dependent on the expansion of the industrial sector for its future growth. Finally, the relatively open economy is heavily dependent on imports and a steady flow of foreign exchange, largely within the framework of several regional and nonregional monetary and customs arrangements.

Agriculture is a major component of the Ivorian economy and the basis of its development. It contributes one-third of GDP, provides around 50 percent of exports, and employs an estimated 75 percent of the labor force, of which 13 percent are immigrants (Fargues, 1981). Ivory Coast is the world's third largest exporter of coffee, and the most important producer of Robusta. It is also the world's largest producer and exporter of cocoa. There are two main agricultural regions in the country. The Southern Forest and the Northern Savannah have different climates, natural endowments, culture and income levels. Traditional cash crops (coffee, cocoa, palm oil and, more recently, rubber) grow in the rich Southern Forest. The more arid and much poorer North is the area of development of cotton and sugar production. Food crops are grown throughout the country.

Table 3 presents details of the structure of agricultural production in Ivory Coast. Food crops and cash crops contribute almost equally to nominal output and value added, while acreage appears to be primarily devoted to cash crops, especially coffee and cocoa. However, the acreage data should be regarded only as indicative because many plantations are

TABLE 1 Structure of the Ivorian Economy in Three Sectors (in 1980)

	Gross Output	Exports	Imports	Domestic Demand	Value Added (at factor prices)
Agriculture (inc. derived industries: sugar, rubber, palm oil)	23.3%	49.4%	5.1%	19.1%	33.1%
Industry (inc. energy, utilities, and construction)	43.1	28.4	78.2	47.8	29.1
Services (inc. transportation)	33.6	22.2	16.7	33.1	37.8
Total	100.0	100.0	100.0	100.0	100.0

Source: Ministere des Finances (1982).

TABLE 2 Structure of Trade (in 1980)

	Share of exports in production	Ratio of imports to domestic supply	Share of imported intermediate inputs in total int. inputs
Agriculture	3.5	39.0	22.6
Industry	30.6	15.4	33.0
Services	11.1	15.4	26.6

Source: Ministere des Finances (1982).

intercropped, and a large part of the area under food cultivation remains unaccounted for due to the absence of extension services for these crops, with the exception of rice.

Since the early 1960s, the government emphasized the development of cash crops through direct intervention in production, consisting of the provision of extension services by public enterprises or of market regulation. Cash crops under regulated prices include coffee, cocoa, cotton, and palm oil. Official producer prices are fixed at the beginning of each season for these products, and a Stabilization Fund (CSSPPA) makes up the difference between the domestic price and the price obtained in export markets. This mechanism provides producers with more stable incomes and it has also generated substantial surpluses for the government. Most coffee and cocoa production comes from smallholders, who typically benefit from the extension services of the Technical Assistance Society for the Agricultural Modernization of Ivory Coast (SATMACI), the regional development agency for the Center Zone. Cotton is produced almost exclusively by small farmers under the auspices of the Ivorian Company for Textile Development (CIDT), the regional development agency for the north, which provides extension services and controls the marketing of the crop. Seventy percent of palm oil originates from the industrial plantations of PALMINDUSTRIE, with village plantations accounting for the rest. Rubber culture is also dominated by public enterprises, and smallholders represent 8 percent of total acreage. Finally, the production of sugar is entirely controlled by SODESUCRE, which is running six sugar complexes in the north and the center of the country.

In the mid-seventies, the government started to give more priority to the development of food crops. However, the food crop sector has generally not experienced direct intervention by the public sector, in sharp contrast with the situation prevailing for most cash crops. The only exception is rice. Producer and consumer prices for rice are regulated through the *Caisse de Perequation,* and extension services are provided by regional development agencies.

TABLE 3 Structure of Agricultural Production

	Food crops	Cash crops	Coffee	Cocoa	Main Cash Crops Cotton	Rice	Source
Share in total cultivated acreage[1]	36%	64%	30%	21%	1%	8%	(1)
Share in the value of agricultural production	56	44	12	20	2	8	(2)
Share in total value added	15.8	13.1	3.6	6	.6	na	(3)
Share in agricultural value added[2]	54	46	12	20	20	2	(2)
Share in total exports[2]	—	36.3	15.1	17.6	—	—	(3)
Share in agricultural exports[2]	—	100	41.6	48.5	—	—	(3)

[1]The acreage is a theoretical one, defined in the RNA as the hectare equivalent in sole stands, as opposed to actual area in association with other crops.

[2]Excluding forestry.

Sources: (1) Recensement National de l'Agriculture (RNA) (1981). (2) Ministere des Finances (1982). (3) Social Accounting Matrix, in G. Michel and M. Noel (1983).

Public enterprises are not limited to the agricultural sector, but play a role in other key parts of the economy with the exception of industry. Although it favors a liberal type of economy, the Ivorian Government has always relied partly on public enterprises to implement its development policies, particularly in areas where private initiative remained inadequate. Public enterprises are important because of their contribution to national production and investment. It has been estimated that one-third of agricultural production is directly dependent on public enterprises. They are also involved in land transportation, shipping, services, construction and electricity. Overall, 15 to 20 percent of GDP can be attributed to parastatal enterprises in Ivory Coast.[1] The contribution of public enterprises to investment is even more important. According to the *Budgets Economiques* (Ministere des Finances, 1983), their share of total investment was 29 percent in 1980, 26 percent in 1981 and 22 percent in 1982, after having reached a peak of 37 percent in 1978. Table 4 gives the sectoral allocation of public enterprise investment in 1980.

A large part of these investments have been financed by foreign capital, which has been attracted by publicly guaranteed investment opportunities. As a result, public enterprises have been instrumental in opening the economy to foreign investors. Accordingly, they account today for 35 to 40 percent of the external public debt. Finally, since public enterprise investments are ultimately controlled at the government level, they represent an important policy variable for the government. With both public enterprise and central government investment, the government controlled as much as 70 percent of total investment in 1980.

Industry has been one of the most dynamic sectors in the Ivorian economy. Since independence, manufacturing activity has grown at the rate of 13 percent per year, and its share in GDP rose from 4 percent in 1960 to 14 percent in 1980. This rapid expansion has been primarily based on import substitution and on the processing of local agricultural raw materials for

TABLE 4 Sectoral Allocation of Public Enterprise Investment in 1980

Percent of Sectoral Allocation	
Agriculture	18.1
Mining-petroleum	29.3
Manufacturing industry	0.9
Utilities	17.7
Construction	5.7
Services	28.3
Total	100.0

Source: Ministere des Finances, 1983.

exports. Until the early 1970s, industrial development took place in the framework of a simple system of incentives, which was essentially based on a moderate tariff schedule that applied equal protection among industrial activities, without quantitative import restrictions. The 1973 tariff reform and, more recently, the proliferation of quantitative import restrictions have introduced increasing distortions in the industrial structure. As a result, inefficient import substituting enterprises have been established and a strong bias against exporting activities has appeared (Noel, 1982).

This sector developed without the direct involvement of public enterprises. Instead, it relied exclusively on private initiative, which was mainly foreign, especially in the first stages of industrialization. Foreign firms were attracted by the stable and liberal framework provided by the government as well as by the incentives provided under the Investment Code.

The manufacturing sector consists of two distinct types of activities: those which are based on the processing of local agricultural or forestry raw materials (food processing, textiles, and construction materials); and those which import raw materials intensively (chemicals and plastics and engineering industries). The former were leaders in the early industrialization process of Ivory Coast and are relatively export-oriented. For food processing and construction materials, imports are mainly goods that are not produced locally. In contrast, textiles directly compete with imports in the domestic market. The second type of industry is much less export-oriented, and relies heavily on imports for its operations (50 percent of intermediate inputs are imported). With the exception of fertilizers, these industries fall far short of satisfying domestic demand, as is shown by the ratio of imports to domestic supply. This is because local production is concentrated on specific product lines, and imports in these areas are essentially complementary to domestic production. Moreover, engineering industries alone represent more than a third of the imports of the country, and 60 percent of its total imports are manufactured goods.

Energy dependence is rapidly decreasing due to the development of hydroelectric production in the 1960s and 1970s and to the current expansion of the oil sector. Although the start of power production by several new dams in the late 1970s has not made Ivory Coast energy self-sufficient, the consumption of fuel oil needed to generate electricity has declined by 57.7 percent since 1979, as a result. The Soubré dam project, expected to become operational in the late 1980s, makes self-sufficiency a reasonable prospect. Moreover, petroleum production is increasing, and one-third of Ivorian consumption of crude oil was produced domestically in 1981. Although the projections were lowered recently, the outlook is still for Ivory Coast to become a net oil exporter by 1987. Finally, an oil refinery with a 4 million ton capacity already meets domestic requirements and also exports to neighboring Upper Volta and Mali.

TABLE 5 Structure of Manufacturing Industry

	Share in industrial GDP (in percent)	Share of total GDP	Share of exports in gross output	Share of total exports	Share of import in intermediate input	Share of total imports	Imports over domestic supply
Food processing	28.3%	3.9%	28.7%	10.1%	21.7%	8.8%	54.4%
Textiles	25.2	3.5	20.2	4.0	29.2	4.1	40.6
Chemicals	9.3	1.3	14.5	1.4	47.1	8.8	62.8
Construction material	15.5	2.1	32.5	3.7	26.7	2.7	54.1
Engineering industries	21.7	3.0	11.8	2.8	51.7	35.5	269.7
TOTAL	100.0	13.8	—	22.0	—	59.9	—

Source: Michel and Noel (1983).

Monetary arrangements for Ivory Coast play an important role in its development. The country is a member of the Monetary Union of West Africa (UMOA) with Benin, Niger, Senegal, Togo and Upper Volta, which centralizes foreign currency reserves, issues a single currency (the CFA Franc) through a common Central Bank, has a common interest rate structure and allows free transfers of funds within the Union. The CFAF is linked to the French Franc by a fixed exchange rate. It is fully convertible with the French Franc, and the French Treasury intervenes through a special "operations account" to maintain parity. Although this limits the countries' autonomous monetary policy and prevents the adoption of an independent exchange rate policy, convertibility with the French Franc and the backing of the French Treasury provide advantages, and on the whole the arrangement seems to have been beneficial for development.

Ivory Coast is also a member of the West Africa Economic Community (CEAO), a customs union with Mali, Mauritania, Niger, Senegal and Upper Volta. As a partner in the Lomé agreements, Ivory Coast receives duty-free treatment for its exports to the EEC. These external ties are reflected in the trade structure of Ivory Coast. Approximately half of the trade of the country is with the EEC, and 6 percent with the CEAO. Thus, more than half of its foreign trade is with countries with which Ivory Coast has special relationships and arrangements.

Recent Economic Developments and Policy Issues: 1976–1982

After the coffee and cocoa boom in 1976 and 1977, a series of external shocks produced a 40 percent decline in the terms of trade through the sharp drop in coffee and cocoa prices in 1978 and the subsequent increase in the price of imported oil, and then sharp increases in real interest rates on international financial markets. These shocks have led to rapid financial

TABLE 6 Structure of Trade in 1981

	Share of total exports	*Share of total imports*
EEC	54.7%	48.4%
of which France	(18.6)	(31.1)
Other European Countries	5.1	4.6
Sub-Saharan Africa	12.3	7.1
USA	11.5	5.4
Asia	2.9	7.7
Others	13.5	26.8
TOTAL	100.0	100.0

Source: Ministère de l'Economie et des Finances (1982).

deterioration, a severe slowdown in economic activity, and two consecutive years of recession in 1981 and 1982, in sharp contrast to the previous twenty–year economic growth.

During the coffee and cocoa boom of the mid-1970s, when world prices multipled by 3.6 and 2.2, respectively, between 1975 and 1977, large surpluses for the Stabilization Fund were generated and the balance of payments situation substantially improved. Under these favorable circumstances, the Government embarked on an ambitious investment program. The share of public investment in GDP increased from 15 to over 25 percent between 1976 and 1978. This program was also financed through external borrowing, which was possible because balance of payments pressures had declined. The share of investment financed by national savings thus fell from 50 percent to less than 20 percent between 1976 and 1978, while gross inflows of public capital increased from CFAF 56 billion to about CFAF 200 billion between 1975 and 1977. GDP grew by almost 10 percent in real terms in 1978.

However, between 1977 and 1978 coffee and cocoa prices declined by 31 percent and 10 percent, respectively, and remained constant at these low levels until the first half of 1980, while the public investment program was maintained at a level corresponding to 20 percent of GDP. This created several concerns. On the one hand, Ivory Coast's terms of trade declined by 15 percent between 1977 and 1978, mainly due to the decline of export prices and by an additional 17 percent between 1978 and 1980, due to sharp increases in import prices. On the other hand, the government increasingly relied on foreign borrowing to finance its investment program. As a result, a public sector deficit of around 10 percent of GDP appeared in 1979, rising to 13 percent in 1980, and the balance of payments turned negative in 1979. The abrupt decline in coffee and cocoa prices that started in the second half of 1980 further aggravated the situation. In 1980, the current account deficit represented 16 percent of GDP, and the net foreign assets of the Central Bank were exhausted, despite continued heavy borrowing abroad. Correspondingly, a CFAF 118 billion overdraft was registered in the operations account of the UMOA with the French Treasury in that year.

In 1981, the government initiated a drastic financial stabilization program within the framework of an Extended Facility agreement with the IMF. The program called for a reduction in the public sector deficit to 8.6 percent of GDP in 1982 and 6.3 percent in 1983; a decrease in the current account deficit to 11.8 percent of GDP in 1982 and 8.3 percent in 1983; and the restoration of overall balance of payments equilibrium by 1983.

Although the fiscal targets of the stabilization program were met by the end of 1982, a series of unfavorable international economic developments resulted in a significantly larger current account deficit than was originally targeted. Indeed, Ivory Coast's terms of trade declined again by 16 percent between 1980 and 1982. Simultaneously, the country became increasingly dependent on nonconcessional loans to finance its public investment program and the public sector deficit, at rapidly increasing interest rates. Finally, oil production did not expand as expected, reaching a level of 1.3 million tons in 1982 against the expected 3.5 million tons. At the same time, a surge in gross foreign borrowings by the public sector from CFAF 277 billion to CFAF 407 billion between 1981 and 1982 contributed to a reduction in the overall balance of payments deficit within the program target. However, it presaged rising debt service ratios in future years, and more deficits of the overall balance are projected at least until 1985. Table 7 summarizes the main macroeconomic indicators for the period.

The sharp deterioration in the internal and external financial situation has affected Ivory Coast at a critical phase in its development. Two decades of growth were essentially based on the exploitation of the most obvious areas of comparative advantage, particularly in agriculture, and on the development of a dynamic, although still limited, industrial base. However, the growth potential of the country progressively deteriorated during the later part of the seventies, primarily because of low economic returns on the expanded public investment program launched in 1977, the rigidity of the system of macroeconomic and sectoral incentives in the face of rapid changes in the country's external environment, and inadequate support for agricultural development.

The rapid expansion of public investment toward the end of the seventies was accompanied by a sharp deterioration in the quality of investment projects. Unlike the 1971–1975 plan, the increase in public investment for the 1976–1980 program was mainly allocated to large

TABLE 7 Macroeconomic Indicators: 1978–1982

	% of GDP				
	1978	*1979*	*1980*	*1981[1]*	*1982[1]*
Growth rate of GDP at constant prices	9.9	5.2	6.3	−1.3	−1.8
Revenue of Stabilization Fund	10.1	7.8	3.8	1.3	2.4
Public investment	25.5	22.8	20.8	15.8	12.7
Gross public savings	13.0	9.3	6.5	6.1	2.0
Public sector deficit	8.5	10.1	12.8	9.3	8.9
Exports f.o.b.	33.1	29.0	29.4	32.4	32.3
Imports f.o.b.	25.9	23.8	24.6	24.5	23.0

Source: Compiled by the authors from the World Bank Data Base (see Michel and Noel, 1983a and 1983b).

[1] Preliminary figures.

projects with high unit costs. In agriculture, for example, most of the increased allocation was for six sugar complexes that had unit operating costs two to three times above world market prices. In education, the investment program has been burdened by several overdesigned higher education facilities, which led to high recurrent costs. The main problem for transportation has been the large scale of highway investment. Overall, it has been estimated that incremental national income from the US $8 billion spent on public investment from 1976–1980 was approximately 40 percent less than it would have been if earlier criteria had been maintained. This figure translates into an annual cost to the economy in terms of foregone earnings of around 5 percent of GDP in the early 1980s, according to World Bank estimates. Furthermore, the underlying growth potential of the economy was already greatly weakened when the recession in 1981 and 1982 began after the stabilization program was imposed.

The rigidity of the system of macroeconomic and sectoral incentives has imposed more constraints on growth and on the flexibility of the country to rapidly changing external conditions. The sharp acceleration of domestic inflation after 1975, and the sharp deterioration in the terms of trade between 1978 and 1982, led to a large overvaluation of the CFA Franc vis-a-vis the currencies of Ivory Coast's main trading partners. This situation revealed fundamental deficiencies in the incentive system. Although major agricultural exports were not hurt by the overvaluation because of their considerable comparative advantage, this was not the case in the industrial sector, where comparative advantage is not as strong. Expansion of the industrial sector was directly affected by the strong bias against exports in the system of industrial incentives. In addition, the most obvious opportunities for exports within the protected CEAO markets have already been exploited. As a result, Ivory Coast is forced to turn to nonregional markets to sustain the growth of its industrial base and to generate the foreign exchange earnings required to balance its external accounts.

Finally, the growth potential of the country has suffered from the inadequate support of agricultural development. Although agriculture has been a key to the country's successful economic performance, agricultural development projects have remained a small part of the public investment program in recent years, apart from the large expenditures for the six sugar complexes. More fundamentally, the definition of a coherent development strategy for the sector, in particular of an adequate system of agricultural incentives to emphasize the medium to long-term comparative advantage of the country has only recently received attention.

THE MODEL

Computable general equilibrium (CGE) models have generated a large literature since the pioneering works of Johansen (1960). The aim of this section is to provide a broad overview of their characteristics, their behavior and their use as well as to focus on the specificities of the Ivorian model. The recent textbook of Dervis, deMelo and Robinson (1982) (referred to hereinafter as DMR) provides a comprehensive presentation of CGEs and describes a general type of CGE on which we based the present study.

CGE models are by essence simulation models designed to investigate the impact of policies that work through the market system, such as taxes, tariffs or subsidies change, or to analyze the impact of direct Government intervention on markets such as the profile and composition of the public investment program, pricing policies or market import restrictions. They are in the tradition of economy-wide multisector models that have been used for development planning over the last two decades. In contrast with traditional input–output and programming models that are best suited for planning in centralized economies, CGE models have been developed for policy simulation in the framework of mixed economies. These are economies where relative prices vary in response to supply and demand decisions by individual agents, and where the Government can affect the outcome of these decisions, either indirectly through fiscal and incentive policies, or directly through intervention in key sectors of the economy.

It is clear in such contexts, that the impact of policy packages can only be assessed in a general equilibrium framework. Indeed, partial equilibrium analysis can certainly provide some enlightening insights into the ways a given particular variable is likely to react to a certain policy change. It is, however, only after having described the full flow of transactions in the economy that the overall compounded effects of the initial measure will be fully quantified. This is, for instance, clear in the case of a tariff reform that not only has an initial impact on import demand through price elasticities but may also affect the savings investment balance through its effects on public finance. Another example would be the case of a devaluation whose consequences work out through the price system but also through the macro effects of the modification of the balance of payments it may induce.

The model[2] is static and was built by adapting the standard model of the type described in DMR. Ultimately the policy analysis should be carried out in the framework of a dynamic model. Comparative static experiments can, however, provide a useful contribution to the understanding of the issues at stake from at least two points of views. First, they allow tracking the economic mechanisms at work and quantifying their effects in a consistent and global framework. Second, they focus on the "first round" effects that may be crucial for the long-term, in that they may either hamper or reinforce the expected long run effects of the policies. We shall not describe the model in detail here (see Michel and Noel, 1983b for a technical presentation) and shall limit ourselves to a presentation of some of its important features, in order to contribute to a better understanding of the results.

The first important element concerns the treatment of foreign trade.

Traditionally, two different approaches have been proposed in the literature for the treatment of foreign trade. On one hand, classical trade theory is built upon the small country assumption, where each country is a price taker on international markets. This assumption introduces a strong distinction between traded goods, which are perfectly substitutable with imports and whose prices are fixed on the international market, and nontraded goods, whose prices are entierly determined on the domestic market. On the other hand, the structuralist school, particularly in the two-gap models, assumes that imports are noncompetitive, so that the degree of substitutability between domestic goods and imports is zero. Imports are perfect complements for domestic goods, resulting in a rigid framework where trade policy has no role to play in closing the foreign exchange gap. The assumption in our model is that imports are neither complete substitutes nor full complements of domestic production. This allows two-way trade at the sectoral level and the possibility of wedges between domestic and import prices. It also implies, instead of a clear-cut distinction between traded and nontraded goods, a continuum of sectors characterized by different degrees of tradeability and a continuum of goods with varying degrees of substitutability. On the export side, we assume that export and domestic prices may differ and that their ratio determines, in each sector, the allocation of production between exports and the domestic market. The volume of exports of the cash crops is, however, assumed to be fixed in the short run.

The second important feature of the model relates to price determination. Although most markets are price clearing, prices being endogenous in such cases, some agricultural prices are fixed, in order to reflect the particular situation observed in major agricultural markets in Ivory Coast because of the Stablization Fund. This institution, whose importance in terms of public finance has been stressed in the first section, is essentially designed to isolate the domestic producers of some agricultural products from the fluctuations of the world markets. This mechanism is taken into account in the model by allowing the possibility of fixing exogenously the nominal price received by the producers. The positive (or negative) difference is then received (or paid) by the Stablization Fund account that, in turn, transfers its surpluses to (or has its deficit financed by) the Government. This captures the essence of the stablization mechanisms of the country. It is also possible to fix some domestic prices in the model, as is often the case in Ivory Coast for the products that are regulated by the Stablization Fund. In such a case, however, it is also necessary to specify how the market clears in case of excess supply or demand, since price clearing is by definition excluded. We supposed that excess supply (demand) on the domestic market of these goods (export crops) was just met by an additional (smaller) volume of exports. Export and domestic prices have been assumed fixed for coffee, cocoa and "other agricultural products" that account for products whose majority are fixed-price ones (palm oil, rubber).

A third important element of the economy that had to be accounted for in the model is the presence of import quotas. The imposition of a limit in the number of import licenses became a common practice for a growing number of imported goods in Ivory Coast, as a way of protecting the domestic industry. Although this has not always led to binding quotas, because the number of allowed licenses could sometimes be larger than those actually desired, the volume of imports is effectively limited for at least two sectors (i.e. textiles and clothing; chemicals and plastics). Quantitative import restrictions amount to a fixed supply of imports in the economy and reverses the logic of the treatment of imports in the model. Indeed, if the availability of imported goods is limited and binding and if there is no mechanism for direct allocation of imports (i.e., quantity rationing) as is the case in Ivory Coast, the only possibility of clearing the demand for imports is to raise the domestic price of imports. Since world prices and tariffs are supposed to be fixed and exogenous, this leads, for a given exchange rate, to generating a pure rent for the importers. Therefore, whereas in the usual case (small country assumption) the domestic price of imports is exogenous and its volume is endogenous, world supply being infinite, the volume of imports is exogenous when quotas are binding, and their domestic price is endogenous. The resulting rents are separately accounted for in the model and distributed to "urban high income" households, which are assumed to include all the importers.

The fourth point to be mentioned concerns a problem CGE modelers generally face, namely the equation of savings and investment. It is an ex-post necessary condition for being in equilibrium, which is not ex-ante warranted given the specifications usually chosen. This is the so-called "closure" problem, which calls for the choice of an ad-hoc way of realizing this equation (see Lysy 1982 for a good survey on this subject). Ivory Coast presents an interesting situation as far as this aspect is concerned, since the weight of public investment as a whole (i.e., central government plus public enterprises), which represented more than three-fourths of total investment in 1980, suggests that the government savings rate and overall public investment can in fact be realistically looked at as policy variables, whereas private investment and private savings rates can be safely considered as fixed and exogenous in the short run. This makes the problem of savings–investment balance a policy choice, which we make explicit in the model. An investment-driven model will therefore be interpreted as a policy choice where the government decides to realize a given public investment program (set either in nominal or real terms) and accepts adjusting its savings rate consequently. Conversely, a savings-driven model must be looked at as a model in which the government decides to adapt the level of public investment to the available savings of the economy. Accordingly, we distinguish in the model public and private investment. Public investment, which in turn is split into central government and public enterprises investment, is scaled such as to make overall investment match available savings in a savings-driven model (with proportional adjustment on its two components). In an investment-driven model the government savings rate adjusts so as to make the overall savings of the economy match the level of investment. In the paper, we present experiments with both types of policy.

Finally, we briefly discuss the estimation of the trade substitution and export supply elasticities. A feasible range of trade substitution elasticities was first determined from cross-sectional evidence based on CGE modelling experience in other developing countries. The productive sectors in the model were then grouped into three different categories corresponding to high, medium, and low trade substitution elasticities, on the basis of our knowledge of the product composition within each individual sector in Ivory Coast. The medium estimate retained for the base model for the trade substitution elasticites is 0.6, indicating that a 1 percent change in the relative price of imported to domestic goods induces a 0.6 percent change in the ratio of imported to domestic goods in domestic demand. Low and high estimates were set at two-tenths of a percentage point on both sides of the medium estimates. Sensitivity analyses were performed in the range of feasible values between 0.3 and 1.1. A similar approach has been followed for the determination of the elasticities of the export supply functions. A central estimate of 0.5 has been retained, indicating that a 1 percent change in the relative price of exports to domestic goods induces a 0.5 percent change in the ratio of exports to sales on the domestic market by exporters. Two alternative estimates were retained for the purposes of sensitivity analyses, corresponding to the high end (1.0) and the low end (0.25) of feasible values.

FLEXIBLE EXCHANGE RATE

The Exchange Rate Issue

As a member of the Franc Zone, Ivory Coast has had a fixed exchange rate vis-a-vis the French Franc since independence. In purchasing-power-parity (PPP) terms, the real exchange rate of the CFAF vis-a-vis its trading partners remained relatively stable until the mid-1970s. Taking 1973 as a base, the index of the real exchange rate averaged 97.6 percent over the 1960–1974 period, fluctuating within a range of about 6 percent on both sides of the average.

After 1975, however, the real exchange rate appreciated sharply, as a result of the acceleration in the rate of domestic inflation, especially following the coffee and cocoa boom in 1974. By comparison with 1973, the rate of appreciation reached 28.7 percent in 1977 and remained at about 25 percent until 1980. A depreciation in real terms with respect to the 1977–1980 situation then started in 1980. It resulted mainly from the slowdown in the rate of domestic inflation after 1980, from movements between the currencies within the European Monetary System and the US dollar and, to a lesser extent, between these currencies themselves. However, in the first quarter of 1983, the degree of overvaluation of the CFAF was still estimated at 17.5 percent compared to the 1960–1974 average.

The price-level-deflated PPP index, which estimates the degree of appreciation of the exchange rate resulting from differences in rates of inflation at home and abroad, is not an adequate indicator of the overvaluation of the domestic currency, as it does not take into account the effects of changes in terms of trade and of transfer movements with the rest of the World on the foreign exchange situation of the country. The relevant measure is the equilibrium exchange rate, defined as the exchange rate that equals the demand and supply of foreign exchange in a given period for a given set of trade taxes and subsidies. Changes in the equilibrium exchange rate can be decomposed into several factors, among which the most important are differential inflation, changes in terms of trade, and changes in transfer movements with the rest of the world (see DMR, 1982, pp. 196–197 and pp. 332–342).

In the case of Ivory Coast, the reduction in differential inflation with respect to the trading partners was accompanied by a sharp deterioration in the terms of trade, estimated at 40.4 percent between 1977 and 1982, of which 16.3 percent was between 1980 and 1982 alone. Between 1977 and 1982, the current account balance deteriorated rapidly, both as a result of rising interest payments on external public debt and of continued increases in salary remittances abroad. The former increased from 4.1 percent of exports of goods and services in 1977 to 21.0 percent in 1982, while the latter grew from 14.3 percent of exports of goods and services in 1977 to 19.2 percent of exports of goods and services in 1982. These factors led to a deterioration of the overall balance, which turned into deficit starting in 1979. By the end of 1982, continued deficit of the overall balance of payments resulted in a negative net foreign assets position of $1,625.4 million. These combined factors suggest that the CFAF has remained largely overvalued, in spite of the apparent recent improvement shown by the PPP index.

Over the rest of the decade, current price projections indicate no further deterioration of Ivory Coast's terms of trade. Moreover, reductions in imports following the increase in domestic oil production, and the possibility of oil export surpluses of the order of 500,000 tons a year after 1985, are likely to lead to an amelioration of the current account balance situation. However, it is not clear whether this improvement will result in a corresponding reduction of the degree of overvaluation of the CFAF, as the availability of oil surpluses could presumably lead to sharp increases in the inflation differential with respect to Ivory Coast's trading partners. Furthermore, despite favorable long-term prospects, continued deficits of the overall balance are projected over the rest of the decade. Under the present set of trade policies, as lower inflows of external public capital result from sharp cuts in the public investment program, the burden of debt with respect to exports of goods and services will not be matched by reductions in the current account balance deficits and will continue to increase at least until 1985.

In this perspective, exchange rate policy may become a major issue over the coming years in Ivory Coast. Many difficulties arise in addressing this issue given the position of the country within the Franc Zone. However, alternative arrangements are possible within the existing institutional framework of the West African Monetary Union. In particular, it should be recognized that there is no conceptual incompatibility between the continuation of the convertibility agreements and the introduction of periodical parity modifications within the Franc Zone.

Principal Economic Mechanisms Involved

The analysis of flexible exchange rate policies presented in the next section is made by simulating the response of the economy to a tightening of foreign exchange constraints. This is done under alternative hypotehses concerning key behavioral parameters of the model, such as the response of exporters to changes in relative prices at home and abroad, or to alternative foreign trade and incentive policies, particularly concerning quantitative import restrictions in key sectors.

Starting from a position of overall balance of payments deficit, a tightening of the foreign exchange constraint calls for a devaluation, which primarily results in a change in the relative price of imported to domestic goods, and in a reduction in the available savings to the economy. The overall net effects will depend on "sectoral tradeability" characteristics and on the pattern of demand adjustment following the reduction in the inflow of foreign savings.

A devaluation raises the relative domestic price of close import substitutes and of exportables and lowers the relative domestic price of less tradeable commodities or commodities that behave as import complements. On the production side, this relative price change induces an expansion in the production of exports and import substitutes, and a contraction in the production of less tradeable commodities and import complements. On the demand side, an expenditure switching effect takes place, following which domestic demand for exportables and import substitutes is reduced, and domestic demand for non-tradeables and import complements increases. Overall, the effects on the structure of sectoral net prices will depend on a number of "sectoral tradeability" characteristics, namely: the share of exports in total production; the share of imports in total domestic demand; the ratio of imports to intermediate inputs; and the trade substitution elasticity. A devaluation can be said to raise the relative net price of sectors with high export shares; have a larger impact on sectoral net prices the higher the share of imports in total demand; lower the relative net price of sectors with a high ratio of imports to intermediate inputs; and tend to raise (lower) the net price in sectors with high (low) trade substitution elasticities, or import substitutes (complements). Tradeability indicators for each sector are given in Table 8. The extent to which these effects mutually reinforce or counterbalance each other can only be found in a general equilibrium framework.

The pattern of demand adjustment following the contraction of the inflow of foreign savings is the other key determinant of the structure of relative net prices under the flexible exchange rate regime. When the model is savings-driven, investment adjusts to match available total savings (i.e., domestic and foreign). Although the expenditure-reducing effect of the devaluation may also induce a contraction in real private and public consumption, the burden of the adjustment falls primarily on investment demand, resulting in a downward pressure in the relative price of capital goods versus consumer goods. On the other hand, when the investment level is assumed to be steady, savings adjust to bring the domestic gap in line with the foreign exchange gap. In this case, the burden of the adjustment falls on consumption, public and private, and the expenditure-reducing effect of devaluation is relatively weaker on investment, resulting in a downward pressure on the relative price of consumer goods versus capital goods.

Finally, the impact of the devaluation will depend on the presence of quantitative import restrictions. The imposition of an import quota will tend to reduce the impact of the devaluation on the net price in the sectors where quantitative import restrictions are binding. The devaluation will result, in this case, in a reduction of the import premium accruing to license holders. Correspondingly, the removal of quotas in conjunction with a move to a flexible exchange rate regime will result in stronger sectoral net price changes by comparison with a scenario where quotas remain binding, as a larger devaluation will be required to reach balance of payments equilibrium, and as its effects will be directly transmitted to import prices.

It should be emphasized that changes in the exchange rate refer to changes beyond the differential between domestic and world inflation. Thus, a change in the nominal exchange rate from period to period just offsetting

TABLE 8 Sectoral Tradeability Indicators

Sector	Share of Exports in Domestic Production (in %)	Ratio of Imports to Domestic Production minus Exports (in %)	Ratio of imports to intermediate inputs (in %)	Trade substitution elasticities		Classification[1]
Food crops	0.24	16.91	21.96	.6	—	MS
Coffee	82.92	0.00	44.03	—	EX	MS
Cocoa	83.11	0.00	60.21	—	EX	MS
Cotton	0.00	0.00	61.26	—	—	MS
Other agric.	33.59	1.30	20.67	.6	EX	MS
Forestry	90.04	0.00	34.62	—	EX	MS
Mining & petroleum	42.14	199.98	61.90	.8	EX	MS
Food process.	28.74	54.42	22.12	.6	EX	MS
Textiles	20.19	67.03	29.31	.8	EX	MS
Chemicals	14.47	238.87	47.61	.8	EX	MS
Construction materials	32.45	54.12	26.73	.8	EX	MS
Engineering industries	11.82	269.76	51.75	.4	EX	MC
Utilities	1.55	0.00	43.93	—	—	NT
Construction	0.14	0.00	35.98	—	—	NT
Services	15.45	20.45	30.52	.4	EX	MC

Source: Michel and Noel [1983].
[1] EX = exportable
MS = import substitute
MC = import complement
NT = non-tradeable

differential world and domestic inflation rates would correspond to a constant real (or price-level deflated) exchange rate.

Analysis of the Experiments

The base experiment consists of simulating a restriction of the balance of payments deficit by one half (i.e., CFAF 70 billion on an overall deficit of CFAF 145 billion in 1980), corresponding to an ex-ante decrease of foreign savings of the order of 3.5 percent of GDP. This undoubtedly represents a drastic stabilization effort, which, however, remains in line with the targets set under the original IMF Program. The model is run under the assumption that investment adjusts to available savings in the economy. The experiment has been made under a median export hypothesis. Quotas have been kept at their base year values.

The balance of payments target is achieved by a devaluation estimated at 11.3 percent. It is accompanied by an overall decrease of 1.2 percent in GDP; substantial improvement in the public finance situation; a marked decrease in household income and consumption; and dramatic shifts in the structure of relative prices and external trade. Results of this experiment are summarized in Table 9.

On the supply side, the decrease in GDP results almost exclusively from the sharp decline in construction value added (-3.3 percent) and to a lesser extent in services value added (-1.0 percent), while agriculture and industry value added remain practically stagnant (-0.1 percent). This change in the structure of GDP is essentially due to the decline in investment in response to the reduction in the inflow of foreign savings in the economy. Similar changes occur in the composition of output.

On the demand side the devaluation increases the domestic currency equivalent of foreign capital inflows, which are labeled in dollars, and thereby offsets the impact of the reduction of the overall balance of payments deficit on total nominal savings. Indeed, when the same balance of payments target is achieved under a fixed exchange rate regime through a tariff-cum-subsidy scheme, construction value added declines by an additional 9.7 percent from its base year value. At the same time, the devaluation induces a substantial increase in tariff receipts and in the revenues from the Stabilization Fund. Although imports decrease by 5.6 percent in volume their CFAF value increases as a result of the devaluation yielding an increase of 5.5 percent in tariff receipts. Likewise, as the differential between the CFAF price of exports and the fixed nominal producer prices is increased by the devaluation, the Stabilization Fund revenues increase by an estimated 38.7 percent.

Since public consumption is kept constant in this experiment, the increase in tariffs and Stablization Fund revenues yield an increase in

TABLE 9 Summary of Major Results for Flexible Exchange Rate Simulations With Real Investment Adjusting to Constant Savings Rates (percentage deviations from Reference Year)

Target
    Reduction of Balance of Payments Deficit by CFAF 70 Billions (50% of 1980 actual level)

Estimated Policy Measures:
    Devaluation: +11.3%

Aggregate Figures (volumes)

GDP of Agriculture	−0.1	Industrial exports (in $)	6.9
Industry	−0.1	Total exports	2.7
Construction	−3.3	Total imports	−5.5
Services	−1.0		
GDP at factor prices	−0.8	Composite goods prices	2.3
GDP at market prices	−1.2	Net prices	−0.7
		Capital goods prices	4.1
Investment	−4.2	Import prices	8.9
Government consumption	−2.8		
Private consumption	−4.5	Import/domestic supply	−3.4
		Exports/domestic output	4.1
Total output	−0.9		
Industrial output	0.6		

Sectoral data for some selected sectors

	Composite prices	Net prices	Output	Exports	Imports
Food crops	−2.9	−5.9	0.0	—	−9.3
Forestry	+14.2	+21.7	0.0	0.0	—
Mining Petroleum	+10.4	+13.2	0.0	+1.4	−7.6
Food Processing	+1.3	+1.6	+0.9	+8.5	−10.4
Textiles	−2.8	+1.2	+0.5	+7.3	−0.5
Chemicals	−2.5	−0.9	−0.6	+5.7	−0.3
Construction Materials	+5.3	+2.7	+1.8	+6.4	−7.1
Engineering Industries	+8.9	−1.7	−2.2	+2.1	−6.0
Utilities	+0.3	−1.8	−1.6	—	—
Construction	+2.1	−1.9	−3.3	—	—
Services	+1.0	−0.7	−1.0	+5.1	−6.6

government savings. This increase in public savings, in fact, offsets the drop in domestic private savings and foreign savings (respectively, −4.8 percent and −8.0 percent) and, overall, the nominal value of savings remains unchanged. This is in sharp contrast with the results obtained with the tariff and subsidy reform. Nominal household income decreases by 2.6 percent as a result of the fall in output; therefore, domestic savings and consumption also decrease respectively (−4.8 percent and −4.3 percent).

The structure of relative value-added prices (net price) is, naturally, substantially altered after the devaluation. Investment goods sectors and relatively less tradeable industrial sectors see their net prices fall, whereas the opposite is true for exported oriented sectors. Because of its very low export share, its low trade substitution elasticity, and the drop in domestic consumption, the net price of the food crop sector is also adversely affected by the devaluation. Finally, the trade structure of the economy is significantly changed, becoming more export oriented and less import dependent as the ratio of imports to domestic supply decreases by 3.4 percent and that of export to domestic output increases by 4.1 percent.

Various sensitivity analysis experiments have been carried out in order to assess the reliability of the results (Michel and Noel, 1983b). This is particularly important given the sometimes poor information on some key parameters. Overall, these experiments showed that the basic tendencies outlined above do not change when different parameters are chosen, although their magnitude can be affected. In particular, the required levels of devaluation estimated under different assumptions on exporters' responses to export incentives, as well as on trade substitution elasticities range between 8 percent and 14 percent, whereas the drop in the real investment level varies from −2.3 percent to −6.3 percent.

A last experiment was performed to simulate the impact of a reduction of the balance of payments deficit by one half under the assumption that overall investment remains constant in real terms, with government savings adjusting to balance the investment-savings gap with the foreign exchange gap. Its results are presented in Table 10.

Under these assumptions, the required devaluation is estimated at 11.1 percent, accompanied by a decline in overall GDP of 0.9 percent, levels that are comparable to those obtained under the base run. The changes in the structure of the economy are, however, very different from that of the base experiment.

On the one hand, the sectoral structure of GDP is markedly changed since agriculture and industry remain practically constant, services decline by 1.3 percent, and construction increases slightly. On the other hand, a clear crowding out of private investment by public investment takes place as a result of the assumption that government savings adjusts to maintain the investment level.

TARIFFS AND EXPORT SUBSIDY REFORM

In this section we analyze the short term effects of changes in the tariff and export incentive structures.

TABLE 10 Summary of Major Results for Flexible Exchange Rate Simulations With Savings Rate Adjusting to Constant Real Investment (percentage deviations from Reference Year)

Target
   Reduction of Balance of Payments Deficit by CFAF 70 Billions

Estimated Policy Measure:
   Devaluation +11.1%

Aggregate Figures (volumes)

GDP of Agriculture	−0.1	Industrial exports	+7.1
Industry	+0.1	Total exports	+2.6
Construction	+0.1	Total imports	−5.4
Services	−1.3		
GDP at factor prices	−0.6	Composite goods prices	+2.3
GDP at market prices	−0.9	Net prices	−0.7
		Capital goods prices	+4.1
Investment	0.0	Import prices	−8.8
Government consumption	−17.6		
Private consumption	−3.9	Import/domestic supply	−3.9
		Exports/domestic output	+3.5
Total output	−0.4		
Industrial output	+0.5		

Sectoral data for some selected sectors

	Composite prices	Net prices	Output	Exports	Imports
Food crops	−2.4	−5.2	0.1	—	−8.8
Forestry	+16.8	+22.4	0.1	−0.2	—
Mining Petroleum	+10.0	+12.1	0.1	+1.6	−3.4
Food Processing	+1.3	+1.4	+1.2	+8.6	−10.0
Textiles	−2.7	+1.2	+0.6	+7.3	−0.7
Chemicals	−2.4	−0.7	−0.6	+5.6	−0.4
Construction Materials	+6.5	+4.4	+3.4	+6.9	−3.5
Engineering Industries	+8.6	−1.4	−1.8	+2.5	−5.6
Utilities	−1.3	−3.9	−2.9	—	—
Construction	+3.0	+0.3	+0.1	—	—
Services	+0.5	−1.2	−1.3	+4.9	−7.0

The Policy Issues Involved

Up to the mid-1970s, the expansion of the Ivorian economy took place in the context of a relatively simple system of incentives. It was essentially based on moderate tariffs that applied fairly uniform protection among different branches of activity, without recourse to quantitative import restrictions.

This situation was modified by the 1973 tariff reform, which resulted in an increase in the escalation of the tariff scale according to degree of processing and in substantial distortions in the degree of effective protection given to particular industrial branches. Average effective tariff protection coefficients (ETP) have been estimated on the basis of average nominal tariff protection coefficients derived both under the pre-1973 and the post-1973 tariff schedules (Noel, 1982). Between 1971 and 1978, the ETP for the industrial sector as a whole increased from 1.23 to 1.76. In 1971, the sectoral ETP varied between 1.19 and 2.06, whereas the interval was widened to between 0.92 and 2.18 in 1978, with an increase in some sectors by as much as 30 percent, as in the case of grain products and canning and food processing.

While the production of manufactured goods for sale on the domestic market expanded in the framework of a distorted system of protection, the Government never implemented an adequate system of export incentives to counterbalance the bias against exports inherent in the system. Until the second half of the seventies, exports of manufactured products grew rapidly within the CEAO zone, and the need for an export incentive system was not directly perceived. However, with the most obvious opportunities for exports within the CEAO region already exploited, further growth of exports will depend crucially on the ability of Ivory Coast to break into nonregional markets. This is particularly true for the EEC, where Ivory Coast enjoys duty-free entry under the Lomé agreements.

Recognizing the inadequacy of the present system of tariffs and the bias against exports generated by the system of incentives, the Government is now preparing a comprehensive reform of the system of industrial incentives. This reform will include the progressive harmonization of effective tariff protection across industrial branches and, within each branch of activity, between the different levels of processing. At the same time, the Government is preparing the implementation of an across-the-board subsidy on value added for manufactured exports to non-CEAO countries. The subsidy will compensate for effective tariff protection on the domestic market, and will also provide an element of compensation for the overvaluation of the CFA franc vis-a-vis Ivory Coast's trading partners.

Economic Mechanisms at Work

The effects of a change in the tariff and export subsidy structure are both direct and indirect, occur at the micro and macro levels and may well counterbalance each other. It is therefore only in a general equilibrium framework that we can measure the overall impact of these compounded effects. However, it may be interesting to detail them one by one first, in order to disentangle the various economic mechanisms at work.

A change in the tariff structure yields a modification of the price structure of the economy that should modify the structure of production and of demand. It is also likely to reduce imports and to have an impact on the investment-savings balance, while, finally, it will have a public finance effect through an increase in tariff revenue.

The first and direct effect of an increase in tariffs on a given good is a substitution effect, decreasing the demand for import of this good and increasing the demand for its domestic substitute. The extent to which this phenomenon occurs depends of course on trade substitutability. Substitution effects occur within final as well as intermediate demand. In the latter case, they affect the net price of various sectors and might therefore modify levels of production. Overall, the price of traded goods relative to nontraded goods increases, shifting demand towards the latter type of goods. However, an income effect will also appear, reducing the volume of demand because of higher prices.

Since imports are going to be reduced by the measure, the amount of foreign savings available in the economy is decreased in the same proportion, and the aggregate investment-savings balance is modified. The effect of this modification depends on the specification of the closure of the model. In a savings-driven model, the level of investment is cut, reducing the overall level of demand of the economy. In an investment-driven model the savings of some agents will increase at the expense of their consumption. The overall demand effect is the same, but its composition differs and therefore the final result does also. However, in both cases the demand for domestic goods and for imports decreases, reinforcing the initial effect.

Finally, a change in the level of tariffs changes the tariff revenue of the government, the direction of the change depending on relative volume/price effects. This change has to be offset by a similar change of another item of the government budget. According to the type of modification that is decided (consumption, transfers, savings), the consequences might also differ significantly.

Contrary to tariff increases, a change in export subsidies does not directly modify the domestic price structure, and these effects work out through the possibilities of arbitrage between domestic and export markets that have been introduced for producers. The value added subsidies make exports much more profitable and will generate a shift of production towards export markets, at the expense of domestic ones. This will be accompanied by a change in the level of production, since the net price for exporters increases. As production increases, households' income and demand increase. The combined effects of changes in production and demand will affect the domestic price structure.

The increase in exports also amounts to a reduction in foreign savings; the investment-savings balance problem will arise in the same terms as with a tariff structure increase. It must be noted that the initial positive effect on the trade balance due to the boost in exports is somewhat dampened by a parallel increase in production and demand, which generates higher demand for imports. As export subsidies are financed by the government, a public finance balance problem arises, similar to the preceding one.

Overall, a change in tariffs and export subsidies is likely to affect substantially the structure of the economy: relative prices, production and demand patterns, income distribution, investment–consumption allocation, savings structure, and government budget are all bound to be affected by the reform.

Analysis of the experiments

The following experiments simulate the impact of introduction of a tariff-cum-subsidy scheme designed to yield a given level of the trade balance, while balancing the public budget; the additional cost of the subsidies is exactly matched by the additional tariff revenue.

The base experiment, the results of which are given in Table 11, consists of a reduction of the balance of payment deficit by CFAF 70 billion (approximately in half for 1980), or 3.5 percent of the GDP in that year. This is achieved by imposing uniform tariff and export subsidy levels and neutral fiscality. The decrease in foreign savings is accompanied by a corresponding decrease in investment (savings-driven). The experiment has been made under a median export elasticity hypothesis. Quotas have been kept at their base year values.

The desired reduction in the balance of trade deficit is achieved in the model by an across the board export subsidy of 42 percent and a uniform tariff level of 36 percent, which represents an average increase in all sectors of about half actual levels, except in food processing. The impact on the economy is: (i) a substantial change in the structure of GDP by origin and by destination, accompanied by a decrease in its level (-1.7 percent at market prices); (ii) a drop in public investment and an increase in the price of capital, resulting in a sharp drop in the overall investment; (iii) a dramatic change in the price structure and in relative sectoral profitabilities.

The structure of GDP by sector of origin is distorted in favor of industry (6.9 percent), mostly at the expense of construction (-13.0 percent). This is due on the one hand to the increase in value-added prices of industrial sectors generated by the export subsidy, which leads them to increase their production, and on the other hand, to the drop in investment that is the main source of demand for the construction sector. The overall decrease in investment is naturally due to the reduction in available savings that is matched by an equal reduction in public investment, but also by the increase in capital goods prices due to their strong import content. Public investment

TABLE 11 Summary of Major Results for Tariff and Export Subsidy Reform Simulation with Real Investment Adjusting to Constant Savings Rates

Target

Reduction of Balance of Payments Deficit by CFAF 70 Billions (50% of 1980 actual level)

Estimated Policy Measures

| Tariff Level | 35.8% | Export Subsidy Level | 42.1% |

(Percent Deviation from 1980)

Aggregate Estimates (volumes in %)

GDP of Agriculture	−0.1		
Industry	6.9		
Construction	−13.0	Industrial exports (in $)	+31.5
Services	−2.7	Total exports (in $)	+3.8
GDP at factor prices	−1.5	Total imports (in $)	−4.7
GDP at market prices	−1.7		
		Composite goods prices	+2.4
Investment	−13.2	Net prices	+2.4
Government consumption	−2.3	Capital goods prices	+2.9
Private consumption	−1.4	Import prices	+7.1
Industrial output	8.8	Imports/domestic supply	−1.8
Total output	−1.2	Exports/Domestic output	+5.7

Sectoral Data for Some Selected Sectors

	Composite Prices	Net Prices	Output	Export	Imports
Food crops	+7.7	+2.8	0.0	—	−15.1
Forestry	+17.0	+0.4	0.0	−1.2	—
Mining petroleum	+6.6	−25.9	0.0	−1.7	−3.6
Food processing	−6.0	−27.3	+18.1	+40.9	+4.2
Textiles	+0.9	+14.8	+5.2	+22.1	−0.1
Chemicals	−2.1	+10.7	+5.4	+24.0	−0.2
Construction material	−2.3	+16.1	+9.1	+30.9	−18.3
Engineering industries	+7.2	+3.2	−0.9	+15.8	−7.8
Utilities	+2.9	+2.3	−1.1	—	—
Construction	−0.7	−5.6	−3.0	—	—
Services	+1.7	+0.1	−2.7	−3.8	−4.7

having a large construction component, this sector is bound to be the most hit by the drop in investment. On the expenditure side, the change in GDP is almost entirely borne by investment (−13.2 percent) and household consumption has only slightly decreased (−1.2 percent).

The introduction of the tariff-cum-subsidy scheme has a strong impact on the structure of relative value added prices across sectors. As shown in Table 11, sharp increases in value added prices are estimated in all subsidized sectors, in particular food processing (27.3 percent), textiles (14.8 percent), and construction materials (16.1 percent). By contrast, value added prices drop substantially in mining and petroleum (−25.9 percent) which is not a subsidized sector and which imports 62 percent of its intermediate inputs, and in construction (−5.6 percent), following the decline in investment demand.

Finally, the trade structure of the economy is, expectedly, also substantially modified. The introduction of the package has made the economy less import-dependent (the ratio of imports over domestic supply decreases by 1.8 percent), and much more export-oriented through an increase of industrial exports of 31.5 percent, which raises the share of exports in domestic output by 5.7 percent.

The effects of a tariff and export subsidy reform as well as the level of the required reform depend on the import elasticities on the one hand, and on the ability of domestic producers to respond to export incentives on the other.

Sensitivity analyses conducted by the authors (Michel and Noel, 1983b), show that, within a reasonable range of values, changes in import elasticities do not significantly alter the order of magnitude of the results. By contrast, results are significantly affected by the hypothesis retained for export supply response. The level of the export subsidy required to achieve the balance of payments objective while keeping the government budget balanced varies from 65 percent under the low export response hypothesis, to 24 percent under the high export response hypothesis, while the corresponding tariff increase varies from 79.8 percent to 33.1 percent, respectively, under the low and the high export response scenarios.

The major macroeconomic effect of the decrease of the trade deficit is that it implies, *ipso facto*, a decrease in foreign savings available to the economy. The basic experiment was made under the assumption that the level of public investment was reduced in accordance with the reduction of savings. This is consistent with what actually happened in 1980–1981. This has effects in the short run via the structure of demand and prices, but also in the long run, since the level and the structure of capital formation is considerably affected. Therefore, we investigated the consequences of a policy maintaining the level of investment (real or nominal) together with implementation of the incentive reform. The results are presented in Table 12.

The results show that the required increase in government savings can be met only if tariffs are substantially increased (49 percent instead of 36 percent) and export subsidies made smaller than in the base experiment (set at 11 percent against 42 percent), in order to raise tariff revenue that offsets the increase in expenditure due to export subsidies. This raises the price of imports and has an adverse effect on net prices, output and employment. The result is a typical crowding-out effect, with investment replacing private consumption, which decreases by 7.7 percent in volume. It is also accompanied by a reversal of the direction of change in the structure of GDP.

QUANTITATIVE IMPORT RESTRICTIONS

The Background

Until the beginning of the 1970s, the Government relied on import licensing and import prohibition on an ad-hoc basis as a protective device for local industry. The first comprehensive list of products subject to import licensing or import prohibition was established in 1975. It contained 310 industrial products, of which 23 were subject to import prohibition.[3] By January 1982, the number of industrial products under import licensing had grown to 426, with the heaviest concentration in textiles, clothing, chemicals, and plastics. In 1981, import of industrial products under licensing represented CFAF 233.6 billion, or 38.4 percent of total imports in that same year. Parallel to the import licensing system, the Ministry of Commerce issues a list of products whose importation is subject to prior import agreement. For the products belonging to that list, "import intentions" are submitted to special import control commissions whose decisions have executive force. In 1981, the number of industrial products subject to prior import agreement amounted to 140, and imports of industrial products under prior agreement amounted to CFAF 53.2 billion, or 8.8 percent of total imports in that same year. Quantitative import restrictions have therefore become a major feature of the system of incentives in Ivory Coast. The Government is now planning to reverse this trend and to replace quantitative restrictions by temporary import surcharges, in conjunction with tariff and subsidy reforms to be implemented in the framework of the structural adjustment program.

Economic Mechanisms at Work

The imposition of import quotas in a given sector generates two types of effects. On the one hand, it protects the domestic economy and on the other,

TABLE 12 Summary of Major Results for Tariff and Export Subsidy Reform Simulations where Savings Rates Adjust to Constant Real Investment (Percentage Deviation from Reference Year)

Target

Reduction of Balance of Payments Deficit by CFAF 70 Billion with Constant Real Investment

Estimated Policy Measures

Tariff Level	48.9%	Export Subsidy Level	11.0%

Aggregate figures:

GDP of Agriculture	−0.1		
Industry	+0.2		
Construction	−0.9	Industrial exports (in $)	5.3
Services	+0.4	Total exports	0.4
GDP at factor prices	−3.6	Total imports	−7.4
GDP at market prices	−2.2	Composite goods prices	3.4
Investment	0.0	Net prices	−4.9
Government consumption	−3.6	Capital goods prices	7.1
Private consumption	−7.7	Import prices	13.4
Industrial output	−1.1	Imports/domestic supply	−5.3
Total output	−1.4	Exports/domestic output	2.1

(Percentage deviation from reference year)

Sectoral Data for Some Selected Sectors:

	Composite Prices	Net Prices	Exports	Imports
Food crops	−2.7	−11.9	—	−26.3
Forestry	+10.7	−2.1	−0.5	—
Mining petroleum	+15.0	−52.3	−3.9	−5.9
Food processing	−0.5	−3.4	+5.1	−12.8
Textiles	−5.8	−1.1	+7.5	+0.1
Chemicals	−3.0	−3.6	+3.8	−2.1
Construction materials	+12.7	−6.5	+8.1	−7.7
Engineering industries	+17.1	−2.4	+0.7	−7.6
Utilities	−0.8	−4.8	—	—
Construction	+5.1	+0.1	—	—
Services	−1.2	−4.7	−2.8	−7.4

it changes the distribution of income. Quantitative barriers to imports are imposed when a domestic industry is not profitable at the price of its foreign competitors, and when the social and political benefits of protecting the industry are believed to be worth its cost in terms of inefficient use of domestic resources. This cost may, however, be larger if quotas are imposed rather than tariffs, assuming that there is always a tariff equivalent of a given quota. First, the administrative management of a system of import quotas may be very heavy. Second, black markets for import licenses may be created, possibly leading to a waste of resources for enterprises looking for those licenses. Third, although such a system is usually presented as temporary, it is often difficult to remove, in particular because of the rents it creates. Indeed a quota system has a distributional effect, as it amounts to a private appropriation of the public revenue that would have been generated by its tariff equivalent.

In the case of Ivory Coast, domestic prices in the textile sectors have been estimated to be higher than world prices plus tariff by 74 percent; the corresponding estimate in the chemical sector is 59 percent. This generates a total rent estimated at CFAF 43 billion which accrues to urban high income households and represents 8.7 percent of total government revenue. It is clear that the effects of such flows on the consumption and output patterns as well as on the prices structure are far from being negligible.

Effects on the Exchange Rate

In order to analyze the effects of the removal of quotas in a flexible exchange rate regime, two alternative experiments have been carried out. First, a tariff surcharge is imposed on textiles and on chemicals and plastics, which are the three sectors where quotas have been estimated to be binding, in order to generate the same protection as in the situation with quotas. In a second experiment, imports in these two sectors are allowed in excess of the previous quotas. Table 13 presents the results of these two experiments.

Under the first experiment, the devaluation required to achieve the reduction in the balance of payments deficit by one-half is estimated at 11.6 percent, almost the same level as obtained under the base experiment. The tariff surcharge needed to yield the same protective effect as the quota is estimated at 36 percent in textiles and 6 percent in chemicals. This results in an 18 percent increase in tariff revenues for the government, from CFAF 158.6 billion to CFAF 188.1 billion. This effect, combined with the increase in stabilization fund revenues induced by the devaluation, yields a 12 percent increase in government earnings. Accordingly, overall investment declines only by 1.4 percent in real terms. As a result, overall GDP declines by 0.8 percent under this experiment, compared with 1.2 percent under the base run. Finally, the structure of foreign trade improves slightly, with industrial exports growing by 7.3 percent (versus 3.6 percent under the base run) and imports declining by 5.3 percent (compared to 5.1 percent under the base run).

TABLE 13 Summary of Major Results for Impact of Quotas on Flexible Exchange Rate Policy with Real Investment Adjusting to Constant Savings Rates (Percentage deviation from reference year)

Target:
    Reduction of Balance of Payments Deficit by CFAF 70 Billion

Additional Requirement *Estimated Policy Measure:*	*Tariff-Equivalent Quotas*	*Removal of Quotas*
Devaluation:	11.6	13.6
Real GDP of Industry	0.1	0.9
Real GDP of Construction	−0.6	−0.9
Real GDP of Services	−0.7	−0.2
Real GDP of Market Prices	−0.8	−0.3
Investment	−1.4	−2.1
Private Consumption	−5.1	−4.1
Industrial Output	0.2	1.1
Total Output	−0.3	0.1
Industrial Exports	7.3	9.4
Total Exports	2.9	3.6
Total Imports	−5.3	−4.6
Composite Goods Prices	2.3	2.3
Net Prices	−0.9	−0.7
Capital Good Prices	4.5	5.1
Import Prices	9.1	9.1
Imports/Domestic Supply	−3.8	−2.9
Exports/Domestic Output	3.7	4.3

With the removal of quotas (experiment 2), the devaluation required to achieve the balance of payments constraint is estimated at 13.6 percent, higher than the 11.3 percent obtained in the base experiment with binding quantity rationing. It is however accompanied by a smaller decrease in the overall GDP (−0.3 compared to its reference year value).

Overall, the measures seems desirable although it must be weighted against the cost of exposing the two sectors originally protected to foreign competition, since the volume of imports of textiles and chemicals increases respectively by 22 percent and 2 percent from their reference year value.

Tariffs and Subsidies Reform

In order to analyze the effects of the removal of quotas on the tariff and subsidy reform, two experiments have been carried out in which a tariff-cum-subsidy scheme is generated without quotas, with the objective of reducing the overall deficit of the balance of payments by one half. First, a tariff surcharge is imposed on textiles and on chemicals and plastics, in order to generate the same level of protection as in the situation with quotas. In the second experiment, imports in these two sectors are allowed in excess of the previous quotas. Table 14 presents the results of these two experiments.

The simultaneous removal of quantitative import restrictions and the imposition of tariff surcharges on goods initially subject to quotas maintains the original level of protection in these two sectors and therefore highlights the distributional effects of quotas. Comparison of the case where quotas are eliminated in the context of tariff and subsidy reform with the results of the latter alone shows that quota elimination is a desirable measure. It allows the

TABLE 14 Impact of Quotas on Tariff and Subsidy Policy with Real Investment Adjusting to Constant Savings Rates (Percentage deviation from reference year)

Target
Reduction of Balance of Payments Deficit by CFAF 70 Billions

Additional Requirement *Estimated Policy Measure*	*Tariff Equivalent*	*Removal of Quotas*
Tariff level	32.3[1]	39.4
Export Subsidy Level	49.2	54.8
Real GDP of Industry	9.2	10.4
Real GDP of Construction	−11.6	−13.4
Real GDP of Services	−2.1	−2.5
Real GDP at Market Prices	−0.8	−0.8
Investment	−12.1	−13.8
Private Consumption	−0.5	0.2
Industrial Output	11.6	13.0
Total Output	−3.4	−0.3
Industrial exports	37.8	41.8
Total exports	4.8	5.2
Total imports	−3.4	−3.5
Composite good prices	2.1	2.5
Net prices	3.9	3.8
Capital good prices	2.3	3.8
Import prices	5.4	6.9
Import/domestic supply	−1.5	−0.7
Export/domestic output	5.8	6.4

[1]Nominal tariff level on industrial goods except on "Textiles" and "Chemicals and Plastics."

reform to take place with a larger real GDP, a reduction in income dispersion, a more dynamic industrial sector and a larger volume of external trade.

By imposing an additional tariff, calculated at the quota equivalent level of tariffs, the government recuperates the trade rent, which originally accrued to importers. Since we impose fiscal neutrality in this experiment (i.e., that additional tariff revenue is exactly offset by additional export subsidies expenditure) this flow is used to finance additional export subsidies. By this operation, the government is thus able to finance more export subsidies than in the original experiment, resulting in larger industrial exports. A second round of effects occurs since additional exports require additional production and imports. Overall, the requirement of fiscal neutrality and the balance of payments target are met with an export subsidy level of 49 percent, against 42 percent in the base experiment. A dramatic increase in the average tariff occurs, which reflects the large increases needed in the textiles and chemicals and plastics sectors.

The export subsidies induce a larger boost of industrial exports than in the reference experiment, and accordingly a larger increase in industrial output and total output. Because of import complementarities, this also generates more imports; overall the economy ends up being more trade-oriented than in the base experiment.

The changes in the level of real GDP and in its structure stem directly from these effects. On the supply side, the GDP of industry soars, because of the export subsidy that raises value added prices in the subsidized sectors. The structural change is therefore more accentuated with this policy package.

The second experiment results in a larger GDP than in the two preceding experiments, as well as larger industrial exports, output and private consumption. However, these positive effects must be weighed against the fact that textiles and chemicals are now exposed to foreign competition and that imports are substantially higher as are import prices (due to tariffs). Therefore the general price level is also higher, resulting in a drop in real investment.

The double objective of fiscal neutrality and of reduction of the balance of payments deficit by one half is achieved with a level of export subsidies substantially higher than in the base year (55 percent as opposed to 42 percent) and an across the board rise in tariff levels. However, the process that led to this outcome is not the same as in the preceding experiment as there is no direct transfer in this case between households and government. The initial effect that triggers the process here is the surge in imports of textiles and chemicals (respectively 22.4 percent and 5.4 percent in volume) that results from the removal of quotas. This generates an additional tariff revenue to the government, as compared with the base experiment. As before, this additional revenue is made available for financing additional export subsidies. Overall, it results in an export subsidy level that is higher than in the preceding experiment. This explains why industrial exports and overall output are higher, as is total GDP, which remains at its base year value. Accordingly, private consumption is also higher than in the two other experiments.

The trade structure of the economy is rather different from what was found in the other cases, since the ratio of imports to domestic supply is close to its base year value (-0.7 percent), whereas the ratio of exports to domestic output is also largely increased (6.4 percent). This is due to the rise in textile and chemical imports, the ratio of imports to domestic supply increasing respectively by 19 percent and 2 percent in these two sectors. This increase is made possible by the fact that the domestic prices of these two goods are lower than in the preceding situation, where quotas or the tariff equivalent of quotas were imposed. Added to the fact that exports of textiles and chemicals also increase, following the introduction of export subsidies, respectively by 19 percent and 31 percent, this suggests that dramatic compositional changes must occur in these two sectors under such a policy package.

CONCLUSIONS

After presenting an overview of the Ivorian economy, we have examined recent economic developments that have led to the present financial difficulties and to two consecutive years of recession, and we have discussed the main constraints bearing on the future growth of Ivorian economy. Among those constraints, distortions in the system of incentives have progressively hampered the growth potential of the country and have reduced its capacity to adjust to rapidly changing external circumstances. The acceleration in the rate of domestic inflation after 1975, and the sharp deterioration in the terms of trade between 1978 and 1982, led to a substantial overvaluation of the CFA Franc vis-à-vis the currencies of Ivory Coast's main trading partners. Although major agricultural products withstood the overvaluation, thanks to the margin provided by their considerable comparative advantage, this was not the case in the industrial sector, where margins are much narrower. In particular, the potential of the industrial sector has been affected by the strong discrimination of the system of industrial incentives against exports, and by widespread distortions in the system of tariff and nontariff protection among and within different branches of activity and among the various stages of product processing. This situation is particularly preoccupying, as the most obvious opportunities for exports within the protected CEAO markets have already been exploited, and as Ivory Coast has to turn to nonregional markets to restore the growth of its industrial base and to generate the foreign exchange earnings required to stabilize its current account situation.

In this context, the policy simulations conducted in the framework of Ivory Coast's CGE model take on a particular significance, as they provide a strong basis for assessing the macroeconomic and sectoral impact of major reforms envisioned by the Government in the framework of its structural adjustment program.

Although the arrangements presently in force within the Franc Zone preclude the implementation of an independent exchange rate policy in Ivory Coast, the flexible exchange rate experiments provide key insights into the magnitude of the adjustments required in the economy following a tightening of its foreign exchange constraint. In the short run, a devaluation induces only a slight decline in overall GDP, as the impact of the reduction in the net inflow of foreign savings is compensated to a large extent by the sharp increase in Stabilization Fund revenues and, to a lesser extent, by the increase in tariff revenues. By contrast, the devaluation has a strong impact on the structure of the economy. Driven by exports, output expands in sectors like food processing, textiles, and construction materials, while it contracts sharply in sectors linked with investment (engineering industries and construction) and in less tradeable sectors (utilities and services). Overall, devaluation induces a sharp change in the trade orientation of the economy, with substantial increases in exports, especially of industrial goods, and reductions in imports that permit the required adjustment of the overall balance.

The second set of experiments provide useful guidelines for the design of a tariff-cum-export subsidy scheme as a second best measure to achieve the required adjustment of the overall balance. As in the case of the flexible exchange rate experiments, the CGE model makes it possible to trace the effects of proposed measures throughout the economy. In particular, the tariff and subsidy level generated by the model are constrained to meet a fiscal neutrality criterion, so that the extra fiscal revenues generated by the tariff reform compensate the outlays needed to finance the export subsidy. By comparison with the flexible exchange rate experiments, the implementation of the tariff-cum-subsidy scheme induces a sharper decline in GDP, as the impact of the reduction in foreign savings is not matched by increased Stabilization Fund revenues. At the same time, exports expand dramatically in all subsidized sectors, in particular in food processing, construction materials, textiles, and chemicals and plastics. Overall, the introduction of the scheme makes the economy less import-dependent and much more export-oriented by comparison with the flexible exchange rate experiment, especially following the sharp increase in industrial exports.

The third set of experiments show that the negative short-run impact on growth of a policy of adjustment through a flexible exchange rate or through a tariff-cum-subsidy scheme can be reduced to a certain extent by implementing those policies in conjunction with the removal of quotas. In this context, the replacement of quotas by import surcharges does not substantially affect the overall growth performance of the economy. It does, however, affect the adjustment required by corresponding sectors, namely textiles and clothing, and chemicals and plastics. In particular, a policy of complete removal of quotas without corresponding import surcharges involves dramatic compositional changes in these two sectors, with sharp increases in both exports and imports in both cases.

Ultimately, the analysis of the policies envisaged in the above experiments should be carried out from a medium- to long-term perspective in the framework of a dynamic general equilibrium model. Indeed, the timing of the supply and demand responses in the economy, as well as the impact of the various policies on investment, are rich in dynamic implications. However, the investigation of the impact of these policies in a static general equilibrium framework presents new and important insights for policy makers faced with the need to design far-reaching reforms in a complex system of interdependent economic relationships.

NOTES

1. Estimates of the share of public enterprises in GDP and investment are based on the Ministère des Finances (1982) definition of public enterprises.

2. The data base used for the model comes from the Ivory Coast Social Accounting Matrix (SAM), which has been built at the World Bank. It contains 15 productive sectors, five labor and household categories, current and capital accounts for households, the central government, the Stabilization Fund (CSSPA), the Amortization Fund (CAA), public enterprises, oil and nonoil private enterprises, and the rest of the world. A detailed description of its construction is given in G. Michel and M. Noel (1983a).

3. The principal sectors affected were food products, adhesives, textiles and clothing, footwear, and certain products of the mechanical and electrical industries. Products under import prohibition included coffee beans (except arabica), roasted coffee, jute bags, and batteries.

5

LESSONS AND CONSTRAINTS OF EXPORT CROP-LED GROWTH: COCOA IN IVORY COAST

Mathurin Gbetibouo and Christopher L. Delgado[1]

Ivory Coast is exceptional in Africa by virtue of its highly successful, agriculturally-based growth strategy in the 1960s and 1970s. From the position of being relatively poor by African standards at independence, Ivory Coast had the highest gross national product per capita in sub-Saharan Africa in 1979, exceeded only by Gabon with its rich mineral deposits and tiny population. Without benefit of mineral revenues, foreign exchange was secured, capital accumulated, and employment generated, largely through expansion of the three principal commodity exports: coffee, cocoa, and timber. Well behind coffee in economic importance at independence, cocoa became Ivory Coast's major export commodity in the late 1970s. Since 1980, the country has been the World's largest producer of cocoa, with a 27 percent market share in 1982. Thus the story of the Ivorian "miracle" is hard to disassociate from the story of cocoa. The experience is rich in lessons and, perhaps, indicates the new difficulties and constraints that export-crop led growth strategies will have to face in the 1980s and 1990s.

One of the most striking aspects about Ivorian agricultural development policy at first glimpse is its apparent similarity to that of other countries in the region. Parastatal interventions in agriculture, predatory price policies that extract surplus from export crops to the benefit of nonagriculture, overvalued exchange rates, and subsidies for food crop production are the rule in Ivory Coast. Similar policies have been diagnosed, in a regional context, as being at the root of economic stagnation in sub-Saharan Africa (World Bank, 1981).

All of this leads us to two sets of questions that are the subject matter of this chapter. First, what is different about Ivory Coast? Why was agricultural development so successful when policies so heavily criticized elsewhere were followed? Second, will the same strategy continue to work in the future, or have internal and external economic conditions changed to the point where this is no longer possible? In the course of addressing these issues, we hope to illustrate both some concerns for the development of the cocoa industry in Ivory Coast and for African agricultural development generally.

To approach these issues, the chapter is divided into five parts. First, the role of export crops is explored in the context of Ivorian economy, with special reference to cocoa. Second, the role of the State in promoting cocoa development is examined, emphasizing differences vis-a-vis other African producers. Third, internal issues affecting the future of cocoa development are explored, with particular attention to relative incentives in the economy. Fourth, external issues are analyzed in the context of a stagnant world market and tough competition from Latin America. Finally, we conclude with some thoughts on research needs with respect to the internal issues and some desirable directions for policy with respect to the external ones.

EXPORT AGRICULTURE IN THE IVORIAN ECONOMY

Agricultural Contributions to the National Economy

One particularly intriguing aspect of the Ivorian economic experience is that an agricultural-oriented growth strategy has been associated with twenty years of declining importance of agriculture in the national economy. Coupled with high rates of overall growth, this serves to indicate the ultimate success of such a strategy and lends support to those theorists, such as Arthur Lewis, who have long argued that primary attention to agriculture is the most sustainable way to industrialize.

Table 1 presents some statistics: the share of agriculture in GDP declined from 43 to 26 percent from 1960 to 1979. The comparable GDP weighted averages for sub-Saharan Africa's eleven middle-income oil importers (including Ivory Coast) show an *increase* of the share of agriculture, from 30 to 36 percent over the same period. This is striking, since the weighted averages are heavily influenced by countries that have followed essentially proindustrialization growth strategies: Ghana, Zambia and Senegal.

At independence, 89 percent of the population in Ivory Coast was engaged in agriculture; this had declined to 79 percent twenty years later. As shown in Table 1, the sources of foreign exchange became steadily more diversified, largely due to deliberate government policy to reinvest export crop related surpluses in other ventures. Most importantly, physical productivity per agricultural worker grew at the rate of 4.4 percent per annum, putting Ivory Coast well ahead of the weighted average of 2.7 percent for middle-income oil importers in sub-Saharan Africa (World Bank,

TABLE 1 Indicators of the Role of Export Agriculture in the Ivorian Economy 1960–1979

	1979 Value	*1960–79 Average Annual Growth Rate*	*Percentage Change 1960–79 (%)*
GNP Per Capita (current $)	$1,040	2.4	61
Share of Agriculture in GDP	26	−2.5	−40
Share of Labor Force in Agriculture	79	−0.6	−13
Share in Total Exports of Three Principal Commodity Exports	68	−0.9	−19
(of which cocoa)	(22)	(0.0)	(0)
Growth Rate of Agricultural Production (by volume)	—	3.8	—
Growth Rate of Agricultural Production (per agricultural worker)	—	4.4	—
Growth Rate of Agricultural Production (per capita total population)	—	−0.8	—
Growth Rate of Cocoa and Coffee Exports by volume	—	3.2	—
Net barter terms of trade	129	0.7	14

[a]1976–1978 average.

Sources: Calculated from data in the statistical appendix of World Bank (1981), except for the share of cocoa in exports, which is from IMF (1982).

1981). Nonetheless, the 5.2 percent per annum growth in overall population over the period, due to massive in-migration from the North going largely to cities, led to an overall decline of agricultural production per capita of 15 percent over the period.

A close look at the net barter terms of trade between Ivorian imports and the principal commodity exports would probably show a decline in Ivory

Coast's position by approximately 25 percent between 1960 and 1983. Nevertheless, there was a net appreciation in Ivory Coast's favor of 14 percent between 1960 and 1979, which is important to bear in mind when assessing long-run outlook on the basis of current data. More importantly, the net income terms of trade, what total Ivorian exports will buy in terms of imports, grew by 7.8 percent per annum between 1960 and 1979 (World Bank, 1981).

The Role of Export Crop Surpluses in Public Investment and Resource Reallocation

The marketing of the major export crops in Ivory Coast—cocoa, coffee, cotton, and palm oil—is regulated by a parastatal organization, the *Caisse de Stabilisation et de Soutien des Prix des Produits Agricoles* (CSSPPA), hereafter referred to as the Stabilization Fund. The Stabilization Fund guarantees a fixed price to planters throughout the crop year and sometimes for several consecutive seasons. Unlike the marketing boards in other West African countries, the Fund does not take physical delivery of the crop. It only regulates internal marketing and issues licenses to exporters who are bound to sell at a price approved by the Fund. Exporters are also guaranteed a FOB price, which is on a cost-plus basis, reflecting the real costs of moving cocoa from producers to the shipping border, plus some margin fixed by the Fund. If the actual selling price on the international market is higher than the guaranteed CIF price, then the Fund retains the difference. If it is lower, the Fund makes up the difference to exporters, although this has rarely been the case.

The Fund typically generates a surplus as a result of its intermediary role in price stabilization. It is widely admitted that cash crop producers have been heavily "taxed" through the marketing board price support scheme. The extent of this taxation is measured by nominal protection coefficients, the ratios of domestic producer prices to the amount farmers would have received had the commodities been sold at the world price net of transfers and marketing costs, converted at a "real" exchange rate that reflects the true value of domestic currency. For Ivory Coast cocoa, the World Bank estimated a coefficient of .56 between 1971 and 1975, and .38 from 1976 to 1980 (den Tuinder, 1978 and World Bank, 1982). Abstracting from the fine points involving transport and handling costs, this implies that Ivory Coast cocoa farmers received 56 percent and 38 percent of the prices they would have received in absence of the marketing board over the respective stated periods.

The surpluses generated by these pricing policies were relatively massive during the 1977 to 1979 coffee and cocoa boom, as indicated in Table 2. In practice, these surpluses are used by the central government for

TABLE 2 Domestic Financing of the Ivorian Capital Investment Budget: 1965–1983

Year	Capital Investment Budget (BSIE)[a] (Billion CFAF)	Amount Financed From Domestic Sources[b] (Billion CFAF)	Share Financed Domestically[c] (%)	Stabilization Fund Surplus[d] (Billion CFAF)	Share of BSIE Financed by Stabilization Fund[e] (%)	Exchange Rate[f] CFAF/$
1965–1966 avg.	14.5	13.6	94	0.5	10	246
1971	41.6	21.4	51	10.1	27	276
1972	34.9	16.6	48	–1.0	5	252
1973	36.9	18.2	49	5.9	—	223
1974	44.2	17.7	40	44.3	—	241
1975	54.0	27.5	51	19.6	15	214
1976	60.1	19.7	33	52.1	—	239
1977	245.0	196.5	80	243.8	—	246
1978	257.2	174.4	68	173.3	—	226
1979	219.7	135.2	62	162.5	—	213
1980	312.8	205.3	66	89.0	—	211
1981	271.3	65.1	24	35.8	—	271
1982	300.9	61.6	21	—	9	320
1983	224.2	39.8	18	—	0	350

Sources: 1965/67: den Tuinder. Other years: (a)–(c), *Marchès Tropicaux et Méditerranéens*, 21 January 1983, p. 136: (d) 1971–1975, den Tuinder; 1976–1981, *Ministère de l'Economie et des Finances*; (e) 1965–1975, den Tuinder; 1982–1983, *Marchès Tropicaux*, Op. Cit.; (f) IMF (1982) up to 1981, guesstimates thereafter.

[a] *Budget Spécial d'Investissement et d'Equipement.*
[b] Including, in addition to Stabilization Fund transfers, resources of public enterprises, local saving, etc.
[d] Net results of stabilization; not published after 1981.
[e] From reserves plus current income.
[f] Market rate, period average. See "sources" for 1982 and 1983.

TABLE 3 Surpluses of the Marketing Board During the Cocoa Boom and Their Uses (Billion CFAF)

	1976–1977	1977–1978	1978–1979
Net surplus	243.8	173.3	162.5
Total transfers to other sectors and central government budget	238.0	171.8	162.3
Direct subsidy to agriculture	0.3	0.2	0.2
Addition to Stabilization Fund reserves	5.5	1.3	0.0
Percentage reinvested in the agricultural sector (%)	15.8	31.2	35.6
Percentage reinvested in other sectors (%)	84.2	68.8	64.4

Source: Ministère de l'Agriculture, 1982.

investment purposes, primarily outside export-crop agriculture. Table 2 only gives figures on the Capital Investment Budget, but the Stabilization Fund also makes transfers to public enterprise budgets and to pay for food production development projects, as in the case of rice in Northern Ivory Coast. As shown in Table 3, however, nonagriculture received the lion's share of cash crop surpluses during the boom years.

Thus the Stabilization Fund played the role of a major resource reallocator during the late 1970s. Had the surplus remained in the producers' hands, it is unlikely that it would have been used in the same manner. A review of recent Capital Budget (BSIE) expenditure shows that priority is typically given to creation of transport and urban infrastructure (*Marches Tropicaux et Mediterraneens*, 1983).

Public investment is the major determinant of the direction of the Ivorian economy. It constituted more than 25 percent of GDP in 1978, a year exhibiting a real growth rate of 10 percent in domestic products (*Ministère de l'Economie et des Finances,* 1974). A period of decline set in after the cocoa and coffee price boom of the mid to late 70s. Starting with a 10 percent drop from 1977 to 1978, cocoa prices fell 25 percent between 1980 and 1981, to experience the steepest drop of a twenty-five year period. This series of declines can be correlated with subsequent poor performance of some macroaggregates. From 25.5 percent in 1978, the ratio of public investment to GDP fell to less than 14 percent in 1981, and the overall balance of payments deteriorated during these same years from a surplus of CFAF 90 billion to a deficit of CFAF 148 billion. The growth rate of domestic product slowed from 10 percent per annum in 1978 to 6.3 percent in 1980, arriving at a net annual decline of 1.6 percent in 1981 (Ministere de l'Economie et des Finances, 1974).

COCOA EXPANSION AND THE DEVELOPMENT OF IVORIAN PLANTER INTERESTS

Historical Pattern of Cocoa Development

Cocoa was introduced into West Africa during the 18th century. The first plantation of cocoa in Ivory Coast was established in 1880. At that time, almost all estates were owned by Europeans. After a period of high prices triggered by the First World War, African planters took interest in cocoa cultivation and production expanded rapidly, starting in the Southeast: from 2,000 metric tons in 1922 to 55,000 in 1939. However, this production effort was frustrated by an embargo on exports during the Second World War. Cocoa output declined thereafter, but picked up momentum with the design of various government programs to increase production. The "cocoa boom" came in the late 1970s, when exports virtually doubled in five years. A chronology of Ivorian cocoa production and exports is contained in Table 4. The appreciable gap noted in Table 4 between production and exports is attributable to a small amount of local processing of beans, storage losses, and external marketing problems explored later in the chapter.

The historical pattern through the 1960s is shared by most African cocoa producing countries. However, the recent boom in the Ivory Coast cocoa industry does not extend to other major African producers. Indeed, while Ivorian cocoa output increased from 180,000 metric tons in the 1970–1971 crop year to 262,000 in 1975–1976, and then to 412,000 in 1980–1981, the Ghanian crop decreased for the same years respectively from 392,000 metric tons to 377,000 tons, and then to 258,000 tons in 1980–1981. The Nigerian crop declined from 308,000 tons in 1970–1971 to 214,000 tons in 1975–1976, and 155,000 tons in 1980–1981 (Gill and Duffus).

Rise of the Cocoa Bourgeoisie

Linked with the economic opportunities offered by cocoa and coffee culture, an African bourgeoisie began to appear in forest zone areas as early as the 1920s. Sawadogo notes that even a mediocre plantation of five hectares, with low average yields of 250 kg/ha, provided a greater income than that of the District Commissioner at the time. Civil servants, teachers, doctors, and other Ivorian professionals rushed to take advantage of the new opportunities offered for a minimal investment (Baulin, 1982).

TABLE 4 Production and Exports of Cocoa Beans in Ivory Coast 1919–1981 (000 metric tons)

Year	Production	Exports
1919	1	1
1922	2	2
1923	4	4
1930	22	22
1939	55	22
1940	46	46
1941	43	43
1942	28	28
1943	18	1
1944	14	14
1945	27	27
1950	53	62
1955	79	75
1960	62	63
1963	148	126
1970	181	143
1975	242	170
1980	400	310
1981	440	340

Source: Gill and Duffus (various issues).

In common with many areas of colonial Africa faced with worldwide depression in the 1930s, policies were instituted to discriminate against African smallholders. Sawadogo notes that African cocoa was classified as "wild" to permit collusion among purchasers to pay lower prices. Smallholders had difficulty in obtaining inputs, and bonus prices were allocated to holdings of over 25 ha, thus excluding 99 percent of African producers. Furthermore, European planters were able to use forced labor (Baulin, 1982).

These conditions provided the barb for political organization among the southern Ivorian planters, united in opposition to forced labor despite the fact that they were personally exempt. The struggle ended in the suppression of forced labor in all French colonies in 1946 after a battle royal led in the French National Assembly by a young deputy who was to give his name to the law: Felix Houphouet-Boigny (Sawadogo, 1980). Thus the history of cocoa in Ivory Coast is closely bound up with the creation of the *Rassemblement Democratique Africain,* an offshoot of which is still the ruling party in Ivory Coast. Membership of the latter, at the highest levels, includes individuals with substantial cocoa interests. President Houphouet-Boigny, for example, maintains a cocoa farm of over 1200 ha in Yamoussoukro (*Afrique Agriculture,* June 1979).

Despite the press attention attracted to the very few large cocoa plantations in Ivory Coast, cocoa is overwhelmingly a smallholder product. The 1974 agricultural census showed that the average size of the nearly 225,000 farms which produced some cocoa in that year was 3.5 ha (*Ministere de l'Agriculture,* 1975). Furthermore, only slightly over one-fifth of these farms were ten ha or larger. Estimating the average smallholder household population (plus permanent hired labor) at seven persons, this implies that just under one person in five in Ivory Coast is directly involved in cocoa farming.

Recently, Gastellu and Affou Yapi have argued, on the basis of anthropological fieldwork, that there is a fundamental class distinction between owners of even large (50 ha or more) cocoa plantations that live on the farm and absentee landlords, for the most part urban people who have invested in cocoa. They argue that the farmers, whom they call "village planters," are not technologically, socially, or politically differentiated from smallholders. Thus they build a case that virtually all of Ivorian cocoa production is produced by a group of individuals that have little common class interest with urban-based political notables; businessmen and administrators that also gain financially from cocoa. Since there is a class-mediated conflict of interest between these two groups of planters in their view, their argument suggests that it is illusory to view the Ivorian power structure as a united front pushing the interests of cocoa development. In fact, there may be an assymetry of interests, since the absentee ("bourgeois") planters benefit indirectly from prourban agricultural policies, whereas rural owner-operators may not. Nevertheless, Gastellu and Affou Yapi's data also serve to make the point essential for our purposes below: a great number of people in the Ivorian power structure, including those in urban areas, have a direct financial stake in the health of the cocoa industry at the producer level. This, we claim, is a significant difference between Ivory Coast and most other West African nations.

ROLE OF THE STATE IN PROMOTING COCOA DEVELOPMENT

Institutions

The very rapid expansion of cocoa production, despite consistently high rates of price taxation, is less a "miracle" than the result of a number of long-term policies designed to promote cocoa development. Scientific research on cocoa has been carried out since colonial times, with an important and current direct input from the *Institut Français du Café, du Cacao et autres Plantes Stimulantes* (IFCC-GERDAT). Extension is the province of the *Société d'Assistance Téchnique pour la Modernisation Agricole de la Côte d'Ivoire* (SATMACI), a parastatal created along crop lines in 1963, in tandem with the Stabilization Fund. The original purpose of SATMACI was to promote coffee and cocoa, but it has since assumed regional responsibility for agricultural development in the forest zone. Specifically, SATMACI assists in disease control for cocoa, provision of subsidized fertilizers, and extension of high-yielding varieties. The 1976–1980 cocoa development plan allocated US $77 million to direct SATMACI action and a $240 cash subsidy to farmers for every new hectare planted in cocoa.

Thus several points in institutional organization stand out. Research has long been a priority and carried out in conjunction with efforts in other cocoa-producing countries. The extension function is distinct from the research function and has a definite crop orientation, yet the two functions are closely coordinated. Output marketing is independent of input supply, and in fact is entirely carried out by private enterpreneurs. As noted above, the Stabilization Fund functions as a regulatory body; all micro level marketing functions and decisions remain in private hands. This last point is in stark contrast to the marketing boards of Anglophone Africa.

Research Results and the Expansion of Production

Cocoa trees generally begin fruiting between three and seven years and yields begin to decline after 25 years. Yields vary principally according to plant material, disease and insect protection, age, and soil fertility (*Afrique Agriculture*, June 1979). Technological progress in cocoa production in Ivory Coast has consisted primarily in improved insect protection, replacement of aging trees, and introduction of Amazonian hybrids, capable of increased photosynthetic activity given changes in farming systems and increased fertilizer use (Liabeuf, 1979). In fact, Ivory Coast is the only major African producer with a tree stock age pyramid wider at the base than at the summit, indicating substantial recent planting activity (Liabeuf, 1979).

Statistics on cocoa area are suspect in most producing countries. Ivorian figures were substantially improved by the 1974 agricultural census (*Ministère de l'Agriculture*, 1975). The survey showed that approximately 19 percent of the Ivorian cocoa tree stock in 1974 was 25 years or older, and 27 percent was five years or younger. Policy is for 90 percent of new plantings to be of the hybrid type by 1984–1985. Whereas only 4 percent of the total area planted to cocoa in 1974 consisted of hybrids, this figure had risen to 14 percent by 1980 (*Ministère de l'Agriculture,* 1980). Since the hybrids begin production earlier and at higher levels, the impact of this policy on Ivorian output in the 1980s is indisputable.

Table 5 brings together the official statistics on area and yield growth for Ivorian cocoa in the 1960s and 1970s. As noted above, some skepticism may be attached to the pre-1974 figures and thus to calculated growth rates. Therefore the results in the table should be taken as best guesses, rather than firm facts. It is clear that the lion's share of expansion of production over the period came from extension of area harvested. Nevertheless, yields have risen appreciably (2.2 percent per annum on the average). This is in contrast to yield declines in the erstwhile major world producer, Ghana, where lack of disease control and aging tree stock are taking their toll.

Incentives Policies

As noted previously, cocoa pricing policy in Ivory Coast has generally been extractive. Table 6 shows that producers typically realized about half of the FOB Abidjan export price from 1960 to 1975. During the cocoa boom of the late seventies this proportion declined to one-third, as world prices soared, reaching a low point of 19 percent in 1977. As of this writing, the comparable ratio for early 1983 is 0.6 percent, due to the maintenance of a stable producer price and the slide in world prices (*Marchés Tropicaux et Méditerranéens,* April 15, 1983).

Ivorian price policies for cocoa during the latter 1970s had the appearance of much in common with other West African producers, as shown by the similarity in the reported nominal protection coefficients of Table 7. However, it is clear that incentives were, in fact, considerably higher in Ivory Coast than in the Anglophone countries due to a much less overvalued and fully convertible currency, an effect that may not be fully reflected in the "adjusted" NPCs for the Anglophone countries. Although data on cocoa smuggling is hard to come by, it is clear that substantial flows have come over the border from Ghana since the late 1970s, even up to the present time, despite harsh measures to police the Ghanaian side of the border since 1981. Nevertheless, it is clear that the main Latin American competitor, Brazil, has been able to subsidize incentives to its producers, due perhaps to lack of a comparable revenue imperative for taxing cocoa exports.

Because yields are very sensitive to application of chemical treatments and fertilizers, and because producers can reduce labor costs by harvesting only a portion of their holdings without harm to the trees, the price elasticity of supply in cocoa production can be surprisingly high for a perennial crop. As shown in Table 7, Ivory Coast has the highest such elasticity among

TABLE 5 Area and Yield Growth in Ivorian Cocoa

Average	Area under cocoa	Area harvested	Harvested/planted	Production	Ivory Coast Average Yields	Ghana Average Yields	Brazil Average Yields
	000 ha.	000 ha.	%	000 m. tons	kg./ha.	kg./ha.	kg./ha.
1960-1961—1964-1965	402.6	281.1	70	104.7	370	250	317
1965-1966—1969-1970	495.1	357.2	72	147.0	410	—	—
1970-1971—1974-1975[a]	694.6	447.1	66	208.0	466	249[b]	448[b]
1975-1976—1979-1980	924.4	583.8	63	297.3	510	214	636
1960-1965—1975-1980	130%	108%	—	+184%	+38%	-14%	+101%
1960-1965—1975-1980[e]							
average annual growth rate	5.7%	5.0%	—	+7.2%	+2.2%	-1.0%	+4.8%

[a]The Ivorian figures for 1974 and 1975 were revised following the 1974 Agricultural Census. Therefore the comparison of pre-1974 and post-1974 figures in the table should be interpreted with caution.

[b]1973–1975 only.

[c]Midpoint to midpoint (15 years).

Sources: Ivory Coast: *Ministère de l'Agriculture,* 1980. Ghana and Brazil: 1960–1975, FAO data from Lee; 1975–80 from *FAO Production Yearbook.*

TABLE 6 Ivorian Cocoa Price 1960–1980 CFAF/kg.

Year	(1) Minimum Guaranteed Producer Price	(2) F.O.B. Export Price, Abidjan	(3) Ratio (1)/(2)	(4) Average Ratio
1960	85	138	0.62	
1961	89	111	0.80	
1962	64	105	0.61	0.67
1963	64	113	0.57	
1964	70	117	0.50	
1965	70	86	0.81	
1966	55	105	0.52	
1967	70	132	0.53	0.45
1968	70	160	0.44	
1969	70	222	0.32	
1970	80	183	0.44	
1971	85	148	0.58	
1972	85	142	0.60	
1973	85	194	0.44	0.52
1974	110	303	0.36	
1975	150	245	0.61	
1976	150	391	0.38	
1977	180	968	0.19	
1978	250	725	0.34	0.34
1979	250	650	0.38	
1980	300	706	0.42	

Sources: Lee to 1974, unpublished figures of the stabilization fund.

TABLE 7 Comparative Price Policy Indicators for Major Cocoa Producers

	Adjusted nominal protection coefficients	Long-run price elasticity of supply	Approximate 1980 world market share
Ivory Coast	.38	.59	23%[a]
Ghana	.40[b]	.126	23%
Nigeria	.50	.113	15%
Cameroon	.31	—	7%
Brazil	1.1	.54	10%

[a]27% in 1982.

[b]Unadjusted for overvalue exchange rate.

Sources: NPC's calculated by the World Bank as background for the *World Development Report*, 1982 except for Nigeria and Ghana which are estimated by the authors from project evaluation documents. The supply elasticities are from World Bank, Commodities and Export Projections Division (1982). The approximate 1980 market share is from the FAO *Trade Yearbook* (1980).

major cocoa producers. This suggests the need for caution in pursuing a positive price policy, in view of the large Ivorian market share and the aggregate price inelasticity of world demand. Ivory Coast may have reached the point where producer price increases become counter-productive with respect to aggregate national revenues, although further research needs to be done in this area.

One aspect of incentives policies that deserves attention, and is frequently overlooked, concerns provision by the State of marketing infrastructure to ensure that producers are able to sell all their output in a timely fashion. The policy of having marketing functions handled by private intermediaries ensures that the bureaucratic bottlenecks characteristic of marketing boards are avoided. Equally important, Ivory Coast has been, in relative terms, one of the world's great investors in roads, which now reach into every corner of the cocoa zone (den Tuinder, 1978). It is striking that in agriculturally-oriented Ivory Coast, agricultural services only accounted for 2.9 percent of central government functional expenditure in 1978, whereas roads accounted for 7.3 percent. The median proportions in Sub-Saharan Africa as a whole are 9 percent for agriculture and 5.5 percent for roads (World Bank, 1981).

Manpower Policies

In addition to administrative public entities, such as the Stabilization Fund, Ivory Coast has at least 19 state corporations such as SATMACI, that reach into every aspect of agricultural production. This has been singled out as a particularly common occurrence in Sub-Saharan Africa, and one that is increasingly criticized by outside observers (World Bank, 1981). Yet Ivory Coast is quite distinct in its efforts to alleviate the logical consequence of a skilled manpower intensive development strategy. Education, including university level training, has been the highest priority of the Ivorian government since independence. While not without problems, educational policy in Ivory Coast over the last twenty years has been primarily directed to alleviating the skilled manpower constraint (den Tuinder, 1978). Furthermore, the government has not hesitated to use expatriates to fulfill the need for professionals and managers *en attendant.* The number of French technical assistants doubled between independence and the mid-1970s. Furthermore, Europeans, Syrians, and Lebanese have been estimated to constitute 2.5 percent of the population in 1975, occupying many managerial positions in the skilled professions, commerce, and administration (den Tuinder, 1978).

On the other hand, rapid expansion of agricultural production based primarily on acreage expansion has aggravated the unskilled labor constraint prevalent in Ivory Coast, as in most African economies. Low paid migrant workers were encouraged to come to Ivory Coast by the government in order to keep labor costs down (Sawadogo, 1980). This group accounted for almost 30 percent of the population in 1975, and most certainly a higher percentage of the agricultural labor force (Lee, 1983).

Thus by deliberate attention to nonprice policies favorable to agriculture, the State has played a vigorous role in promoting export crop agriculture over the last twenty years. These nonprice policies have consisted of institutional experimentation in mixing private and public decision-making, agricultural research, extension, roadbuilding, and manpower policies designed to improve the quality of managerial decision-making, while keeping unskilled labor costs relatively low. Whereas many other African nations have also been quick to tax export agriculture, it is an open question as to whether their nonprice policies have been as favorable to its expansion. The next section will explore some of the internal issues affecting the future of export crop agriculture in Ivory Coast, the principal one of which may be the attempt to apply the same sort of interventionist strategy to other sectors enjoying less of a comparable advantage.

INTERNAL ISSUES AFFECTING THE FUTURE OF COCOA: RELATIVE INCENTIVES AND EQUITY

Trade-offs Between Food and Export Crops at the Producer Level

Since the late 1970s, concerns have been expressed both inside and outside the Ivorian government that cocoa and coffee farmers had begun shifting resources out of traditional export commodities and into food crop production, in which Ivory Coast presumably has less of a comparative advantage. Maintaining the internal terms of trade of agriculture in favor of cocoa in the forest zone may have been one of the principal motivations for raising the guaranteed producer price to 300 CFAF in 1980, and for maintaining it since then in spite of sliding world prices.

In any event, examination of acreage and production data for the principal cocoa-producing zones in 1980 shows little reason for concern on this score with respect to the future of cocoa production, although other questions could be raised with respect to food policies. As indicated in Table 8, cocoa acreage and production shot up by 60 and 66 percent, respectively, in the late 1970s. However, the major food crops did not do nearly as well. Although area harvested increased at the probable (but unknown) rate of population increase in the zone, production per capita in 1980 was almost certainly lower than in 1970. Even allowing for the influence of using a year of poor yields as an endpoint, it is still clear that the relative importance of cocoa in forest zone farming systems increased during the late 1970s. In fact, more recent setbacks in cocoa output in the early 1980s may be attributable to farmers giving increased attention to food crops and less to cocoa, but the data to measure this are not yet available.

Examination of available price data confirms the plausibility of the results in Table 8. Table 9 shows that the nominal producer price of cocoa increased faster after the 1970s than did those of all major food crops, with the exception of plantain. Since plantain is typically grown in association with cocoa, relatively higher prices for this crop may constitute an incentive to divert labor away from the export commodity, other things being equal. With respect to field crops such as maize and yams, calculations of net returns per man-day made in the mid-1970s show that cocoa returns are five to ten times higher than returns to these crops. Only irrigated rice with subsidized mechanization and subsidized producer prices comes anywhere close to equality with low-yielding "traditional" cultivation of cocoa (den Tuinder, 1978). However, increases in production costs and a decline in output price for rice since then makes even this activity a poor second-best, especially in the context of dynamic technological progress in cocoa production.

Intersectoral Trade-offs: Agriculture vs. Nonagriculture

The indexes in Table 9 do serve to indicate a major shift in market incentives that may have serious implications for cocoa. The Abidjan "African" consumer price index (CPI), however unsuited to the task, may be the best measure available to deflate nominal agricultural prices in order to examine the terms of trade between agriculture and nonagriculture. A comparison of the producer price index for cocoa with the CPI shows that there was more than a 20 percent decline in the real producer price of cocoa between 1975 and 1980, even though there was a one-third improvement in favor of cocoa between 1970 and 1975. Assuming that inflation since 1980 has continued at about 10 percent per annum and given that the producer price of cocoa is unchanged, the real producer price of this commodity in 1983 is only 60 percent of its 1975 value.

On the cost side, the price and labor situation up through the cocoa boom was such that growing urban demand for labor did not adversely affect cocoa producers. Output prices for cocoa were rising rapidly and the steady flow of labor from poorer areas in the North kept labor costs down. Table 10 shows that the ratio of cocoa output prices to wage costs more than doubled between the late 1960s and the late 1970s. However, the situation has turned around since then, due to both a stagnant producer price and a rapid rise in the cost of labor, which increased 28 percent between 1978 and 1980, and is probably about 80 percent above 1978 levels as of mid-1983 (based on an estimated 600 CFAF/day wage rate). If correct, the current ratio of cocoa producer prices to wage rates is back to 1960s levels and falling.

The primary explanation of increases in the cost of agricultural labor appears to lie in competition with urban areas. During the early to mid-1970s, nonagricultural wages increased from about three times as high to about four times as high as agricultural wages (den Tuinder, 1978). As the urban sector begins to account for a relatively larger share of the labor force, it is likely that this gap will decrease, due to both increased competition for work among the urban unemployed and more widespread upward pressure on agricultural wage rates as workers leave or prefer to migrate directly to Abidjan from northern areas without stopping in the cocoa zones. The 8 percent per annum rate of urbanization in Ivory Coast tends to support these conclusions.

The likelihood that these trends will continue, to the detriment of export crop agriculture, is increased by a series of fundamental policy changes implemented in Ivory Coast during the 1970s. As argued by Michel and Noel, the 1973 tariff reform and subsequent imposition of a host of protective import quotas was a new departure in industrial protection. In effect, there appears to have been a shift in development emphasis from export-crop growth strategies towards import-substituting industrialization behind tariff

TABLE 8 Relative Performance of Cocoa and Food Crops in Major Ivorian Cocoa Areas[a]

	1970[b]	1975	1980	% Change[b] 1970–1980	% Change 1975–1980
Area Harvested in Major Cocoa Districts (000 ha.)					
Rice	112	174	223	98%	28%
Maize	122	273	339	117%	24%
Yams	115	166	199	74%	20%
Rice, Maize and Yams combined	349	612	760	118%	24%
Cocoa[c]	387	471	752	94%	60%
Production in Major Cocoa/Districts (000 ha.)					
Rice	145	217	209	44%	–4%
Maize	102	125	145	42%	16%
Yams	1,139	1,595	1,559	37%	–2%
Cassava	413	715	861	109%	20%
Plantain	540	970	1,004	85%	3%

132

All major food crops above	2,342	3,623	3,777	61%	4%
Average Cereal Yields in Major Cocoa Districts[a] (kg./ha.)					
Rice	1,290	1,250	940	—[e]	—
Maize	840	460	430	—	—
Average Cereal Yields Nationally[d]					
Rice	1,090	1,270	1,110	—	—
Maize	710	520	430	—	—

[a]Major cocoa areas are defined as those administrative departments that produced at least 10,000 metric tons of dry cocoa beans during the 1979–1980 season. This classification includes the Abengourou, Abidjan, Aboisso, Adzope, Bondoukou, Bouafle, Bouake, Daloa, Dimbokro, Divo, Gagnoa and Sassandra administrative units.

[b]The 1970 data may not be fully comparable to years after 1974, since the first detailed national census of agriculture occurred in that year.

[c]Includes all Ivorian cocoa. The major cocoa districts retained here accounted for 93 percent of Ivorian cocoa area cultivated in 1980.

[d]Computed from data in the table.

[e]Not given since trends in yields between two single years are particularly misleading.

Source: Compiled from disaggregated data in *Ministère de l'Agriculture* (1980).

133

TABLE 9 Major Agricultural Price Movements 1970–1980

	Abidjan Region Retail			1980 National Retail (season/location)		
	1970	1975	1980	Lowest	Average	Highest
Rice (millet)						
CFAF/kg.	74	110	128	121	136	162
Index	67.3	100.0	116.4	—	—	—
Maize						
CFAF/kg.	42	73	98	50	72	113
Index	57.5	100.0	134.2	—	—	—
Yams (late)						
CFAF/kg.	36	51	74	48	68	88
Index	70.6	100.0	145.1	—	—	—
Cassava						
CFAF/kg.	34	54	45	16	29	48
Index	63.0	100.0	83.3	—	—	—
Plantain						
CFAF/kg.	22	33	62	19	51	84
Index	66.7	100.0	187.9	—	—	—
	45.7	100.0	171.4	—	300 CFAF/kg.	—
Cocoa (Index of Producer Prices)	63.3	100.0	100.0	—	150 CFAF/kg.	—
Coffee (Index of Producer Prices)						
Consumer Price Index (Abidjan, low income)	69.7	100.0	215.7	—	—	—

Sources: den Tuinder 1978; *Ministère de l'Agriculture*, 1980; IMF, 1982.

TABLE 10 Major Changes in the Cost of Agricultural Labor 1961–1980 (current CFAF/day)

| Year[a] | Minimum Agricultural Wage | | Actual Agricultural Wage, Major Cocoa Producing Areas[b] | | Indices | | | | |
	Cocoa, housed and fed	Timber, not housed or fed	housed and fed	not housed or fed	Abidjan African Consumer Price Index	Cocoa Minimum Produce Price	Minimum Cocoa Wage, housed and fed	Minimum Timber Wage, not housed or fed	Actual Agricultural Wage in Cocoa Zones[b] housed and fed
1961	156	302	—	—	33	36	57	59	—
1963	156	320	—	—	33	26	57	62	—
1968	156	320	—	—	38	28	57	62	—
1970	156	290	—	—	43	32	57	56	—
1973	160	325	—	—	48	34	58	63	—
1974	200	356	—	—	56	44	73	69	—
1976	250	424	—	—	69	60	91	82	—
1977	250	445	—	—	89	72	91	86	—
1978	275	516	328	488	100	100	100	100	100
1979	275	516	351	523	116	100	100	100	107
1980	275	516	420	622	134	120	100	100	128

[a]Wage rates are for end of period; other items are period averages.

[b]Average of rates reported by extension agents in the administrative districts of: Abengourou, Abidjan, Aboisso, Adzope, Bondoukou, Boufle, Bouake, Daloa, Dimbokro, Divo, Gagnoa, and Sassandra.

Sources: Compiled from data in *Ministère de l'Agriculture*, 1980 and Table 6.

barriers. In addition to implications for investment priorities and other direct policies, such a shift would have important consequences on incentives to produce cocoa. This would occur through market processes, akin to the labor and price trends described above, that shift a higher proportion of national resources into nonagriculture than would have been the case otherwise. Other things being equal, outputs in the relatively efficient cocoa sector are shifted to less efficient sectors, where world prices are taken as true opportunity costs for the purpose of determining efficiency. In other words, the relative incentives between cocoa and manufacturing have shifted in favor of the latter to the detriment of the former. An issue, then, that needs further research is how reducing effective taxation of cocoa production can correct the "distortion" without unduly harming other policy goals.

Interaction Between Cocoa Growth Strategies and Equity Considerations

The trade-off between growth and equity is one of the perennial debates in development economics, particularly in the context of export crop growth. In this regard, it is useful to distinguish four concepts of equity: interpersonal, regional, sectoral, and absolute. Interpersonal equity concerns the economic differentiation of individuals and is properly investigated using such measures as the size distribution of personal incomes. Regional equity is defined to encompass the host of concerns felt by governments with respect to the distribution of wealth in different geographic areas of the country. Sectoral equity means the relative positions of agriculture and nonagriculture, whereas absolute equity is taken to mean the chance for an individual to realize his or her highest opportunities. Alternately, absolute equity could be defined as interpersonal equity defined across national borders, at least certainly when discussing relatively poor African farmers.

Sectoral and absolute equity considerations are likely to be the most important long-run issues in promoting Ivorian cocoa development, especially if the trends outlined in the previous section persist. Nevertheless, policy attention for the forseeable future is likely to be focused on interpersonal and regional issues. We shall accordingly confine our attention to these two sets of questions in assessing the implications for future cocoa development.

Writers concerned with interpersonal equity in Ivory Coast tend to focus on income differences among specific groups of people, such as forest zone smallholders. Thus Lee argues that cocoa-based growth strategies have been achieved at the cost of increased social and economic differentiation arising from the creation of an elite of larger farmers employing hired labor.

Lee correctly argues that the World Bank estimates of agricultural income distribution (den Tuinder, 1978) are, in fact, measurements of differences in income per capita in different administrative districts. They do not convey information about the size distribution of personal incomes, and should not be used to make inferences about income inequality across households within any given area. Therefore, Lee falls back on "partial indicators" of rural inequality, principally the size distribution of landholdings in Southern and Northern Ivory Coast, based on 1974 agricultural census data. He calculates a Gini coefficient of 0.450 for Southern Ivory Coast in this regard, which by implication is synonymous with the forest zone. This coefficient is found to be "a high figure [denoting greater inequality] compared with those of most Sub-Saharan African countries for which estimates are available, as well as some Asian countries . . . " (den Tuinder, 1978, p. 114).

In fact, this measure of income inequality is totally inappropriate to areas with large amounts of unused land, as was the case in Ivory Coast in the mid-1970s. Larger farms tend to be associated with larger families. Although Lee does note this latter fact he does not formally incorporate it into his calculations. Table 11 contains reworked calculations of Lee's data to estimate the size distribution of farm income per capita in the forest zone. This necessarily involves some simplifying assumptions. Average family size in each land size category is substituted for actual household family sizes. Household income is assumed to be equally shared by household members. Furthermore, the income groups chosen probably include significant income disparities within them, as in the case of two versus 4.9 hectare farms. Finally, income includes imputed subsistence income, which is hard to measure. Nevertheless, the conceptual improvement is felt to justify losses in precision.

The data in Table 11 yield an estimated Gini coefficient for the size distribution of personal farm income of 0.195, indicating a comparatively high degree of equality in the forest zone. Given the bias that can result in this form of calculation from using income bands that are too wide, Lee's more disaggregated data on the size distribution of landholdings was reworked in the larger land size categories of Table 11. The results show only a very small decline in the estimated Gini coefficient, from 0.45 to 0.43.

The question therefore arises as to why income distribution within forest zone farms appears to be so much more equal than the distribution of landholdings. The definitive answer to this puzzle must await further microeconomic fieldwork. However, Lee's data suggest an answer that provides guidelines on further work. Farms of under two hectares are seen to have land/labor ratios of the order of one-third hectare per agricultural worker. The comparable ratio for farms over 10 hectares exceeds two hectares per worker. Thus it would seem that small farms are worked much more intensively. While this may at first suggest land scarcity, it is also consistent with relative labor scarcity. Some farmers prefer to cultivate a

TABLE 11 Rough Measures of Farm Income Distribution in the Ivorian Forest Zone

Size of Landholding	Distribution of Farms	Distribution of Resident Population	Distribution of Population	Cumulative Population	Cash Income Per Capita by Farm Size	Cumulative Income	Cumulative Distribution of Income	Cumulative Distribution of Population
(Ha.)	(%)	(persons)	(%)	(persons)	(CFAF)	(million CFAF)	(%)	(%)
0.0– 1.99	24	588,600	16.5	588,600	9,622	19,201	9	16
2.0– 4.99	37	1,158,240	32.0	1,746,840	25,000	74,797	34	48
5.0– 9.99	27	1,066,420	29.5	2,813,260	44,633	146,923	66	78
10.0–19.99	10	619,040	17.0	3,432,300	59,236	197,830	89	95
20.0–99.99	2	189,040	5.0	3,621,340	114,824	222,926	100	100

Gini coefficient: 0.195.
Source: Calculated from "Unpublished estimates, *Direction du Plan*", given in Lee, Table 35.

small area of high-value crops intensively, while others form a larger area extensively. Both may in fact have similar incomes. In sum, the available data are not consistent with the view that there is substantial income inequality among farmers in the forest zone. The major qualifier, of course, is that heads of larger households may carry disproportionate economic and political influence; this is akin to the distinction between managerial and ownership power in the industrial world.

Despite the relative equality of income within forest zone farming areas, major differences between personal wealth in the North and South of the Ivory Coast is likely to have important implications for the future of cocoa development. Lee reports a 1981 estimate of as high as 7 to 1 for the ratio of average incomes between the two areas, although this is undoubtedly on the high side, due to the disproportionate influence of Abidjan. Ivorian government policy has stressed redistribution of income from forest to savannah zones for some time. This essentially takes the form of directly taxing coffee and cocoa production and earmarking the proceeds for development of agriculture and agroindustry in the North.

The southern crops of cocoa and coffee accounted for over 90 percent of government tax receipts from agriculture in the 1980–1981 crop season, not including the surplus generated by the Stabilization Fund, as shown in Table 12. Direct export taxes on cocoa were equivalent to about one-third to one-quarter of payments to producers in the mid-seventies (den Tuinder, 1978). Sugar, cotton, and rice accounted for 93 percent of government subsidies to agriculture in 1980–1981. Sugar and cotton are grown entirely in the North; the main focus of government attention to rice production is also there.

It can be argued that the source and use of government funds are two completely separate entities, therefore the data in Table 12 are not relevant to the impact of cocoa production on equity or of equity concerns on the future of cocoa. However, it is clear that the transfer of income from cocoa and coffee to sugar, cotton, and rice is a conscious objective of Ivorian policy, and thought of in this manner. Furthermore, it is also clear that the overriding objectives in promoting the last three crops are to provide a source of income to the North; diversification and increased food production are only secondary objectives. Therefore, the evolution of policy with respect to high cost domestic sugar and rice production cannot fail to be of interest in assessing probable policies towards cocoa. In this sense, regional equity considerations are likely to severely constrain cocoa production policies, be they price or direct intervention based.

This is especially true today, with lower world prices for the southern export crops and the fact that a major agroindustrial infrastructure for sugar is now in place in the North, requiring a high recurrent subsidy from the central government. Ivorian sugar production was 168,000 tons during the 1981–1982 season, of which 108,000 tons were exported during the first

TABLE 12 Government Balance Sheet for Major Agricultural Projects in 1980/81 (in million CFAF)

Products	Tax Receipts	Percentage of Total Tax Receipts	Subsidies	Percentage Total Subsidies	Balance
Coffee	43,136	45	—	—	43,136
Cocoa	44,712	46	—	—	44,712
Cotton	6,826	7	8,856	18	−2,030
Palm oil	792	1	792	2	0
Coconut	538	1	264	—	274
Fresh Pineapple	381	—	734	2	−353
Canned Pineapple	—	—	859	2	−859
Banana	264	—	694	1	−430
Sugar	—	—	29,210	61	−29,210
Rice	—	—	6,749	14	−6,749
Soybean	—	—	92	—	−92
Total	96,649	100	48,250	100	48,399

Source: Ministère de l'Agriculture, 1982.

nine months of 1982 at the average price of 57.4 CFAF/kg., substantially below production costs (*Marchés Tropicaux et Méditerranéens,* April 22, 1983). The future of cocoa production may depend upon delinking cocoa and sugar policies.

In sum, the rising relative value of foodstuffs such as plantain, increases in labor costs and shifts in the intersectoral terms of trade against agriculture, and discriminatory policies motivated by regional equity concerns all raise questions with respect to the sustainability in the 1980s and 1990s of export-crop led growth of the type provided by cocoa in the 1970s. Two items could turn this situation around. First, bright prospects for technological change in Ivorian cocoa production could substantially improve the relative profitability of cocoa cultivation. Second, a significant rise in the relative world price of cocoa would have the same affect, *ceteris paribus.* The next section investigates the external issues facing Ivorian cocoa production, raises some serious concerns in this respect, and provides the framework for some operational recommendations with respect to future cocoa export strategies.

EXTERNAL ISSUES AFFECTING THE FUTURE OF IVORIAN COCOA: INCREASED COMPETITION FOR A STAGNANT MARKET[2]

A Stagnant World Market, the International Cocoa Agreement, and Lack of Producer Cooperation

The world cocoa market is dominated by a small number of sellers and purchasers. Aggregate demand is price inelastic in most importing countries, of the order of 0.3 (Gbetibouo, 1982). This a minor stock decline of 29,000 metric tons in 1975–1976 was the main influence on the doubling of world prices in 1976–1988. Conversely, supply increases from good weather or technological change severely depress both world prices and producer revenues. Thus, there was an historically high excess quantity of beans of 148,000 metric tons in 1979–1980, setting the pace for a gradual decrease in real prices to their current low levels. This situation provides a powerful incentive to producers to attempt to limit world supply, driving prices up.

Capriciousness of supply and inelasticity of demand combine to give cocoa prices the highest degree of instability among the major commodities surveyed by UNCTAD. This fact has motivated attempts to regulate and stabilize the world cocoa market. One such attempt is the International Cocoa Organization (ICCO), bringing cocoa producing and consuming countries together for the purpose of signing and implementing a pact, the International Cocoa Agreement.

Three agreements have been signed since 1972. The Ivory Coast signed the 1975 agreement reluctantly, and refused to sign the current one on the grounds that the floor intervention price was too low and that, as the Ivorian Minister of Agriculture put it, the price adjustment scheme "held the germ of speculation" (*African Business,* January 1981). There was a clause in the original agreement stipulating that countries representing at least 80 percent of the market had to sign before the pact entered into force. Without Ivory Coast, 23 percent of the market at the time of signature, the agreement could not be operative.

The Ivory Coast still could not be persuaded to join after many attempts in this vein from other cocoa market participants, producers and consumers alike. Therefore, the agreement was signed anyway without the participation of the world's largest producer. On the import market side the world's leading buyer, the United States, also refused to participate on the grounds that the floor intervention price was too high. However, the absence of Ivory Coast in the current agreement probably has more to do with the current difficulties of the agreement than the absence of the United States (Kirschen, 1983). In 1980, the average (ICCO) market price was $1.18/lb and in 1981 it was $.94/lb. In June 1981, just before the third agreement was signed, prices were as low as $.75/lb. When traders anticipated the entry into force of the pact in September of the same year, prices jumped to $1.06/lb based on a planned floor intervention price of $1.00/lb. Later, when traders realized that the agreement was not going to be effective without the participation of Ivory Coast, and without enough money from the buffer stock management to buy up the surplus cocoa, prices fell back to their previous low levels, reaching $.79/lb in 1982.

During the previous two agreements, market prices never went outside the intervention price band, hence the effectiveness of the ICCO had not been tested. The organization was able to accumulate $230 million from the export levy paid by member countries. The buffer stock manager used the money to purchase 100,000 metric tons of cocoa and thus push prices up to a modestly higher level. However, more money was needed to soak up an estimated 210,000 tons excess supply. Ivory Coast, which had contributed over $30 million to ICCO previously, was no longer a member and was threatening to withdraw financial participation. In view of the visible financial difficulties facing buffer stock management with respect to buying excess cocoa, prices went down further.

Besides less money for the ICCO and its price support activity, the absence of Ivory Coast from the agreement means lack of leadership on the producer's side. An influential trade journal reported:

> Oddly enough, during the life of the preceding Agreement, and despite the Ivorian–Brazilian frictions, the producers seemed orientated and gener-

ally united on what they wanted. That what they wanted was beyond their grasp is another matter. But because of the Ivory Coast leadership at that time, it seems that it was this leadership that infused a great amount of coherence, determination, and discipline in the majority producer camp (Kirschen, 1983, p. 44).

Since Ivory Coast is no longer paying levy, the members of the current agreement have to share an undue burden to finance the buffer fund. On the other hand, by supporting a rival Cocoa Producers' Alliance, but not ICCO, Ivory Coast is making it very difficult to reach a common strategy for producers.

Given the current lack of a unified producer strategy, the main issue facing the Ivory Coast cocoa industry is trade warfare with competing producing countries. For a while in the late 1970s, Ivory Coast and Brazil were engaged in a battle for leadership of the cocoa market. Huge and almost equal quantities of cocoa produced by both countries became the primary cause of the abundant world supply and consequent price decline during the years that followed. A market in which two major participants play that game of status is conducive to a special type of market outcome, Stackelberg disequilibrium, a scenario that makes everyone worse off than in competitive market conditions. In effect, the cocoa exporters' market options resembles the typical prisoners dilemma: the more one exporter puts on the market, the more revenue accrues to that exporter—provided that other exporters do not also flood the market. Yet it is rational for each single exporter acting independently to flood the market. When every exporter acts as stated, then no one gains, because of falling prices subsequent to the induced abundant supply.

The Costs of Going It Alone: the 1979–1980 Ivorian Cocoa Gamble

Frustrated with the inability to press its point of view in the ICCO, worried by the oversupply of cocoa in the world market in the late 1970s, and brushing aside complications arising from conditions in other producing countries and in the principal export markets, Ivory Coast decided to act unilaterally to support world prices. During the 1979–1980 harvest, it withdrew a huge 150,000 metric tons of cocoa from the market. This was equivalent to only 10,000 tons less than the entire crop of Nigeria, the world's fourth largest producer.

The gamble failed. Prices continued to slip downwards, due to the ability of Brazil and others, to quickly dispose of its crop and to the fact that manufacturers in the importing countries had built up record stocks in the previous two years. Thus the Ivory Coast was left with cocoa of declining quality and had no other alternative than to eventually sell it at a price far below the market price prevailing when the stockpiling started. The storage facilities owned by the government and 33 licensed export companies were crammed as storage costs in the tropical climate rose. Eventually, 100,000 tons of the stockpile was disposed of in a single operation, the largest single cocoa transaction ever made (*African Business*, June 1980). It has been estimated that the gamble cost Ivory Coast $95 million in storage costs, losses, and foregone opportunity costs of more timely sales, because of delaying from September 1979 to June 1980 (*African Business*, June 1980).

Changing Characteristics of Import Markets

A detailed simulation study of the world cocoa market by one of the present authors found that it was best characterized as oligopolists facing oligopsonists (Gbetibouo, 1982). The study showed that for the forseeable future, Ivorian exports of 375,000 metric tons to its current trade partners would maximize Ivorian revenue. In the absence of domestic distortions, this would be consistent with an implicit 150 percent ad-valorem tax on Ivorian domestic producers (i.e., producers getting about two-thirds of the world prices). This implies that for growth to occur, either new markets must be found in other LDCs or in the Eastern Block, or else efforts must be made to differentiate the Ivorian product.

In the latter regard, some changing features of the traditional import market have to be reckoned with. Processing industries in major importing countries tend to require less cocoa beans, but more cocoa products such as cocoa butter and powder. In 1970, the United Kingdom imported 80,000 metric tons of cocoa beans and 21,000 metric tons of cocoa butter. In 1980 the same figures were, respectively, 69,000 and 30,000. The United States cocoa import structure follows the same pattern: bean import decreased from 277,000 metric tons in 1970 to 144,000 in 1980, while cocoa butter imports increased from 15,000 metric tons in 1970 to 35,000 metric tons in 1980. If this trend persists, exporters should increase their local processing capacity. Currently, Ivory Coast processes only less than one-tenth of its total crop, whereas Brazil processes more than half.

LESSONS AND CONSTRAINTS FOR FUTURE GROWTH IN THE IVORIAN COCOA SECTOR

Lessons and Constraints of Internal Cocoa Policies

The primary economic lesson from the Ivorian cocoa experience with respect to "getting agriculture moving" is how quickly the smallholder sector can respond if agricultural production costs are kept low, relative to output prices. Although Ivorian cocoa planters are heavily taxed with respect to world prices, technological improvements, quality extension, good roads, skilled manpower decision-making at the technical and policy level, and cheap unskilled manpower all serve to keep cocoa production a growth industry. This is particularly noteworthy in the context of the current attention given to output price policies in many quarters, often with inadequate attention both to agricultural opportunity costs and to the length of time required for cost-cutting innovations to occur in the absence of specific policies to that effect.

The obvious political counterpart to the preceding point is that there is a congruence between the occurrence of policies favorable to low agricultural costs and the closeness of the power structure to agricultural interests. This is particularly noteworthy in regard to other countries in West Africa, where power structures are typically closely tied to urban interests. A question that arises for Ivory Coast in the future is what will happen to relative agricultural incentives as the Ivorian power structure becomes increasingly urban based. The latter phenomena can be expected to occur both with expansion of the urban sector and as university graduates with primarily urban allegiances begin to run the administration.

The most apparent internal constraint on the future of Ivorian cocoa production is the one plaguing agriculture in West Africa in general, namely the growing competition for resources of the nonagricultural sector. Possibly cocoa has held out for so long as a going venture by comparison with urban pursuits because of Ivory Coast's very great comparative advantage in this commodity. However, factor costs rising faster than productivity due to distortions in factor markets threaten to kill the goose that laid the golden egg.

Gbetibouo's work shows that in the presence of an undistorted internal factor market, Ivorian cocoa growth is maximized when producers pay no more than one-third of the world price of cocoa in implicit and explicit export taxes. Regional equity considerations and the slide in world prices threaten to produce suboptimal levels of taxation, as occurred around 1980. Furthermore, a new orientation towards import substitution in both manufacturing and food production will distort internal factor markets. In this case, the optimal export tax for cocoa will certainly be lower still.

Lessons and Constraints of External Cocoa Strategies

"Adam Smith" suggests that "when you are tempted to speculate in cocoa, lie down until the feeling goes away." However, this may not be easy advice to follow for a producer who is always in physical possession of the commodity. In view of the impact of the performance of the cocoa industry on the Ivory Coast economy and the recent misfortune in managing current cocoa overproduction—misfortune attributable to local and external factors—it is necessary to seek new export strategies.

First, it may seem judicious to stem the current plunge of prices by signing the cocoa agreement. The failure of the gamble has shown that a single producer, even the largest one, cannot go it alone. Unilateral stockpiling cannot work against a trend of the market. Only cooperative measures can. However, these latter solutions are equally hard to agree upon. Many attempts by the Ivory Coast prior to and during the 1979–1980 cocoa gamble failed to elicit cooperation from the other main producers. Ghana was experiencing serious economic difficulties and could not afford the luxury of withholding cocoa, then the only reliable and substantial source of badly needed foreign exchange. There were also rumors that Ivory Coast made side payments to other leading African cocoa producers to make them momentarily less dependent on cocoa revenues and to persuade them to comply with collective stockpiling. But the side payments could not be made for long; Ivory Coast discontinued them and was soon left to face the down sliding market alone.

Unilateral storage is only successful if it is used as an offensive weapon to artificially accentuate a shortage that already exists. It cannot work as a defensive strategy to correct a structural trend of the market. Stock accumulation in a lasting state of supply glut is generally very costly for any single producer, and of little benefit for the country undertaking it. It may, however, be of some benefit to competitors who get a free ride. Of course, one way for the country to get something from unilateral stockpiling is to use the "mad man strategy": build the reputation of irrationality and make a credible threat of flooding the market to extract concessions from competitors in international agreements. This is likely to be costly and difficult to repeat.

Local processing is another avenue to contemplate. Current processing capacity should be expanded and encouraged with adequate tax incentives, similar to those in Brazil and Ecuador, where exports of cocoa beans are taxed at a much higher rate than cocoa-derived products. This discriminatory taxation would help create more local value-added and help cope with changing import composition in major consuming countries.

Production capacity should be limited to a "reasonable" quantity. Given the supply response patterns that prevailed in the last two decades and the demand characteristics of the major importing countries, an optimum crop for Ivory Coast was estimated at 375,000 metric tons. This figure may be adjusted slightly upwards if the declining production trends in Ghana and Nigeria outweigh the production increases in new producing countries, such as Malaysia.

New marketing techniques should also be considered. Hedging is one way, but research should be done to find the optimal proportion of crop to hedge, since this technique may not be universally appropriate when there are both price and quantity variations (Rolfo, 1980; Gbetibouo, 1982), as in the case of cocoa.

New markets and expansion of old cocoa markets should be explored, especially in Africa and Asia. Promotion campaigns by the Ivorian Center for International Trade should be content with periodic exhibits, but be more aggressive and use the foreign media. Colombia, for example, advertizes mountain-grown coffee on U.S. television networks.

If an international agreement is reached, it should contain provisions for export quotas for force producing countries to limit supply. International buffer stocks in lieu of export quotas as the sole supply control mechanism in the agreement, as was the case in 1980, engenders managerial and financial problems. It may also lead to overproduction in the long run, with disastrous implications for the future of cocoa-based growth strategies.

NOTES

1. The views expressed in this paper are the sole responsibility of the authors, and should not be interpreted as reflecting the position of any organization with which they are affiliated. Gbetibouo took primary responsibility for the analysis of external issues while Delgado concentrated on internal factors. Senior authorship is not assigned.

2. The general reference for analysis and figures in this section is Gbetibouo (1982), unless otherwise indicated.

6

FOREIGN BUSINESS AND ECONOMIC DEVELOPMENT

Lynn Krieger Mytelka*

This chapter analyzes the changing role of the state, foreign and domestic capital in the development of industry in Ivory Coast. It begins by examining the emergence of the colonial state as the locus of collaboration between an Ivorian planter bourgeoisie, whose basis for capital accumulation lay in the production of export crops, and French capital, whose interests were then primarily centered in commerce. By independence, it is argued, this symbiotic relationship between foreign and Ivorian capital had been formalized in a division of labor according to which the agricultural sector was reserved to Ivorian capital, private and later state, while foreign capital was encouraged to expand into processing and secondary manufacturing.

During the 1960s and 1970s, contradictions appeared in this economic growth strategy and the state's role in the economy became more direct as it sought to develop policies to overcome these contradictions. In so doing it broke down the old division of labor by opening new opportunities for Ivorian capital in industry and it propelled the economy into greater reliance on export markets through the encouragement of export-oriented agricultural processing and manufacturing.

Despite these initiatives, by the late 1970s it was apparent that the Ivorian economy was in crisis. In contrast to prevailing analyses, it is argued here that this crisis is not merely the result of conjunctural factors, such as a fall in the world price for Ivory Coast's principal exports. Rather it is a manifestation of far deeper structural problems whose resolution will require more than a marginal adjustment to the existing development model.

*The research assistance provided by Antoine Azar is most gratefully acknowledged.

THE STATE, FOREIGN CAPITAL,
AND THE PLANTER BOURGEOISIE

From the onset of French colonialism to the present, foreign capital and the state have been major forces shaping the pattern of economic growth in Ivory Coast. Colonial state policies favored French capital over emerging indigenous capital and were aimed primarily at mediating the effects of world price fluctuations and foreign competition. These twin roles of state intervention were well illustrated by the colonial state's support for French forestry interests in Ivory Coast in 1952.

In 1952 the forestry industry underwent a major crisis owing to a sharp fall in the price of timber and to increased competition in European markets from other African woods. The colonial state came to the rescue of French forestry concessionnaires and exporters "by guaranteeing a sizable loan to this industry and by reducing the export duty on its output from 6 percent to 2 percent" (Thompson 1962 p. 258). An incentive was thereby created to increase wood exports, which came to rank among the top three Ivorian exports throughout the 1970s.

Towards the end of the colonial era there emerged an indigenous class of commercial farmers located mainly in the south and based in the production of cocoa and coffee for export. Gradually this "planter bourgeoisie" (Amin 1967) replaced French planters as the dominant political force in the rural areas.[1] Organized first into the Syndicat Agricole Africain (S.A.A.) to protest the use of corvee labor by French planters, with whom they were in competition, these indigenous capitalists subsequently formed the Parti Democratique de Cote d'Ivoire (PDCI) as their principal political arm.

As indigenous cocoa and coffee planters gained access to the colonial state in the 1950s, the nature of the state and its policies began to alter. This change was most evident in the 1954 coffee crisis. In the past, economic crises had tended to exacerbate tensions between Africans and the French. By 1954, however, Europeans were no longer in direct competition with African primary producers but rather were engaged in complementary activities—notably processing and commercialization. The sharp drop in the price of Ivorian coffee on the world market that occurred in 1954, therefore, fostered a new unity between French and Ivorian capital. Thus the President of the Chamber of Commerce, a Frenchman, demanded in the Assembly that

> the French government reinstate the 20 percent tariff protection against foreign coffee that had existed before World War II and establish restrictive quotas . . . [and] Houphouet-Boigny wielded his majority in the assembly to obtain unanimous approval of the motion . . . (Zolberg 1969, 166–67)

The Battle of Coffee, as it was locally called, gave rise to further collaboration between African and French capital when in 1955 "African and European members of the Assembly, who had unanimously resisted all past attempts to withhold a portion of the income derived from coffee to build up a stabilization fund . . . agreed to reverse their position" on condition that France subsidize this fund (Zolberg, 1969). In this manner the French state provided a new link in this emerging partnership.

With the *Loi Cadre* reforms of 1956, Felix Houphouet-Boigny's policy of union with French capital was brought to fruition at the level of the Ivorian state in the form of shared governmental authority or dyarchy. Over the next several years the state, thus, became the locus of collaboration between Ivorian planters, whose basis for capital accumulation lay in the production of export crops, and French capital, whose interests were then centered primarily in commerce and to a lesser extent in export-oriented primary processing, such as coffee shelling and sawmilling.

This complementarity of interests was reinforced by the agrarian-based Ivorian leadership's ideological predisposition to regard agriculture as the natural vocation of Ivory Coast's peasantry and development of capitalist farming as the necessary prerequisite to the emergence of indigenous capitalism in industry (Zolberg, 1969; Stryker, 1971; Anyang Nyongo, 1978). The availability of French funds for infrastructure and expanded agricultural export production during the colonial period, moreover, encouraged this drive to develop Ivorian capitalism in agriculture rather than in industry. In the period 1946–1959 the *Fonds d'Investissement et de Développement Economique et Social* made few investments in Ivorian industry (Hayter, 1966). Until the mid-1970s, the *Fonds d'Aide et de Coopération,* the European Development fund of the EEC, and other major foreign aid donors maintained this disinclination to fund investments in industry. Of total grants and loans received by Ivory Coast from 1960–1974, less than four percent was earmarked for industry (CIC, 1976).

Thus the symbiotic relationship forged between foreign and Ivorian capital under dyarchy led to an explicit division of economic spheres of activity in the postindependence period. Under this division of labor, the agricultural sector was reserved to Ivorian capital while foreign capital was induced to invest in industry. It fell to the state to design policies that would facilitate capital accumulation by both partners, each in his respective sphere.

CONTRADICTIONS IN THE IVORIAN GROWTH STRATEGY

The Ivorian growth strategy as set out in the years immediately preceding independence and in the first Ivorian Development plans, contained a number of policies designed to implement this division of labor and to ensure the profitability of investments in each sphere. For the Ivorian planters there were three key policies. First, in its wage policy, the Ivorian state eschewed the establishment of a minimum wage for agricultural workers thereby, under conditions of abundant labour, permitting rural wages to fall. This reduced production costs for Ivorian planters. Second, open immigration policies ensured a plentiful supply of labor at these low wages as young Ivorians, with limited access to good agricultural lands (Mazoyer, 1976), preferred to seek jobs in urban areas. Third, a *Caisse de Stabilisation et de Soutien des Prix* mediated the impact of price fluctuations in export crops and thus provided a monetary incentive to cocoa and coffee farmers to produce for export.

These national policies were reinforced by the bilateral trading arrangements contained in the Franco-Ivorian protocol of 1961. Under this protocol France agreed to maintain preferential tariffs for coffee, cocoa, wood, banana and pineapple exports from Ivory Coast and to subsidize prices for coffee and bananas in the French market. In exchange, however. the Ivorian government agreed to limit Ivorian exports of coffee to France to 100,000 tons per year—all of which would then be covered by French subsidies—and to maintain their 1960 level of French imports for wheat, printed cotton cloth,[2] and a variety of mechanical and electrical goods (Lawson, 1976; Mytelka and Dolan, 1980). Discriminatory tariffs, moreover, would favor French imports over competitors, notably the Japanese.

Ivorian planters were notable beneficiaries of this trade protocol. George Lawson calculated that the price supports given to Ivorian coffee and bananas increased the price of these products CIF at le Havre by some 25 percent over their CIF price at London, Hamburg, or New York.

> One can thus crudely estimate the subsidy by multiplying the volume of sales by the amount of this subsidy. For the harvest years 1960–1961, for example, the subsidy, thus calculated, was on the order of 4.94 billion francs CFA (Lawson, 1975, p. 208).

In actual fact, as the subsidy in 1960–1961 amounted to some 65 percent over world prices, the total subsidy was far higher (Lawson 1975, p. 208). In September 1960 when Houphouet-Boigny finally gave in to union demands for increased wages, workers on plantations and in the forestry sector were excluded from the agreement (Thompson, 1962, pp. 267–8). With artificially depressed wages and large price supports, a substantial surplus was created for primary producers in this period.

For foreign capital investing in industry, four policies were implemented to ensure the profitability of their investments. First, Loi No. 59–134 of

September 3, 1959 contained an investment code that guaranteed industrial investments against the risk of nationalization, of nontransferability of profits and capital, and of nonconvertibility of currency. The investment code also provided a firm with priority status according to which it could receive numerous tax concessions—exemptions from corporate income taxes, property taxes and import duties on transportation equipment, intermediate goods, and machinery used in the production process. In addition, a *convention d'etablissement* could be signed ensuring an enterprise fiscal stability over a 25 year period. Second, state lending mechanisms, such as the *Banque Ivorienne de Development Industriel* (BIDI) and the *Society Nationale de Financement* (SONAFI), were created in the 1960s to provide loans, loan guarantees, and interest subsidies to industrial investors, most of whom were foreign (Mytelka 1981). Third, high external tariffs were maintained and indeed had been sought by foreign investors as a means to protect the domestic market. Fourth, a system of price fixing (*homologation des prix*) was introduced thereby making it possible for producers to pass their high costs along to domestic consumers in higher prices.

Although the first independence decade brought about a dramatic rise in agricultural and industrial output and Ivory Coast came to have among the highest per capita income in sub-Saharan Africa by the end of the 1960s, there were numerous disquieting signs that the Ivorian growth strategy was in difficulty.

Although income in Ivory Coast is more evenly distributed when compared to other African countries (den Tuinder 1978, p. 135), during the decade of the 1960s income appears to have become more concentrated with the share of national income accruing to the poorest 60 percent of the population falling from 30 to 22 percent (Lecaillon and Germidis 1977, p. 45). The slow growth of the domestic market that this implied threatened to undermine import-substituting opportunities in such consumer-oriented industries as textiles.[2b]

Ivorian efforts to attract foreign investment had proved so successful that foreign capital dominated in all industrial sectors. By 1971, as Table 1 reveals, 71 percent of the capital invested in the food industry, 86 percent of the wood industry, 92 percent of textiles, shoes and clothing, 81 percent of chemicals, and 89 percent of the metalworking industry was foreign-owned. Intersectoral linkages established by foreign firms in Ivory Coast, however, were exceedingly weak, even in industries that made use of local inputs. Thus domestic value added, as a percentage of sector turnover in 1971 was only 37 percent for the food industry, 47 percent for wood, 40 percent for textiles, and 31 percent for metalworking (Chevassu and Valette, 1975a, pp. 3, 5; 1975b, pp. 14). The extent to which Ivorians influenced the direction of industrial and technological change, moreover, was severely limited by the

TABLE 1 Foreign and National Investment in Ivorian Industry by Sector in 1971, 1975, 1979 (millions of CFAF)

Sector & No of firms	Year	Social Capital	Ivorian State	Capital Private	%	Foreign French	%	Capital Other	%
tobacco, na	1971	12696	3265	445	29.2	8010		976	70.8
food 147[a]	1975	20375	5354	1624	34.2	8511		4886	65.8
191[b]	1979	44424	20195	5303	57.4	11217		7709	42.6
wood na	1971	2830	0	401	14.2	1917		512	85.8
95[c]	1975	na	na	na	na	na		na	na
114	1979	10500	0	2500	23.8	5700		2300	76.2
textiles, na	1971	3221	212	54	8.3	1885		1070	91.7
clothing, 34	1975	12499	2156	2611	38.1	3869		3863	61.9
shoes 72	1979	17381	4174	2361	37.6	4802		6044	62.4
chemicals, na	1971	10101	1935	26	19.4	7020		1120	80.6
petrochemicals 55	1975	9167	2741	624	36.7	4584		1218	63.3
rubber 64	1979	21292	7930	1178	42.8	6677		5507	57.2
construction na	1971	726	215	0	29.6	439		72	70.4

						%a			%b
materials	12	1975	1270	344	33	28.9	534	369	71.1
	22	1979	3869	566	1067	41.9	1002	1244	58.1
metalworking,	na	1971	2343	199	68	11.4	1284	792	88.6
mechanical,	51	1975	6129	701	828	24.9	2869	1731	75.1
electrical	104	1979	14233	1245	2061	22.9	6658	4314	77.1
diverse	na	1971	330	54	126	54.6	122	28	45.4
	40[d]	1975	1213	610	193	66.2	238	172	33.8
	91[e]	1979	3022	759	788	51.2	931	544	48.8
TOTAL		1971	32247	5880	1120	21.7	20677	4570	78.3
		1975	50653	11896	5913	35.2	20605	12239	64.8
		1979	114711	34859	15213	43.7	36987	27662	56.3

[a]Includes 101 bakeries (boulangeries).
[b]Includes 137 bakeries.
[c]Mostly sawmills.
[d]Includes 31 printing shops (imprimeries).
[e]Includes 79 printing shops.

Sources: (1971) J. Chevassu and A. Valette, Les industries de la Côte d'Ivoire: Qui et Pourquoi (Abidjan: ORSTOM. 1975). (1975) La Côte d'Ivoire en Chiffres, 1977–78 edition. (1979) La Côte d'Ivoire en Chiffres, 1980–81 edition.

very low level of Ivorian participation in managerial positions. Of 798 executives and technicians in industry as of 1971, only 10 percent were Ivorian (Chevassu and Valette, 1975b, p. 16).

Finally, and most immediately pressing from a political perspective, was the rising rate of urban unemployment. By 1969 demonstrations of the unemployed, rent strikes, tax boycotts, and student unrest had become too prevalent to ignore (Cohen, 1974). In that year Houphouet-Biogny initiated a process of "dialogue" with various segments of Ivorian society leading to the adoption of a new economic strategy for the 1970s.

The new strategy represented an effort to deal with the multiple contradictions that had emerged out of the attempt to build indigenous capitalism in agriculture while attracting foreign capital into industry. It did so in two principle ways—creating the conditions for greater efficiencies in production and opening new opportunities for Ivorian capital. The new economic strategy thus encouraged foreign capital in import-substituting industries to move towards export-oriented manufacturing in order to overcome the narrowness of the domestic market and the lack of backward linkages within the economy. All new industrial investment should similarly be geared towards larger-scale, export-oriented production, as the 1971–1975 Five Year plan stressed:

> We must therefore begin and achieve a second phase of our industrialization, and for that seek the installation of a new type of industry based on large units of production oriented principally toward foreign markets. (Republique de la Cote d'Ivoire 1971, p 12)

The state, moreover, would now accelerate the development of export-oriented agriculture, notably by moving from the phase of state sponsored production, as in the SODEPALM plantation scheme (Amagou and Gleizes 1975) to agroindustrial processing through, for example, the State sugar complexes—SODESUCRE. Thus an active role for the state was envisaged and indeed the Ministry of Plan acknowledged that despite its "liberal" economic philosophy the state would not play a laisser-faire role but rather

> Through larger and larger resources which it would obtain from rapidly expanding production, the State to the contrary found itself in a position to create the conditions of rapid growth. (Republique de la Cote d'Ivoire 1971, p. 6)[3]

The modified economic strategy also sought to open new opportunities for Ivorian capital in sectors that had hitherto been the preserve of foreign firms. Thus the need to Ivorianize capital in manufacturing and in the timber industry was emphasized. Finally the plan promoted the Ivorianization of managerial and technical personnel in industry as a means to absorb the growing number of university educated Ivorians.

As the modified economic strategy unfolded, however, it soon became apparent that new inflows of direct foreign investment (DFI) would not be sufficient to realize these industrial objectives. In 1971 and 1972 direct foreign investment in Ivory Coast amounted to only 4.4 billion CFAF each year whereas new investment in industry totalled 14 billion in 1971 and 39 billion in 1972 (Table 5). Although DFI rose in the period after 1973, in large part this was due to an increased resort by foreign firms to reinvested earnings, which in the period 1973–1979 amounted to over 80 percent of total foreign private investment (see Table 2).

TABLE 2 Direct Foreign Investment in the Ivory Coast: 1963–1979
(billions CFAF)[a]

Year	Amount
1963	2.6
1964	2.9
1965	4.7
1966	−0.4
1967	1.6
1968	3.0
1969	4.1
1970	8.5
1971	4.4
1972	4.4
1973	12.2*
1974	7.4*
1975	17.5*
1976	9.3*
1977	0.6*
1978	12.9*
1979	21.1*

[a]For the years 1969–1979 SDRs were converted directly into francs using series aa (end of period) exchange rates as indicated in *International Financial Statistics.*

*During the period 1973–1979 of a total direct foreign investment in Ivory Coast of 304.2 million SDRs, 246 million SDRs or 80.9 percent consisted of reinvested earnings. In 1977, in fact, there was a net disinvestment of −11.8 million SDRs offset by reinvested earnings of 27.2 million SDRs.

Source: IMF, *Balance of Payments Statistics Yearbook,* Vol. 18 (January 1976); Vol. 21 (January 1970); Vol. 25 (August 1974) and Vol. 30 (1981).

A more directly interventionist role in the economy was clearly needed to sustain the growth process. In industry this was reflected in the dramatic rise in state ownership. State participation in industry rose from 18.2 percent of social capital in 1971 to 23.5 percent in 1975 and 30.4 percent in 1979 (see Table 1). By 1981, the state's share of industrial social capital had reached 52.2 percent (BAN, 1149, 9-9-82). Yet in the context of continued reliance on foreign capital and technology suppliers this new role for the state only served to heighten the contradictions of the Ivorian growth strategy.

With insufficient domestic savings and limited amounts of new direct foreign investment, foreign borrowing accelerated in the 1970s as both the state and foreign investors turned to foreign banks for loans and to foreign suppliers for credits. For the foreign investor, in the context of increased state equity participation coupled with loans guaranteed by the state, the resort to foreign borrowing constituted a key element in a strategy of risk reduction. But this substantial increase in external financing added a new dimension to the vulnerability of the Ivorian economy—already highly dependent on foreign markets and prices for the cocoa, coffee, and wood, which in 1981 still constituted 70 percent of total exports (BAN, 1153, 7-10-81). To those who had long regarded Ivory Coast as Africa's economic miracle, that country's difficulties did not become apparent until the end of the 1970s and even then were interpreted as a conjunctural payments crisis, i.e., a crisis derived solely from the sharp drop in world prices for Ivorian exports.[4]

In 1979 and again in 1980 a marked worsening in the Ivorian balance of payments occurred. Significantly this period was noted for its large deficit on the balance of trade—an anomaly in the Ivorian case where exports have traditionally exceeded imports. In part this deficit was attributed to the rising price of oil, which accounted for 17 percent of the Ivorian import bill in 1980 as compared with 14 percent in 1979 (BAN, 1125, 11-2-82). A year later, however, the trade deficit began to disappear as falling domestic demand and rising petroleum production led to a 22.5 percent drop in the volume of oil imports in 1981 and a considerably smaller trade deficit (BAN, 1147, 29-7-82). The overall balance of payments, however, was scarcely affected because the payments deficit was primarily due not to commodity trade but to capital flows. These included the exceedingly high negative balance on services—running at −210.5 billion CFAF in 1980—and the negative balance on unrequitted transfers, that is, repatriated earnings and payments for technical assistance, which amounted to a further −132 billion CFAF (BAN, 1125, 11-2-82). Much of this deficit, then, resulted from a combination of debt servicing, which in 1980 amounted to 26 percent of exports (BAN 1124, 11-2-82) and capital outflows generated by foreign investment, which over the entire ten year period, 1969–1979, had only amounted to 110.9 billion CFAF (see Table 1). The late 1970s thus marked a period of considerable decapitalization in Ivory Coast.

The payments crisis, in turn, led to the imposition of austerity measures recommended by the IMF. These tended to accentuate the already declining rate of final domestic demand. Real consumption of households, which had increased by 8.5 percent in 1979 over the previous year, rose only 4 percent in 1980 and fell in 1981 (BAN, 1121, 1-1-82). As the government itself noted, this contraction in domestic demand further exacerbated the difficulties faced by Ivory Coast's import-substituting industries. Only the export-oriented agroindustrial sector appeared to be thriving and even here the rate of growth was uneven, depending, as it did, upon external market conditions. Thus output increased in coffee shelling but falling world demand for canned pineapple left that industry operating at only 52 percent of capacity in 1980 (BAN, 1124, 4-2-82).

As the above analysis suggests, the payments crisis is only the most salient manifestation of more fundamental contradictions in the Ivorian political economy. These contradictions are most evident in the industrial sector.

THE TARNISHED MIRACLE

Despite efforts to Ivorianize industry, the industrial sector remains heavily dominated by foreign capital although the state has been playing a larger role in agricultural processing and in the provision of electricity, water, and other social goods. Of the five largest Ivorian firms, only the Ivorian electrical company (EECI) has the state as a majority partner. The Ivorian oil refinery (SIR) has an Ivorian state share of 47.5 percent but UNICAFE and UTPA, two large coffee processing firms are 100 percent foreign owned while the major soap and oil firm, Blohorn, is 80 percent foreign owned. Of the three next largest firms, SODESUCRE, Palmindustrie and CIDT, all three in the agroindustrial sector, the state is majoritarian. Private Ivorian capital has increased its share in industry over the decade, as Table 1 indicated, but among the top 34 industrial firms, which account for over 70 percent of industrial turnover (BAN, 1150, 16-9-82), private capital is nowhere in the majority. Rising levels of Ivorian state and private ownership, moreover, cannot be equated with increased Ivorian decisional authority and control as shall be shown in the two case studies below.

As the data in Table 3 reveal, the Ivorian industrial sector is also highly concentrated. Nineteen firms produced 56.8 percent of total industrial turnover that amounted to 540.3 billion CFAF in 1980–1981 (BAN, 1150,

TABLE 3 Ivory Coast's Top 34 Industrial Firms Ownership, Value Added and Turnover in 1979–1980

| | | Ownership | | | (millions CFAF) | | |
| | | IC | IC | | Value Added | Turn-Over | VA/ CA |
Size of Firm	Sector	State	Pvt	Forg.	(VA)	(CA)	percent
Turnover >30 billion CFAF							
SIR	refining	47.5	—	52.5	7,700	61,300	12.6
EECI	electricity	81.0	—	14.0	31,779	40,868[a]	77.7
UNICAFE	agro-industry	—	—	100.0	2,634	na	—
Blohorn	soap, oils	—	20.0	80.0	6,376	na	—
UTPA	agro-industry	—	—	100.0	na	na	—
Turnover 20 ≤ 30 billion CFAF							
SODESUCRE	agro-industry	100.0	—	—	9,793	na	—
Palmindustrie	agro-industry	100.0	—	—	13,891	26,000[b]	53.4
CIDT	agro-industry	55.0	—	45.0	9,662	35,000	27.6
Turnover 10 ≤ 20 billion CFAF							
SITAB	cigarettes	19.0	21.0	60.0	11,683	18.900	61.8
Gonfreville	textiles	33.0	22.0	45.0	7,955	16,000	49.7
SOLIBRA	beer	—	20.0	80.0	8,619	15,875	54.3
SACO (cocoa)	agro-industry	35.0	—	65.0	1,787	11,200	16.0
BRACODI	beer	—	22.0	78.0	5,500	9,398	58.5
SODECI	water	52.4	45.0	2.6	11,485	na	—
GMA(milling)	agro-industry	—	25.0	75.0	2,100	11,500	18.3
CAPRAL (coffee)	agro-industry	24.0	9.0	67.0	3,911	11,053	35.4
Decorticaf	agro-industry	—	—	100.0	na	na	—
COGEXIM	agro-industry	na	na	na	na	na	—
Turnover 5 ≤ 10 billion CFAF							
SCA	cement	40.0	—	60.0	1,700	6,200	27.4
SMB	Petrochem	93.0	—	7.0	1,872	4,265	43.9
SICM	cement	—	—	100.0	1,688	9,572	17.6
ICODI	textiles	16.0	16.0	68.0	1,010	9,000	11.2
API(cocoa)	agro-industry	77.0	—	23.0	1,033	na	—
COTIVO	textiles	29.0	—	71.0	4,076	6,548	62.2
SOTEXI	textiles	20.0	15.0	65.0	1,927	na	—
SAFAR	car assembly	—	—	100.0	1,094	9,900	11.1
UTEXI	textiles	20.0	—	80.0	3,965	na	—
SALCI	agro-industry	24.0	—	76.0	na	7,862	—
SIEM	metal boxes	12.0	—	88.0	1,344	6,000	22.4

TABLE 3 (*continued*)

Size of Firm	Sector	Ownership IC State	IC Pvt	Forg.	Value Added (VA)	Turn-Over (CA)	VA/ CA percent
					(millions CFAF)		
SONACO	paper carton	90.0	—	10.0	1,761	6,438	27.4
PROCACI	agro-industry	60.0	—	40.0	na	na	—
Tôles Ivoire	steel	—	24.0	76.0	2,360	6,300	37.5
SIFAL	lubricants	—	—	100.0	na	6,764	—
Trituraf	agro-industry	79.0	—	21.0	1,969	5,220	37.7

[a]"sales" as opposed to "turnover."

[b]"value of production" as opposed to "turnover."

Sources: For size of the firm—statistics are from La Chambre d'industrie de Côte d'Ivoire as reported in the *Bulletin d'Afrique Noire,* No. 1150 of 16 September 1982. Value Added figures are from *La Centrale de bilans 1980 de la Côtè d'Ivoire,* Ministère de l'Economie, des Finances et du Plan as Reported in *Bulletin de l'Afrique Noire,* No. 1138 of 20 Mai, 1982 and *Ban* No. 1140 of 30 juin 1982. Turnover Figures are from EDIAFRIC, *L'Industrie Africaine en 1982,* 8 edition, Tome 2 (Paris: Ediafric, 1982).

16-9-82). An additional 19 firms contributed a further 15 percent to total industrial turnover.

Although industrial output grew rapidly in the 1960s and 1970s (see Table 4), the industrial sector provided surprisingly few jobs. Thus with industrial turnover, as measured in constant 1975 CFA francs, increasing at an average annual rate of 12.8 percent from 1967–1971, industrial employment rose on average by only 10.8 percent. In the next five year period, 1972–1976, industrial turnover rose by an annual average of 21.1 percent but employment incresed by an annual average of only 8.4 percent. In the most recent period, 1977–1981, industrial turnover rose by an annual average of 7 percent whereas employment rose by only 3.8 percent per year on average (Table 4).

These disparities are largely due to the increasing capital-intensity of industry in Ivory Coast. Thus Table 5 reveals that total investment per job rose steadily over the period 1966–1981. In looking at the textile industry an explanation for this choice of capital-intensive technology will be offered.

Finally, it should be pointed out that value-added by industry has remained low and this is indicative of the continued high import-content of Ivorian industry and the relative lack of inter- and intra-sectoral linkages. Some indication of the limited domestic integration of Ivorian industry can

TABLE 4 Annual percentage Increases in Industrial Turnover and in Industrial Employment

	Turnover in billions of 1975 CFAF		Employment	
	Total	Percent increase	Total	Percent increase
1966	91	—	23,600	—
1967	105	14.3	26,000	10
1968	118	12.4	29,100	12
1969	130	10.2	31,900	10
1970	143	10.1	36,300	14
1971	167	16.8	39,100	5
1972	196	16.7	40,900	5
1973	214	9.2	32,800	
1974	283	32.2	46,300	6
1975	303	7.1	52,762	14
1976	289	−4.6	57,915	10
1977	321	11.1	63,005	8.8
1978	341	6.2	64,007	1.2
1979	345	1.2	67,443	5.4
1980	368	6.7	71,373	6.0
1981	405	9.9	69,595	−2.0

[a]Figures were deflated by the index of consumer prices as published in the *International Financial Statistics Yearbook* (1982) pp. 264–265.

Sources: La Cote d'Ivoire en Chiffre, Edition 1976, p. 158 and statistics compiled by the Chambre d'Industrie as published in BAN, No. 1102 (22 juillet 1981), p. 8 for 1980 and BAN, No. 1150 (16 September 1982), p. 4 for 1981.

be seen from the figures on value added as a percentage of turnover for some of Ivory Coast's largest firms (Table 3). High-import content of Ivorian manufacturing is also a factor that increases the vulnerability of Ivorian economy to external price and market conditions. This vulnerability is reflected in the growing emphasis on export-agriculture and agricultural processing within the manufacturing sector. Between 1975 and 1980 agricultural exports rose from 133 billion CFAF to 312 billion and processed agricultural exports increased from 57.9 billion CFAF to 136.5 billion CFAF. As a share of total exports, primary products thus moved from 62.7 percent to 63.6 percent while manufactured exports, despite the substantial increase in processed agricultural products, fell slightly from 34.4 percent to 34.1 percent of total exports (BAN, 1161, 2-12-82).

Clearly Ivory Coast is not on the way to becoming a "newly industrializing country." Rather the late 1970s marked the beginning of a process of deindustrialization and a growing need to reemphasize the agricultural sector. A more detailed analysis of two of the Ivory Coast's

TABLE 5 Growing Capital Intensity of Industry
(millions CFAF)

Year	Cumulative investment in industry before depreciation (year end) current CFAF	in 1975 CFAF[a]	Number of workers employed in industry	Total investment per job in 1975 CFAF
1966	47,000	83,039	23,600	3,519
1967	52,000	89,810	26,000	3,454
1968	57,000	93,596	29,100	3,216
1969	72,000	113,029	31,900	3,543
1970	84,000	120,516	36,300	3,320
1971	92,000	134,111	39,100	3,430
1972	106,000	154,070	40,900	3,767
1973	145,000	189,543	43,800	4,327
1974	186,000	207,358	46,300	4,479
1975	217,000	217,000	52,762	4,113
1976	250,000	206,441	47,915	3,257
1977	293,000	205,182	63,005	3,257
1978	329,000	203,841	64,007	3,185
1979	459,770	243,889	67,443	3,616
1980	701,000	324,988	71,373	4,553
1981	871,000	370,954	69,595	5,330

[a]Figures were deflated by the index of consumer prices as published in the *International Financial Statistics Yearbook* (1982) pp. 264–265.
Sources: Calculated from figures presented in *La Cote d'Ivoire en Chiffre,* edition 1978–1979, p. 150, BAN, No. 1102, 22 juillet 1981, p. 10 and BAN, No. 1149, 9 September 1982, p. 7.

flagship industries—textiles and agriculture processing—will serve to illustrate this process.

Textiles

Three generations of textile firms are active in the Ivory Coast and in each, foreign capital plays a predominant role (Table 6). Of these firms, Gonfreville is the most diversified. Established in 1921 by a colonial official, it was taken over later by a French commercial company, OPTORG, the engineering division of a large French textile company, Texunion, and a set of foreign banks. This combination of foreign commercial companies, technology suppliers, and banking capital became the typical pattern of ownership pattern in the Ivorian textile industry. In contrast to Gonfreville, ICODI, UNIWAX, and SOCITAS were primarily import-substituting

TABLE 6 Ivorian Textile Firms: Year of Establishment, Ownership Structures, Turnover, Employment, Profitability and Activities in 1977–1978
Ownership as a % of share capital

Company	Year of Establishment	State	Private Ivorian	Foreign	Turnover m CFAF	Profitability[1]	Employment Total	Percent Ivorian	Activities
Textiles									
Gonfreville	1921	33.0	21.8	33.0	11,700	6.1	3268	92.0[2]	S,W,P,C,
Socitas[3]	1966	56.6	7.0	36.5	2,956	11.0	228	92.0	S,W,
Icodi	1962	31.8	—	68.2	6,100	12.3	378	90.0	P
Cotivo	1973	28.6	—	71.4	4,631	(losses)	n.d.	n.d.	S,W,
Sotexi	1966	35.0	—	68.0	8,000	0.6	464	83.0	P
Utexi	1972	20.3	—	79.7	4,316	-6.4	1529	96.9	S,W,
Uniwax	1966	—	15.0	85.0	7,000	9.0[4]	666	97.0	P
Sivoitex	1977	—	7.2	92.8	600	-24.7[5]	106	90.6	W,P,

Key: S = spinning; W = weaving; P = printing; C = clothing.
[1]Profitability is measured as the average "net result" as a percentage of turnover in 1973–1977.
[2]The remaining employees are primarily expatriates in the skilled worker, supervisory and management categories. Few non-Ivorian Africans are employed in the textile industry.
[3]Indented firms are affiliates of the firm preceeding. Gonfreville owns 32% of SOCITAS and ICODI owns 90% of COTIVO.
[4]Declared after-tax profits as a percentage of turnover.
[5]Few of the firms in this survey were subject to corporate profits taxes. SIVOITEX, however, was and this might have led to a deflation of "gross results" in order to reduce taxable income.

Source: Government and company interviews.

ventures induced into the Ivorian market by a favorable investment climate created by the state. Each was established by a commercial firm already present in Ivory Coast and anxious to maintain its share of the Ivorian market. These commercial companies recruited the technology suppliers who were also responsible for managing the new subsidiary. ICODI, for example, was founded by three large commercial companies (SCOA, CFAO, and CFCI [Unilever]), the Schaeffer engineering division of a major French textile company, and a number of private banks and national aid agencies. Subsequently, Riegel, the American manufacturer of Wrangler's blue jeans, also became a partner. What distinguishes the third generation textile firms, COTIVO, UTEXI, and the Gonfreville Grand Ensemble is that they are export-oriented. COTIVO, for example, was designed to produce denim for an upstream export-oriented blue jeans manufacturing firm (Blue Bell) established by Riegel Textiles, while UTEXI and Gonfreville Grand Ensemble were intended to export mass-market textiles, such as bedsheets, to Europe.

The state has played a substantial role in the development of the textile industry. Traditionally the state provided guarantees for loans from local banks. More recently, as foreign firms were reluctant to bring in new capital[5] the state has invested in new firms alongside foreign capital.

State intervention in the industrialization process has been designed to reduce the risks to foreign investors, but such policies also cheapened the cost of capital to foreign partners. While this made expansion into export-oriented activities more attractive, it also increased the tendency for technology suppliers, who were minority shareholders and managers of the firm, to choose capital-intensive technology and to overbuild these plants. This occured both because funds were readily available and because the technology suppliers, although they were shareholders, received a commission on the sale of technology that was generally a function of total investment costs.

Choice of sophisticated production technology limited the growth of Ivorian industrial employment and inflated the wage bill because of the need to employ expatriate personnel. Heavy borrowing to meet this inflated investment program, moreover, led to high interest payments. These two factors have contributed to the relatively higher costs of production in each of the Ivorian textile firms, as compared with their Asian competitors. Yet by guaranteeing the profitability of these investments through the provisions of the Investment Code, the tariff structure and the process of price harmonization practiced with respect to textiles, the state diminished the incentive in these firms to move towards more efficient production. As relatively inefficient producers, the output of these European affiliates needed the margin of protection provided by the Lomé Convention as against the General System of Preferences (GSP). These firms, thus, became vulnerable to even small shifts in demand or in the level of competition within the West European market to which the bulk of their output was directed. ICODI–COTIVO is a case in point.[6]

Technology suppliers in Ivory coast generally capitalized their technology and held up to 10 percent of the equity shares in these textile companies. Their major sources of income, however, were not dividends but commissions on the sale of capital goods whose purchase they organized, salaries to managerial and technical personnel and technical assistance payments. Schaeffer, for example, received a 3 pecent commission on total investment costs and was paid 2.5 percent of turnover annually for technical assistance.[7] In 1964 and again in 1970, 1974, and 1976, Schaeffer chose the most sophisticated printing machinery for ICODI, as it later would do for COTIVO, thus significantly increasing the capital intensity of production.

In 1970, Mohamed Diaware, then Minister of Plan, approached ICODI with a view to persuading its owners to integrate backwards towards spinning and weaving, in keeping with the newly adopted export-oriented growth strategy. As ICODI's "priority status" was soon to expire and the firm would no longer be permitted to import the grey cloth it printed free of customs duties, backward integration was now in its interest. The state agreed to grant the new firm, COTIVO, priority status under the Investment Code and it took an equity share of 28.6 percent. Schaeffer, which managed ICODI, would manage the new spinning and weaving plant and would assume all responsibility for the choice of technology. COTIVO, established in 1973, was designed to produce grey cloth for both UNIWAX and ICODI's printing and finishing plant, thus ensuring that the spinning and weaving operations would be able to take advantage of economies of scale.[8] It was also intended to produce denim for Riegel's new blue jeans subsidiary in Ivory Coast. COTIVO received a 1500 million CFAF loan from the European Investment Bank and additional long-term loans amounting to some 1700 million CFAF from the Ivorian Industrial Development Bank (BIDI), the German Aid Agency, DEG (also a partner in ICODI/ COTIVO), and other national and international public lending agencies. In addition, COTIVO has a medium term loan amounting to 3,200 million CFAF from a banking consortium led by the Banque Nationale de Paris' Ivorian affiliate, the BICICI. Loans constituted 67.2 percent of the capital invested and financial charges ran at 15 percent of turnover in 1979. In 1980–1981 the BIDI was obliged to open a further line for short term credit amounting to 135 million CFAF for COTIVO (BAN 1158, 12-11-82).

Not only is COTIVO heavily in debt and thus vulnerable to shifts in demand for blue jeans and the imposition of voluntary export restraints by importing countries, but the choice of product and the choice of technology can both be questioned. Denim is a product with high technical specifications. It permits only very limited tolerances in dyeing, streaking and twisting. Although COTIVO's quality has improved, most denim firms operate with a 2 to 3 percent "second choice" whereas COTIVO's output still includes 15 percent or more "second choice." In addition to high quality standards, denim production requires high volume and low cost to compete effectively with Asian producers who currently set world prices. COTIVO cannot meet these conditions.

COTIVO is also plagued by a number of inappropriate technological choices. The Saurer looms initially purchased by Schaeffer are not appropriate for heavy denim cloth and they have now been converted to the production of cotton grey cloth for sale to ICODI and UNIWAX. But the use of expensive looms for such a simple product pushes the cost of grey cloth well above that of imports and increases the price of printed cloth produced by these two firms.[9] UNIWAX, which has traditionally exported its "Indonesian 'Dutch'" style wax-prints to neighboring West African countries, has been particularly affected and initiated talks with the government to import cheaper Asian grey cloth rather than fulfill its commitment to use COTIVO's output.

COTIVO's denim spinners and other related equipment, moreover, are designed to produce enough input to weave 9 million yards of cloth, but COTIVO is only producing 2.3 million yards of cloth. Hence all spinners operate only two days per week and indigo baths similarly function at less than one-third capacity.[10] This further increases the cost of producing denim. As Blue Bell is having difficulty selling its output in Europe and has cut back production, further difficulties at COTIVO can be anticipated.

When pressures to reduce textile imports from the Third World intensified in the EEC during 1975 and 1976, it became politically expedient to place ceilings on ACP textile imports even though these were not the source of market disruption. In effect, the EEC was signaling its decision to abandon a strategy of African industrialization just as negotiations leading to Lomé II were getting underway. By 1978, as a result, a halt was called to planned second and third stage investments in Ivorian export-oriented textile ventures, and in line with World Bank and EC policies now favorable to an expansion of primary production in Africa, Ivorian energies and resources were redirected to increasing productivity in the export-oriented *agricultural* sector.

Agroindustry

Coffee and sugar production provide further illustrations of the complex set of contradictions to which the Ivorian economic strategy has given rise. Coffee growing in Ivory Coast is overwhelmingly a planter and peasant activity. As planters have been the backbone of Houphouet-Boigny's political support since the 1950s, state policies, unlike in most other third world countries, have been designed to ensure that planters received a relatively high rate of return from agriculture.

On the input side this meant guaranteeing planters low rural wages through the continued provision of cheap foreign migrant labor. This policy has, however, had a number of important contradictory consequences. First, in times of economic contraction, foreign labor becomes a target for antagonism. Second, where no or very low minimum wages are fixed for agriculture and where Ivorians are expected to transform themselves from peasants into planters, landless Ivorians are disinclined to enter rural wage employment. By the late 1960s, land concentration and a highly unequal distribution of monetary income from village coffee and cocoa plantations (Mazoyer, 1976) thus led younger members of a community either to invade forestry zones in order to establish farms—a process that has significantly depleted forestry reserves and currently threatens the future of the wood processing industry (Mytelka, 1981)—or migrate to the cities in search of jobs—swelling the state sector when the growing capital intensity of industry (see Table 5) limited the availability of industrial jobs.

Third, where wages are kept artificially low, there is little incentive for farmers to invest in techniques of production that improve productivity. Limitations on productivity within the traditional mode of production reduced the rate of growth in output in both food crops and in export agriculture at a time when imports were rising rapidly.

On the output side, planter profits were maintained by the relatively high purchase price offered by the Caisse de Stabilisation et de Soutien des Prix to coffee growers. The purchase price of green coffee, in fact, doubled over the five harvest years 1974–1975 through 1979–1980 (BAN, 1123, 4-2-82). Under these conditions planters with access to larger holdings of more fertile land tended to accumulate considerable profits. Yet as they accumulated capital, they found few investment opportunities available to them. In large part this was due to the entrenchment of local French and foreign-based import-export houses in coffee deshelling and commercialization activities.[11] Of some 232 coffee exporters registered in the early 1970s, Africans had "shares in less than five handling a negligible volume of coffee every year" (Anyang Nyongo 1978). The manufacture of soluble coffee was similarly controlled by foreign interests—in this case a subsidiary of the Swiss corporation, Nestlé.

In response to these multiple pressures of land hunger, unemployment, low agricultural productivity, and limited opportunities for indigenous capital accumulation, the state proposed a number of solutions. In the agricultural sector, modernization would be pursued by the consolidation of land holdings into medium-sized family farms, and the extension of plantation cultivation thereby permitting a greater use of fertilizers and higher levels of mechanization (Bra Kanon: 1978, pp. 18–19; BAN, 996, 21-3-79 and BAN, 1041,

19-3-80). By reducing still further the land available for the expansion of a capitalist class based in agriculture and by limiting the growth of employment opportunities through mechanization, the new agricultural strategy was, however, likely to increase pressures for job creation in urban areas. Yet, as we have seen, employment in the secondary sector was expanding less rapidly than anticipated. The new agricultural strategy, thus, required the proletarianization of the Ivorian peasantry, that is, the transformation of peasant farmers not into wealthy planters but into laborers. The 1976–1980 Five Year Plan acknowledged this deviation from the model of smallholder capitalism when it announced that "the ivorianization of agricultural employment has now become a necessity and this implies a substantial change in the incomes, status and way of life of the peasantry" as well as "an increase in agricultural salaries" to induce Ivorians to enter rural wage employment as opposed to migrating to urban areas (BAN, 896, 12-1-76). Both the "ivorianization of salaried agricultural jobs" and "agricultural modernization" were emphasized again in the 1981–1985 Five Year Plan (BAN, 1163, 16-12-82).

Ivorianization of agricultural labor was accompanied by policies to assist Ivorian planters to move into processing activities in such older agroindustrial activities as wood and coffee processing. In 1970 the *Societe d'Etudes et de Realisation pour l'Industrie Caféière et Cacaoyère* (SERIC) was established to reorganize coffee treatment and trade. The state held 55 percent of SERIC's capital while the remainder was held by a number of French import-export houses. As in other agroindustrial ventures, management of the coffee deshelling plant, which SERIC owned at Toumbokro, was left in the hands of a French firm, Ets. Jean Abille Gal (*Afrique Industrie*, 1 Oct. 1977). During the 1970s, other foreign firms continued to enter the coffee processing industry. UNICAFE is typical. Established in 1977, its owners include a number of local subsidiaries of foreign banks and foreign commercial enterprises (see Table 3). As late as 1981, and despite major campaigns to Ivorianize capital and management in industry, Ivorians were infrequently found in an industry as basic to the development of agrobusiness as the coffee processing sector. Thus in 1981 when COGEXIM, an export-import company owned by Ivorian coffee and cocoa planters, took over the state-owned processing plant at Toumbokro, it, too, sought out French partners (S.A., Louis Dreyfus) and formed a joint venture (Agrivoire) to manage this coffee processing plant.

Finally the new agroindustrial strategy called for the diversification of agricultural production away from coffee and cocoa and into other commodities suitable either for export or as feeder stocks into local industry via the development of state-peasant plantation schemes such as SODEPALM in the south, or SODESUCRE, CIDT, and SODERIZ in the north. Two features of this drive to diversify are particularly unique. First, as Bonnie

Campbell has pointed out, the state chose to favor large plantations run by European concessionaires rather than village cooperatives or village plantations operated by the peasantry, as the former were administratively easier to manage and more likely to produce quick returns (Campbell, 1978a, p. 95). This approach has accelerated the proletarianization of the peasantry, swelled the importance of the tertiary sector (Mazoyer, 1981) and widened the gap between planters and wage laborers as "many civil servants have bought farms" becoming "weekend planters" (Bra Kanon as reported in Le Courier, 1982, p. 14).

Second, these schemes are remarkable for the high involvement of foreign capital in partnership with the state and the reliance on foreign firms to manage production and processing activities. As Jean Oulanie, Director General of SODERIZ, in 1977 pointed out, the state only undertook to play a major role in the development of agricultural export production and processing because of the need to secure foreign financing; even then the state turned to foreign firms to manage these agroindustrial companies (*Afrique Industrie,* No. 147, 1-10-17, p. 44). The consequences of this reliance on foreign technology suppliers are evident from a brief examination of the development of sugar refining in the 1970s.

With sugar imports running at 60,000 tons per year in the early 1970s, the development of sugar production and refining as an import substituting industry appeared to be a logical extension of the Ivory Coast's policy of agricultural diversification. Initially 10 sugar complexes were envisaged, each to be supplied by an adjacent plantation. Although the state was a major investor providing more than one-third of the funds (BAN, No. 1037, 20-2-80) it played only a minimal role in designing or managing these complexes. Rather, for each of the six complexes operating in 1982, a different foreign firm was designated to plan and manage the enterprise. Table 7 provides data on these firms and points as well to the excessive reliance on foreign borrowing incurred in the development of this sector. Loans from foreign banking consortia and aid agencies constituted over 60 percent of the capital invested.

Reliance on foreign banks and technology suppliers had a number of negative consequences for the sugar industry, particularly insofar as costs and prices were concerned. When it became apparent to the Ivorian government that Redpath and other foreign collaborators were building up serious cost overruns, an independent Egyptian agency was hired to audit these firms. Of four complexes built after Ferkéssédougou I, only the Borotou complex fell roughly within the projected cost range. In the remaining three, a total of 34 billion CFAF in "overpricing" was discovered (BAN 1053, 25-6-80 and 1069, 19-11-80). In comparison with the Carmeroon, where the CAMSUCO plant, built by SOMDIAA, produces sugar at 100 CFAF per kilo, Ivorian sugar cost over 250 CFAF per kilo to

TABLE 7 Ivorian Sugar Complexes: Total Investment, Loans and Foreign Partners

	Total Investment (billion CFAF)	*Loans (billion CFAF)*		*Foreign Partner*
Ferkéssédougou I	31	Ivorian State: Eximbank & First Nat'l city	11.0 19.5	LONRHO (UK)
Ferkéssédougou II	56	Ivorian State: Cdn. Banks:	22.4 32.8	Redpath (Canadian)
Borotou	43	FAC: CCCE: COFACE: Ivorian Banks:	2.5 12.5 13.6 na	ADRA-RENAULT (FR)
Sérébour	41	Ivorian State: Foreign Bank Consortium: German Supplier Credits: COFACE	10 10 11 10	SOMDIAA & SODETEG-BUCKAU Wolf (Krupp) (FRG)
Katiola	58	Belgian Supplier Credit: Austrian Supplier Credit: Forg. Bank Consortium:	18.3 10.8 10.1	SOMDIAA & SOPEX-BAUER (Belg & Austrian)
Zuénoula	54	Ivorian State Foreign Banks	5 35.4	ABR (Belgium) Vereinigde HVA Masstschappij (Netherlands)

Source: Ediafric, *L'Industrie Africaine en 1982,* 8 edition, Tome 2, "Côte d'Ivoire" (Paris: 1982).

produce—well above world prices in the eal y 1980s (Ediafric, 1982, pp. 24–25).

As in the textile case much of the failure to develop efficient sugar production in the Ivory Coast must be attributed to the heavy foreign involvement in the design and management of these firms. As President Houphouet-Boigny himself pointed out, it was the "inattention with which the negotiations were carried out" that led to the "overly short periods for the repayment of loans, overbilling, poor planning, shortage of replacement parts, improper management priorities" and other failings (BAN, 1069, 19-11-80). Though the state owned the firms, it was the foreign technology supplier who actually controlled all aspects of the choice of technique, construction and production phases. The availability of capital provided by the state or through state guaranteed loans, the absence of financial risks and of constraints resulting from a situation in which management fees are paid without regard to the profitability of the firm or its efficiency, once again, proved to be a highly negative combination for Ivorian industrial development. The development of the sugar industry, moreover, served to accelerate the proletarianization of Ivory Coast's would-be independent farmers while opening few opportunities for the growth of Ivorian Capital or the development of indigenous technological capabilities.

CONCLUSIONS

In sum, the coffee, sugar and textile cases illustrate a fundamental transformation in the initial Ivorian economic strategy, as those in the state sought to cope with contradictions generated by the need to mesh the interests of domestic and foreign capital. In so doing they sacrificed the goal of "everyman an independent farmer" in favor of an Ivorian wage labor force in agriculture and the continued concentration of land and wealth in the rural areas. The development of export-agriculture, including agricultural processing, merely accelerated this process while providing new opportunities for foreign capital to profitably restructure Ivorian production without assuming the risks involved in direct investment. The creation of joint ventures between the state and foreign capital in new agroindustries and in the textile sector, thus, have not enhanced Ivorian control over the direction of industrial change. Rather, the interests of international capital, as reflected in product and process choices made by foreign investors and technology suppliers, the fluctuations of world prices and the contraction or expansion of external markets continue to be decisive in shaping the pattern of Ivorian economic growth. In the contemporary period of world economic depression, the absence of an internal dynamic has meant massive decapitalization, deindustrialization and a major structural crisis in Ivory Coast.

NOTES

1. Both Suret-Canale (1972) and Campbell (1975 and 1978) reaffirm the existence and continued hegemonic role of this planter bourgeoisie within the constellation of social forces

dominant in the state. Castellu and Affou Yapi (1982), however, argue that the bulk of the Ivory Coast's commercial farmers are small-scale peasant farmers. While this is clearly the case, the narrowness of the class of planters who constitute a "planter bourgeoisie" in no way determines its relative importance within the political economy. That the importance of this planter bourgeoisie may be changing is suggested by Cohen (1974) who argues that by the early 1970s it had become apparent that holders of positions in the state were as determinant in the policy formulation process as the planter bourgeoisie whose ability to influence policy largely lay in their role within the single political party—the Parti Démocratique de la Côte d'Ivoire (PDCI). The present study casts some light on this debate insofar as it illustrates the key role of the state in fostering new links between Ivorian and foreign capital in the industrial sector during the 1970s.

2. The French textile industry traditionally depended upon sales in protected colonial and domestic markets. In the 1950s with the loss of markets in Indochina, the French state in collaboration with the cotton textile industry, reoriented production and sales to Africa (Mytelka, 1982).

2b. This led the government to sharply increase agricultural prices to coffee, cocoa and cotton producers. Between 1970 and 1974 there was, thus, a notable improvement in income distribution with the share of national income going to the lowest 40 percent of the population rising from 10.8 to 19.7 percent (den Tuinder 1978).

3. There is considerable evidence that the ability of the state to capture an increasingly large proportion of the surplus generated by agricultural and industrial production, moreover, has contributed to the dramatic inequalities in rural–urban incomes and access to services while sustaining a burgeoning tertiary sector (Campbell, 1978; Mazoyer, 1981).

4. A recent issue of the European Economic Community–Africa, Caribbean and Pacific publication, *The Courier,* devoted considerable coverage to the current Ivorian economic crisis in precisely these terms (No. 74, July–August 1982, pp. 10–25).

5. For balance of payments reasons, the French Treasury in the early 1970s restricted the outflow of capital and encouraged French firms to borrow abroad to finance their investments.

6. For a detailed discussion of the Gonfreville and the SOTEXI-UTEXI cases see Mytelka 1981.

7. Data on ICODI–COTIVO were obtained through interviews with M. Knoph, Director, Schaeffer Impression (Vieux Thann, France 13 December 1978); M. Hubert, Director, ICODI (Abidjan 31 January 1979); and M. Boremans, Director, COTIVO (Agboville 12 February 1979); and from Republique de Cote d'Ivoire, *Le Centrale des Bilans,* 1977 (Abidjan 1978); and *Memorandum Textile Pour la Communauté Economique Européenne* (Abidjan Ministere de l'Economie, des Finances et du Plan, Decembre 1978).

8. Unilever, which owned 85 percent of UNIWAX, is a shareholder in both ICODI and COTIVO.

9. Originally the Grand Ensemble in Gonfreville was intended to produce export quality cloth and hence chose very costly Sulzer looms. The high costs of production and the protectionist tendencies of the EEC countries during the late 1970s made it difficult for Gonfreville to market its output in Europe. In 1979 these machines were converted to the production of polyester shirt fabric for the domestic market where tastes and incomes do not require production to such high technical specifications. As in COTIVO, the high costs of production are passed on to the consumer through the process of "price harminization."

10. Underutilized capacity is quite typical in African industries for reasons having to do with the choice of product and the choice of technique discussed above. See also, Frances Stewart, *Technology and Underdevelopment* (London: McMillan, 1977).

11. Investment opportunities in the timber and wood processing industries as well as more generally in secondary manufacturing were similarly limited by the established presence of foreign capital.

7

REGIONAL ECONOMIC INTEGRATION AND FOREIGN POLICY

Achi Atsain

INTRODUCTION

In the middle of the twentieth century economic integration has become one of the leading aspirations of international economic policy. Integration has been defined in different ways by economists. However, the general consensus is that economic integration is a process involving the elimination of discriminatory barriers between economic units of nation states. Distinction should also be made between integration and cooperation. This difference is qualitative as well as quantitative. Whereas cooperation includes activities aimed at lessening discrimination, the process of economic integration comprises measures that lead to the elimination of all forms of discrimination. For example, international agreements on trade policies belong to the area of international economic cooperation, while the abolition of trade barriers constitutes an act of integration. Nevertheless, it is to be noted that no single definition of economic integration is accepted by economists outright. Policymakers use the terms: "integration, cooperation and community," interchangeably. In the literature on international trade policy economic integration has been categorized as steps evolving from a preferential trading club to an economic union.[1] Recently the theory of economic integration has enlarged the field of international trade by exploring the impact of a fusion of national markets on growth and by examining requirements for coordination of economic policies in the union. Furthermore it is argued that economic integration theory should include elements of location theory. The underlying idea is that economic integration tends to be synonymous with rapid economic development and accelerated growth.

Thus, Europe in the mid-1950s witnessed the formation of several economic groupings such as the European Economic Community (EEC), the European Free Trade Area, and the Council for Mutual Economic Assistance (COMECOM). In the less developed countries, integration and cooperation schemes have been encouraged largely by the United Nations and its various agencies. In Latin America the Central American Common Market and the Latin American Free Trade Area may be cited.

Various forms of economic integration have been attempted in Asia. No attempt at economic integration has been made so far in the Middle East for political reasons. Over the past twenty years Africa has experienced several attempts in the area of economic integration and cooperation. These schemes have been inspired by the United Nations Economic Commission for Africa and by the desire of political leaders in these countries to accelerate economic growth and to increase the level of welfare of their populations. Unfortunately, however, the progress that these countries had made in the 1960s has been largely limited to the area of politics.

This attitude changed in the early 1970s. The contrast with the 1960s lies primarily in that African leaders are more convinced and conscious that economic integration constitutes a solution to the development of their economies. As President Ahmed Sekou Touré clearly pointed out in his speech delivered at the Colloquium on Economic Integration in April 1980 in Conakry (Guinea), leaders in Africa "are indeed convinced, and luckily so, that economic integration remains one of the essential conditions and one of the dynamic factors that will enable our young states to free themselves from economic dependency to develop and to evolve consistently with assurance towards the rapid economic progress expected by our people." This awareness results from the failure, in most cases, of the traditional economic development strategies that these countries have followed. Not only were these strategies not logically operational, but also their theoretical framework was ill conceived. The concept of a world economy in which economic growth in the developed countries would automatically and necessarily lead to growth in the developing countries, thanks to the flow of products, technologies and capital, happened to be totally erroneous. These strategies, suitable to the economic structure of the developed countries, have caused in several instances more damage than good.

As a result, heads of state and governments, policy makers, and economists in Africa have come to agree that a wider economic market extending beyond national boundaries will make it possible to harmonize and coordinate economic activities in all sectors; to eliminate regional disparities in economic development; and to exploit resources in order to meet the challenge that these countries face today. It is against this background that the West Africa Economic Community (CEAO), the East African Economic Community, the Mano River Union, and the Economic Community of the West African States (ECOWAS) were formed to constitute the most comprehensive response to the need of economic integration. On a continental basis the Lagos Plan of Action, which seeks to establish an African common market by the year 2000, is the latest attempt in the process of economic integration. Despite their shortcomings, these schemes are shaping the future of African states and it is worth investigating how they will succeed or fail to accelerate growth of their economies. In this study we limit ourself to the West Africa area in order to examine the contributions made by CEAO and ECOWAS to economic cooperation and integration in the subregion.

The remainder of this chapter is as follows. In section II, we examine the past attempts at economic integration in West Africa and the reasons of their failure. Section III attempts to assess the contributions, economic as well as political, of CEAO and ECOWAS to the process of integration. The reasons for maintaining CEAO within ECOWAS are also discussed. In section VI we highlight the main problems that these two economic unions face today. The final section will draw some concluding remarks.

HISTORICAL EVOLUTION OF THE PROCESS OF ECONOMIC INTEGRATION IN WEST AFRICA

It is fully agreed that the African countries, in order to accelerate their rate of economic growth, have to integrate their economies gradually. It is against this background on the one hand, and the worldwide growing enthusiasm for economic integration on the other, that countries in West Africa have come to take steps that ultimately led to the formation of the West African Economic Community (CEAO), the Mano River Union (MANU) and the Economic Community of the West African States (ECOWAS). These entities have not come into existence easily. In this section we explore the rationale for economic integration in West Africa, then we survey the past attempts at integration in the area.

The Reasons for an Economic Union in West Africa

At the moment Africa is divided into more than fifty independent political entities, each of them operating as a sovereign state with its own administration, armed forces, etc. Moreover, most of the countries have rather small populations. In the case of the West African region comprising sixteen states, population varies from .5 million (Cap Verde) to 85 million inhabitants (Nigeria). The problem of small populations is further complicated by low incomes per capita in the area. Ten of the sixteen countries are ranked among the poorest in the world. The annual per capita income of the region as a whole is about $700 (1980) and compares unfavorably with the average per capita income of the developed nations that is about fourteen times as high. In short, West Africa is among the poorest regions in the world. Other social and economic indicators such as literacy and urbanization rates, energy consumption per capita, number of inhabitants per doctor, life expectancy rate, population having access to clean water, and infrastructure confirm this conclusion. Small populations, combined with low income per capita result in very limited purchasing power within each country, and the small size of the domestic markets prevents the effective development of natural resources. This would require large investments of capital that these countries can ill afford. Comparative economic indicators for the countries in CEAO and ECOWAS are contained in Table 1.

The traditional theory of economic integration argues that industries, in order to be efficient and benefit from economies of scale, need to operate on a relatively large scale. This means that industries in West Africa have to operate in markets larger than one nation. By all accounts, the prospects of growth in these countries over the next two decades are not encouraging.[2] Experience of the last two decades indicate that the two major sectors, agriculture and industry, have performed poorly. Whereas in some countries agricultural output stagnated or increased little; others recorded negative rates of growth. Many factors accounted for this poor performance, among them the lack of adequate agricultural policies that favored the cash crop sector to the detriment of the food sector, the problems of transport that added to costs, the absence of an adequate and efficient marketing network and other incentives to stimulate growth in the agricultural sector. As far as the industrial sector is concerned, the prospects are not any brighter given the lack of foreign exchange and inadequate demand. Industrial development in the countries of this area took the form of import substitution. This strategy inevitably led most countries to specialize in light industries, mainly local agricultural processing industries and textiles, the outlets of which are in foreign markets. With persistent worldwide inflation and low growth in the industrialized nations the prospects of industrial growth are bleak.

Simply increasing protectionism in individual countries offers no hope for West Africa to increase significantly its manufactured exports. In order to stimulate industrial exports, should past patterns be pursued, the countries have to shift policies toward heavy industries that will use the natural resources of the region. However, this strategy calls for large amounts of capital and advanced technologies that these countries cannot afford if they pursue separate industrial polices. What is needed is a comprehensive integrated policy. This scheme should depart from traditional trade theory based on static assumptions. While gains from trade should be an important concern of this scheme, it is necessary to look beyond existing patterns of production at what is likely to emerge in the future when comparative advantage and trade patterns are likely to be different. Then arguments for

TABLE 1 Relative Economic Indicators for CEAO and ECOWAS Countries

	Population (million)	GNP per capita ($)	GDP (million $)	Production (percent of GDP)		
				Agriculture	Industry	Services
Ivory Coast	8.2	1040	9130	26	23	51
Upper Volta	5.6	180	860	38	20	42
Mali	6.8	140	1220	42	11	47
Niger	5.2	270	1710	44	32	24
Mauritania	1.6	320	470	27	33	40
Senegal	5.5	430	2480	29	24	47
TOTAL CEAO	32.9	449**	15780			
Ivory Coast (% total CEAO)	24.9		57.5			
Benin	3.4	250	850	43	12	45
Cape Verde						
Gambia	0.6	250	132	46	9	46
Ghana	11.3	400	10160	66	21	13
Guinea	5.3	280	1540	41	26	33
Guinea Bissau	0.8	170	137	54	9	34
Liberia	1.8	500	940	35	26	39
Nigeria	82.6	670	75170	22	45	33
Sierra Leone	3.4	250	790	36	23	41
Togo	2.4	350	1000	25	33	52
TOTAL ECOWAS	144.5	552**	106589			
Nigeria (% Total ECOWAS)	57.2		70.5			
Ivory Coast (% total ECOWAS)	5.7		8.6			

*All the figures are for 1979, except for the budget as percent of GDP which refers to 1977 and exports and imports marked * which are for 1978.
**Weighted means.
Source: World Bank, 1981.

179

TABLE 1 Relative Economic Indicators for CEAO and ECOWAS Countries (*cont.*)

	Production (in million $US)		Gross domestic investment as percent of GDP (million $)		Exports (million $)	Importations (millions US $)	Budget as percent of GDP	Investment budget as percent of GDP
	Agriculture	Industry						
Ivory Coast	2374	3000 (65)	31	2830	2515	2491	34.0	13.0
Upper Volta	315	172	24	206	81	254	16.8	2.8
Mali	512	134	13	195	177	180	20.3	1.6
Niger	752	547	29	479	—	—	15.3	2.7
Mauritania	127	155	51	240	147	259		
Senegal	719	592	21	521	421*	756*		
TOTAL CEAO	4799	4600		4471**				
Ivory Coast as % total CEAO								

Benin	365	102	21	179	190	357		
Cape Verde					—	—		
Gambia	61	12	22	29	—	—		
Ghana	6705	2137	5	508	1096*	993*		
Guinea	631	308	15	231	373	347		
Guinea Bissau	74	12	32	44	14	61	40.3	11.1
Liberia	329	244	27	253	506	487	23.8	7.3
Nigeria	16537	33826	31	23303	18073	12399	30.8	11.6
Sierra Leone	181	181	15	118	205	297	23.2	4.6
Togo	250	230	39	390	251	441	33.2	5.6
TOTAL ECOWAS	29932	41652		29526**				
Nigeria as % total ECOWAS	55.2	81.2		78.9				
Ivory Coast as % total ECOWAS	7.9	7.2		9.6				

integration are relative contributions to economic growth and the structural transformation of the countries in the West Africa region. This dynamic approach, in the sense that factors of production, capital, and labor are taken to be variable, is what is required for a harmonized and balanced development. It also focuses on the positive effects of the creation of regional markets on the pace of development in member countries. In this process the leading factor is the widening of markets. In the context of West Africa, creation of a regional market may increase opportunities for profitable foreign and domestic investment, mobilize unemployed resources, broaden the export base, and acclerate the rate of growth. Taking into account the desire of these countries to industrialize rapidly, it seems to be far more advantageous, in terms of efficient and sustained growth, to industrialize in an orderly and coordinated fashion at the regional level rather than to duplicate within small markets industrial ventures that could be over-burdened by financial difficulties.

Initially the elimination of trade barriers within the CEAO and ECOWAS will have little effect on the agricultural sector. Our analysis shows that the available exportable surplus of foodstuffs of the region as a whole was almost nil over the last two decades. More importantly the West African states have come to rely increasingly on food aid and/or imports to meet internal demand. Cash crops have typically found their outlets in foreign markets. The impact on the manufacturing sector will also be limited in the preintegration period, as the countries duplicate plants producing similar goods. However, widening the market may encourage in the long-run, some existing plants to increase capacity to close to optimal levels, and inefficient plants will probably close down, bringing more efficient use of the resources. New plants may be established and hence, unemployed resources mobilized. Investment opportunities for both domestic and foreign enter-preneurs may further improve as new outlets appear and investment patterns may change through the use or introduction of new processes and new distribution methods. The combination of internal and external economies of scale is likely to lower unit costs, enhance the profitability of existing firms, and further raise the expectations of prospective investors. Rising incomes in the region may stimulate aggregate demand and induce further changes in the productive structure.

The two treaties establishing CEAO and ECOWAS both sought to address these issues in particular: but the manner in which they translated them into a concrete implementation will be the subject of another section. Before that it may improve understanding to review the historical steps that led to the formation of the two economic unions under study.

Historical Evolution of the Process of Economic Integration in West Africa

The origins of the movement towards economic integration and cooperation in the West Africa go back as far as the late 19th century. In the former British territories of West Africa, Wilmot Blyden, Casely Hayford, and Kobina Sekyi pioneered the idea of an economic union.[3] This idea was further reinforced by Kwame N'Krumah around 1940, when he advocated the idea of an economic union that would include French, Portuguese and Spanish territories of West Africa. His idea led to the Pan-African Conference in Manchester in 1945. The Manchester spirit was transformed into a concrete proposition in 1961 by Nnamdi Azikwe, then Governor of the Federation of Nigeria. Despite the enthusiasm of the mid-1950s, English-speaking West African countries have never come close to an economic association after independence, partly because they are geographically scattered and partly because the British administrative structure did not give much impetus to economic unity.

As to the French-speaking countries of West Africa, for more than a century they had close economic and political links with the administrative federation of French West Africa.[4] Under the French administration, the territories forming the French West African Federation (AOF) established in 1895 had achieved a remarkable degree of integration. The Federation had formed a customs union providing free movement of goods and services among territories; it had also adopted a common external tariff. Since 1904, the Federation had maintained a general budget in addition to the territorial ones. Monetary matters were placed under the authority of the West African Bank (*Banque de l'Afrique Occidentale*), a commercial bank that was the common bank of issue until 1955, when that right was transferred to the *Institut d'Emission de l'Afrique Occidentale Francaise et du Togo*. On April 4, 1959 this institution was converted into the *Banque Centrale des Etats de l'Afrique de l'Quest* (BCEAO). The Federation was dissolved in 1959 under French initiative when the territories could not agree to continue federal links within the area. However, aware of unifying factors such as language, educational system, and transportation, the former members of AOF with the exception of Guinea, after their accession to independence in 1960, decided to establish a number of common arrangements and institutions in order to promote mutual economic cooperation. Thus on June 9, 1959 the leaders of the states of Dahomey (now Benin), Ivory Coast, Mali, Mauritania, Niger, Senegal, and Upper Volta convened in Paris to sign a convention establishing the first West African Customs Union (Union

Douanière Occidentale, de l'Afrique UDAO). The most important of the objectives sought by UDAO were to maintain the customs union in effect before independence, and to harmonize import taxation among member countries. Under the provisions of this convention, neither customs nor fiscal duty would be levied on trade among members states. Furthermore, an equitable distribution of the proceeds from duties and import and export operations was envisaged.

Customs duties were levied for fiscal as well as protective purposes but were not applicable to imports from France. Duties also varied between goods imported from countries receiving most favored nation treatment (goods subject to the minimum tariff) and goods imported from other countries (goods subject to the general tariff). The general tariff, curiously, was applied to only a few countries. Moreover, fiscal duties did not differ according to the origin of imports, thus they were also applied to imports from France. There were also certain surcharges and a turnover tax on import transactions. Countries also differed as to the composition of duties and taxes on imports. Nevertheless, the UDAO treaty sought to establish a customs union. In particular it called for the elimination of tariff and nontariff barriers between members states. By establishing a common external tariff and providing for the harmonization of tax legislation in member countries, it contained the basic characteristics of the traditional integration theory. However, it failed to achieve a full customs union for two main reasons.

First, the goals set by UDAO were overambitious under the prevailing circumstances, and secondly, the procedures and unifying machinery were complicated. Moreover the countries were not prepared to meet all the requirements in administering fiscal matters. Although the convention provided for compensation, the modalities were not properly described and some questions, namely the problem of origin of import, were not addressed. It should be recalled that import duties and taxes accounted for betwen 40 and 65 percent of total budget revenues. UDAO did not set up separate and permanent institutions such as a general Secretariat, an Executive Committee, and a council of Ministers of Heads of State. In the absence of these institutions, the member countries could not find ways to simplify the procedures of revenue distribution and set up other common services. No progress was made in fiscal harmonization. The convention did not provide for adequate consultation between its members. Above all UDAO countries had the urgent problem of nation building in the aftermath of the colonial period and there was not a deep belief in the virtues of economic association.

In the light of these disappointing results, the member countries met in Paris in 1966 to search for a more elaborate solution. As a result of the Paris meeting a new convention was signed on June 3, 1966 in Abidjan establishing the West African Customs Union (Union Douanière des Etats de l'Afrique de l'Ouest, UDEAO) as of December 15, 1966). Although

UDEAO sought to correct for the weaknesses of UDAO, it turned out to be a looser customs grouping. It failed to establish a common external tariff. Tariffs varied from one country to another. No significant progress was undertaken in the area of fiscal harmonization. The institutions created were understaffed owing to insufficient financial resources and were not able to carry out their tasks fully. On the other hand, the member countries were pursuing separate national development policies. UDEAO did not provide for any regional long-term development strategy. Finally, UDEAO did not gain the wider political support necessary to carry out its objectives.

In short, UDEAO was but a legal creation without any real impact on the urgent economic problems of the countries of the area. More importantly the balkanization of West Africa which followed the colonial period contributed to the failure of UDAO and UDEAO. In Francophone West Africa, the paternalist foreign policy instituted by De Gaulle did not favor an economic association. It was not an accident that UDAO and UDEAO were "born" and "died" in Paris or after Paris, a clear indication that any economic grouping which did not favor French interest would not survive. This was the essence of the policy of "divide and reign" practiced by De Gaulle that contributed to the limited progress towards integration to date made by English- and French-speaking countries in West Africa. Therefore, it was apparent that UDEAO under such circumstances could not survive; it was transformed on June 3, 1972 into another economic union, the West African Economic Community for CEAO.

The most comprehensive economic grouping yet envisaged in the region, the Economic Community of West African States (ECOWAS), was discussed in April 1968 in Monrovia by fourteen of the current sixteen members of ECOWAS. This was the first arena where the Anglophone and Francophone states of the region discussed their common economic problems. However, this movement towards a wider economic integration was not consummated until April 1972, when Togo and Nigeria took the initiative to revive the Monrovia spirit. Practical steps were then taken that led ultimately to the establishment of ECOWAS in May 1975 in Lagos.

In concluding this section it should be observed that political, as well as economic, problems were the main factors that accounted for the limited progress achieved by West Africa in the process of economic integration.

CONTRIBUTION OF CEAO AND ECOWAS TO ECONOMIC INTEGRATION AND COOPERATION IN WEST AFRICA

In the foregoing discussion we examined the economic situation of the West African countries and surveyed the historial path towards the establishment of the West African Economic Community (CEAO) and the

Economic Community of West African States (ECOWAS). There it was argued that given the narrowness of the individual domestic markets and the weak purchasing power within each country, the only strategy that will have a greater impact will be through collective efforts. This approach will create new opportunities and conditions for a faster economic, social and political development in the area.

If the West African States are "convinced that a more rapid and better balanced growth of their economies requires the implementation among their states of an organized zone of exchanges and the setting up of an active policy of economic cooperation at a regional level,"[5] is it really worth setting up two separate economic communities aimed at the same objectives? What makes CEAO different from ECOWAS? What significant contribution did they make to economic cooperation in West Africa? These questions and others are those we intend to answer in this section. In so doing, it is worth examining the two treaties establishing CEAO and ECOWAS in order to draw out the similarities and/or the differences.

The CEAO and ECOWAS Treaties

The West African Economic Community (CEAO) comprises the former members of UDEAO, namely Ivory Coast, Mali, Mauritania, Niger, Senegal, and Upper Volta with a total population of nearly 40 million inhabitants; while the Economic Community of West African States regroups all CEAO members plus Benin, Cape Verde, Gambia, Ghana, Guinea, Guinea-Bissau, Liberia, Nigeria, Sierra-Leone, and Togo with a total population of 150 million inhabitants. The main objectives of CEAO as stipulated in Title 1, Article 4 are: (1) to elaborate an active policy of economic integration and cooperation particularly in matters of industrial and agricultural development, and to set up a better system of communications and transportation; and (2) the development of trade of agricultural and industrial products through the establishment of an organized trade area among the member states and through a Regional Cooperation Tax. In particular, the treaty aims at creating among CEAO members a unified customs zone characterized by a common import duty and tariff within twelve years in their relations with third countries from January 1, 1974 and a free trade area among member states. Thus, CEAO objectives are fundamentally different from those of UDEAO.

The CEAO treaty also provided the missing institutions, namely a Conference of Heads of State, a Council of Ministers and a General Secretariat. The treaty sought also to resolve the problem of compensation through three development institutions: The Regional Cooperation Tax, the Community Development Fund, and the Solidarity Intervention Fund for

Community Development. By these three institutions CEAO looked more like a "solidarity" association rather than a typical customs union.

The Economic Community of West African States, like CEAO, aims at "promoting cooperation and development in all fields of economic activity, particularly industry, transport, communication, agriculture, natural resources, trade, monetary and financial matters, and in the field of social and cultural affairs for the purpose of raising the standard of living of its peoples" (Manu 1982). It also aims at increasing and maintaining economic stability, at fostering closer relations among its members, and at contributing to the progress and development of the African continent. In order to achieve this objective the ECOWAS members envisage progressively (a) the elimination of customs and all forms of taxes levied on merchandise imports and exports between member states, (b) to abolish administrative and quantitative restrictions on trade between member countries, (c) to establish a common external tariff and commercial policy with respect to third countries, (d) to suppress barriers to free movement of persons, goods and capital and services among member countries and, (e) to harmonize development policies in the fields of agriculture, transport, communication, trade, energy, and industry. Likewise, harmonization is sought in financial and monetary matters and in all forms of activities aimed at community objectives that the member states undertake collectively, at all times. It is the responsibility of each member state to create the necessary conditions within its borders by restructuring where necessary, its economic, social and cultural policies for the attainment of ECOWAS objectives. The treaty went into effect in November 1976 when the Heads of State and Government approved the five protocols annexed to the treaty in Lome.

Thus, the ECOWAS treaty seeks to establish progressively a customs union within fifteen years following its ratification. The process is as follows: within two years after the treaty went into effect, member countries could not institute additional import duties and taxes nor increase the existing ones. Within two to ten years they are to undertake the gradual elimination of duties between members; within 10 to 15 years member states are to institute a common tariff in their relationship with third parties. After fifteen years, there is to be formation of a common market among the West African states. Although it fell short of the West African economic and political unification that Kwame N'Krumah fought for in the 1940s, ECOWAS is the second major attempt to bring together the French, Portuguese, and English speaking countries in an economic association. Like CEAO, the Economic Community of the West African states has established several institutions including a Conference of Heads of State or Government, a Council of Ministers, an Executive Secretariat and four technical and specialized commissions that cover all the fields that ECOWAS seek to deal with. The

Lagos treaty provides furthermore for compensation for losses incurred by member countries as a result of treaty implementation and sets up a fund for community development projects. Finally, it seeks to guarantee foreign loans obtained by member states for developmental purposes.

Comparative Performance of CEAO

While CEAO institutions have come to perform quite satisfactorily, progress in implementing the ECOWAS treaty is mainly limited to a set of decisions reached in political ethusiasm, the application of which remains hypothetical. In both treaties raw products and products of traditional handicrafts originating from member states are free of all duties and taxes normally levied at entry, but not from internal taxes equally levied on domestic goods; industrial products originating from member states are subject to the Regional Cooperation Tax (RCT) in CEAO countries and admitted to a general preferential tax regime in ECOWAS. The Regional Cooperation Tax is a special preferential regime, which is substituted for all duties and taxes levied on imports from member states. An industrial good is admitted to the RCT regime when at least sixty percent of the raw materials used in the processing originates from member countries, or the value added exceeds 40 percent of the final value of production. Industrial products originating from member states and not admitted under the RCT regime are subject to the import tax that would be applicable to them if they originated from a third party country.

The difference between the amount of import proceeds accruing to a member country as the result of the applicability of the Regional Cooperation Tax and the amount that would result from the application to the same products of the import taxes, which would be applicable if they originated in a third country, gives rise to the payment of compensation from the Community Development Fund. The difference constitutes the capital loss incurred by member countries.

The amount of the Community Development Fund is determined by the annual Conference of Heads of state in terms of the total amount of capital losses that are likely to be incurred by each member state as a result of the application of the Regional Cooperation Tax. Member states' contributions to the Fund are proportional to their share of intracommunity trade in industrial products. Two thirds of the Fund are allocated to importing countries in compensation for their capital losses, the remainder is shared among the least developed countries in CEAO and is intended to finance development projects. From 1974 to 1981, member states contributions to the fund, as shown in Table 2, amounted to 20,320 million CFA Francs, of which Ivory Coast's contribution represented 11,333 million and Senegal's share was 8,212 million. In terms of compensatory disbursement, Upper

TABLE 2 Contributions to the CEAO Community Development Fund (Millions CFA Francs)

Country	1974	1975	1976	1977	1978	1979	1980	1981
Ivory Coast	52.6	524.8	1385.7	791.4	1140.9	1276.2	2280.8	3880.4
Mali	12.7	56.7	35.5	17.0	21.5	20.7	121.2	112.9
Mauritania	7.9	0.5	0.2	0.5	0.4	0.5	1.1	0.7
Niger	14.4	6.1	9.7	6.9	6.4	6.5	12.9	12.8
Senegal	52.6	300.4	819.3	426.5	1109.3	1121.1	1754.4	2628.4
Upper Volta	9.6	16.3	30.1	45.3	21.5	21.7	32.5	112.9
TOTAL	149.8	904.8	2280.5	1287.6	2300	2446.7	4202.9	6748.1

Source: *Communautè des Etats de l'Afrique de l'Ouest, no. 15 December, 1982.*

TABLE 3 CEAO Compensatory Disbursements (Millions CFA francs)

	1976	1977	1978	1979	Percent
Ivory Coast	226	77	110	413	11.2
Mali	92	195	242	529	14.4
Mauritania	96	152	116	364	9.9
Niger	90	188	231	509	13.8
Senegal	8	219	615	842	28.9
Upper Volta	219	307	489	1015	27.6
TOTAL	731	1138	1803	3672	100

Source: *Communauté des Etats l'Afrique de l'Ouest*, no. 11 September, 1982.

Volta and Senegal received 56.5 percent, 14.4 percent went to Mali, and 13.8 to Niger; Mauritania, the last in intracommunity trade, received 9.9 percent while Ivory Coast, the major trading partner, received only 11.2 percent, as shown in Table 3. As to community development from 1974 to 1979, priority was given to national projects in the least developed countries in CEAO: Upper Volta, Mali, Mauritania, and Niger. Community development projects have taken the lead since 1979 as it is reflected in Table 4.

By sectors of activity from 1974 to 1979, agricultural and cattlebreeding constituted the main areas where Fund intervention was the most visible, representing 34.3 and 26.4 percent of the committed activities on the last third of the Community Development Fund. These two factors are followed in decreasing order by equipment and infrastructures (13.4 percent), training and research (7 percent), and trade (7 percent). The transport and communications sector which so far constitutes a major obstacle to intracommunity trade received only 1.6 percent of the fund allocated for developmental projects from 1974 to 1979, whereas fisheries accounted for 3.1, and energy and industry 5.7 percent.

The third institution established by CEAO, is a financial institution called the Solidarity Intervention Fund for the Community Development. The main objectives are to provide guarantees and counter-guarantees to loans contracted by member countries under specific rules, to grant loans to member countries under certain conditions, and to provide subsidies for feasibility studies when countries are applying for loans in international financial markets. The resources of the Fund include ordinary and special contributions made by member countries. The capital of the Fund is fixed at 5 million CFR Francs and annual contributions are set at 1.5 billion CFA Francs of which the Ivory Coast accounts for half and Senegal for 250 million CFA Francs. In May 1980, the Fund Guarantee potential was put at 30 billion.

TABLE 4 Activities Undertaken on One Third of the CEAO Community Development Fund 1974–1979 (Millions CFA francs)

Sector	Ivory Coast	Mali	Mauritania	Niger	Senegal	Upper Volta	Community	Total by Sector	Percent
Agriculture	51.8		312.6	540.0	117.2	196.8	115	1281.6	34
Cattle breeding		253.4	204.4	98.6	70.6	198.7	113.5	991.0	26.4
Fishery							114.9	114.9	3.1
Industry		176.1	11.0				26.1	213.2	5.7
Energy									
Transport									
Telecommuni- cations							58	58	1.6
Infrastructure		50		100	35.7	315		500.7	13.4
Training									
Research	12.4	14.5	12.9	14.4	14.5	12.9	203.8	286.4	7.6
Trade	1	61.1	3	15.7	2	12	200.6	295	7.9
TOTAL	65.2	555.1	543.9	768.8	240	735.4	831.9	3740.8	99.7*
Percent	1.8	14.8	14.5	20.6	6.4	19.7	22.2	100	

*Total different from 100 percent due to rounding.
Source: Integration Africaine, No. 11 September 1982.

The CEAO countries in search for a better economic community have established these institutions that operate quite efficiently despite their shortcomings. It is clear that Ivory Coast, as the major trading partner and the most advanced country in the area, provides more than half the financial contributions to the Fund. Therefore, accomplishment of CEAO objectives in terms of Community agriculture, industry, trade, transport and communication, cattle breeding and fishery development will be largely influenced by Ivorian economic conditions. This was particularly felt at the sixth conference of Heads of State in October 1981 in Niamey (Niger) at which Ivory Coast and Senegal came under attack by the four other members when they were reluctant to pay their contribution to the Community Development Fund, arguing that data on which the calculations are based have never been accurate. The main reason was that the two major CEAO exporters have recorded declines in budget revenues against increasing expenditures. The situation was more alarming in that the countries' past dues amounted to 5 billion CFA Francs, or 1.33 times the total received by all the sectors in terms of national and community development programs over the 1974–1979 period. It should be noted that CEAO also provides a secured outlet to the Ivorian manufacturing industry. In 1975, 75 percent of the manufactured products exchanged in CEAO were of Ivorian origin, against 54.4 percent in 1978. The gains for Ivory Coast from intracommunity trade must be contrasted with its contribution to find out whether CEAO represents a net loss to the country.

The establishment of the preferential tax regime is seen to be a positive step on the path towards a full customs union, a CEAO objective for 1990. UDAO and UDEAO did not survive because the founders failed to properly resolve the problem of compensation as a result of elimination of tariff barriers within the former French Federation of West Africa. At the time UDEAO was formed, revenues from trade accounted for more than fifty percent of the budget revenues of most of the countries. Given the internal tax structure and tax base, no significant revenues could be derived from the domestic market. This is still true today and no economic integration scheme would survive if the treaties did not provide for compensation for member countries' losses.

The Regional Cooperation Tax can be critized on the grounds that it provides opportunities only to the firms operating in the formal sector. Even in this sector firms may not qualify to benefit from the special tax regime. As shown in Table 5, in mid-1980 212 enterprises within CEAO were admitted to the RCT regime compared to 91 in 1975. Ivory Coast accounted for 115 enterprises, compared to 1 for Mauritania, 64 for Senegal, 14 for Upper Volta, 13 for Mali, and 5 in Niger. In 1980, 450 enterprises operated in the Ivorian manufacturing sector. If one excludes bakeries, repairs shops and other activities that do not lead to exports, it is estimated that 350 enterprises

TABLE 5 Number of Firms and Products Admitted to the Regional Cooperation Tax Regime

| | Firms | | | | | | Products | | | | | |
	1975	1976–1977	1978	1979	1980*	1975	1976–1977	1978	1979	1980*
Ivory Coast	46	81	94	113	115	127	209	235	271	273
Mali	8	10	12	12	13	23	35	37	38	41
Mauritania	0	0	0	1	1	0	0	0	3	3
Niger	3	5	5	5	5	10	13	13	13	13
Senegal	30	52	58	61	64	88	156	171	176	179
Upper Volta	4	6	10	12	14	5	14	42	47	54

*Six months data.
Source: Communauté des Etats de l'Afrique de l'Ouest, no. 11 September, 1980.

manufacture exportable goods. Still, only 115 firms were admitted to the Regional Cooperation tax system, or about one-third. It is not certain how many firms will engage in intracommunity trade, but it can be argued that RCT requirements prevent a number of them from regional trade.

Three additional problems may be identified with the RCT system. First, the system may lead to fraud. In CEAO countries, except for Ivory Coast and Senegal, data collection agencies are nascent. Statistical information is hardly reliable and fraud cannot be discounted in examining compliance with the RCT criteria. If this occurred, importing countries would be penalized because of the loss of revenues that would be derived if the goods imported were not admitted under the RCT system. Second, the system may be criticized in that it amounts to a subsidy on manufactured exports by exporting countries. In fact, the RCT system protects industries within CEAO against outside competition. In the long run firms under the RCT regime may find it difficult to adjust to new combinations of factors and lose substantial shares of their markets. Third, the RCT system may tend to prevent the institution of effective domestic fiscal policies to generate budget revenues in importing countries. Since contributions to the Community Development Fund are proportional to the volume of regional trade, it can be argued that more active trade policies will increase Fund resources for compensation. These resources constitute real budget revenues to the least developed countries that may work against internal fiscal policy reform.

Therefore, the RCT practice would be counterproductive in the long run if CEAO countries did not undertake steps to eliminate gradually the RCT system before 1990, when a full customs union is expected. More concerted regional development combined with national development strategies geared to growth will increase the opportunities to generate more fiscal revenues internally. This policy must be viewed as a long term objective. At the present moment, most CEAO countries have little hope to generate budget revenues except through trade taxes and for aid.

A look at CEAO over the past ten years indicates that a degree of integration has been achieved within Francophone West Africa. The institutions established, despite some inherent difficulties, operate quite efficiently. The countries have harmonized their customs laws and regulations and adopted common customs nomenclature. Thus, despite its shortcomings, the Regional Cooperation Tax constitutes a major innovation in the preintegration era.

In the area of rural development the countries have set regional development programs according to factor endowments of member countries. More cooperation is expected in agriculture and cattle breeding. The objective of CEAO countries is to achieve selfsufficiency in food production.

In the field of industrialization, more cooperation is needed in order to avoid duplication that distorts resource allocation.

Comparative Performance of ECOWAS

Although progress made by CEAO in the area of economic cooperation cannot be ignored, there remain numerous problems that lie in the way of complete economic integration. Although the coexistence of CEAO and ECOWAS has raised the issue of the future of these two integration schemes, some English-speaking countries tend to blame CEAO for the timid start of ECOWAS. This fact was illustrated at the conference in Cotonou (Benin) in May 1982, at which President Mathieu Kerekou in his opening speech acknowledged that "ECOWAS' fundamental problem is not that of important decisions to reach. It is an imperative duty," he went on, to "take all steps in order to strengthen and save at all cost our political will and the spirit of solidarity and cooperation that we all express by beginning to implement all the decisions that we have already reached at our previous conferences." This appeal is a clear indication that after seven years of existence, ECOWAS still remains a project fueled by good intentions and proclamations without a concrete achievement. Apart from the adopted communications for which the Executive Secretariat was instructed to search for funding, it is very hard to find evidence of any concrete implementation of the provisions of ECOWAS treaty.

Despite the theoretical similarities, the two communities exhibit very important practical differences that may explain the lack of progress made by ECOWAS. While CEAO has adopted a step by step procedure in order to achieve a real economic integration and cooperation, ECOWAS appears to be an integration scheme which envisages an outright elimination of all forms of barriers between the economic units of its members by ignoring the social and economic conditions of its members. Historical evidence has shown that such overambitious schemes have not survivied for many reasons, among them the problem of distribution of gains from intra-community trade. In the ECOWAS treaty, although there are provisions to compensate for the losses incurred by importing countries as a result of the implementation of the treaty, it is still not clear how those countries will be compensated in practice. The treaty only says that the Council of Ministers, upon the Report of the Executive Secretariat and on the recommendation of the competent commissions, decides the compensation to make to a member that has incurred losses. It does not suggest a basis for calculating the amount. This practice is in sharp contrast with CEAO provisions according to which two-thirds of the Community Development Fund compensates for capital losses incurred by importing countries. In that respect, CEAO sought to safeguard its community from the most serious problem that afflicted its predecessors. If the problem of compensation is not properly resolved, the ECOWAS treaty may remain a paper economic community for a long time. The rule of proportionality may serve as a basis of calculation. This rule will favor the least developed countries, which would then be induced to implement the ECOWAS treaty.

Although the ECOWAS treaty went into affect in 1975, no country has yet implemented the provision on trade liberalization. While the protocol on the definition of the origin of the products from the community is specific as to imported raw materials, it leaves some loopholes as far as manufactured goods are concerned. The ECOWAS treaty admits all industrial products to the general preferential regime. These products are considered to originate from the community if they pass at least one of three tests: (1) they are manufactured in the community and the CIF value of noncommunity inputs does not contribute more than 60 percent of the total value of intermediate inputs, (2) they are manufactured in the community with at least 40 percent local content of raw materials, or (3) at least sixty percent of the raw materials in the product, in quantity terms, originate from the community. For exported manufactured goods, community value-added must at least be equal to 35 percent of the net exfactory price of the final product.

Thus, products processed within ECOWAS may use materials from foreign or undetermined origin. The treaty does not specify what it means by undetermined origin. In addition it gives two independent forms of calculation, by value and by quantity. The interpretation of this provision alone slowed down progress on the Trade Liberalization Program, which was adopted only in May 1980 in conformity with article 12 and 13 of the treaty. The program prescribed the total elimination of all tariff barriers to unprocessed goods as from May 28, 1981, contrary to the original date of November 1978 originally planned. The ECOWAS treaty needs to choose one basis for calculation in order to properly set the compensation fund criteria. Finally, it is important to clarify the term "undetermined." This overshadows the protocol and may give rise to different interpretations, making the implementation of the provisions unlikely. Trade barriers may be eliminated, but if the terms are not clarified, this scheme may not generate manufactured exports within ECOWAS.

A further difficulty is implied by the definition of product origin in the Trade Liberalization Program adopted in May 1980. According to this article, manufacturing enterprises must comply with acceptable levels of national participation. In other words, the treaty requires that firms producing goods for export within the community must be primarily owned by nationals. The program specifies that the degree of national control over manufacturing industries is proportional to its participation in the capital base. By May 1989, 51 percent of the capital of any enterprise exporting manufactured goods to the ECOWAS market will be held by nationals against 20 percent in 1981 and 35 percent in 1983. This provision, although idealistic, is hardly realistic. In ECOWAS countries national participation in the capital of manufacturing firms is weak or nil. In these countries with the exception of Nigeria to some extent, the industrial enterprises established are subsidiaries of foreign firms. National entrepreneurship is not much in evidence and firms are largely owned by the government with heavy foreign influence and interest. The implementation of the treaty, if it becomes a reality, will not foster trade and development in this regard. The bulk of manufacturing firms for export will not qualify for intracommunity trade, which ECOWAS badly wants to foster.

Thus from the pure point of view of the treaties, CEAO appears to be more realistic and pragmatic. There is no doubt that its more liberal approach to the problems of the West Africa region was a major factor in its limited success. But this success may be short-lived if the fundamental contradiction between the two treaties is not resolved in the near future. According to article 59, paragraph two, of the ECOWAS treaty, rights and obligations of members resulting from previous treaties are not affected by the provisions of the present treaty. On the other hand, paragraph three of the same article states that whenever these agreements become incompatible with the ECOWAS treaty, the members are to take appropriate measures to eliminate the incompatibilities. Interpreted correctly, this provision means that under article 20 of the ECOWAS treaty (the most favored nation provision), CEAO members would have to extend the same priviledges to all ECOWAS countries. Then the CEAO customs union will logically come to an end and be dissolved within ECOWAS. This conflict has prompted CEAO and ECOWAS to seek more collaboration. A committee is established to deal with this problem for a better working of the two institutions. Whether CEAO or ECOWAS fail will not necessary depend on the contradiction of these treaties. An assessment of the prospects of success of these two schemes of integration must be based on real economic and political facts in West Africa.

PROBLEMS OF ECONOMIC INTEGRATION IN WEST AFRICA

In the previous section we investigated the causes of the limited success of CEAO and the reasons that accounted for the slow start of ECOWAS. There, we also raised some of the issues that may endanger the process of integration in the West Africa region. In this section we take a close look at these problems, which may be categorized as economic and noneconomic.

Economic problems to Economic Integration and Cooperation

To a large extent the economic barriers are real but they are not likely to endanger the process towards a full economic integration and cooperation in West Africa, the major obstacles being the noneconomic factors to which we will return shortly. Initially, the elimination of trade barriers within West Africa may have little effect on the agricultural sector and industrial sectors. As noted, over the last decade the available exportable surplus of foodstuffs was nil in many countries; some countries even recorded negative rates of growth of food production and had to rely on imports of foodstuffs. Widening the market will not also create the expected effects in the industrial sector, in the short-run, because of the tendency of the West Africa countries to duplicate plants. Only in the long term, when costs of production are cut down and inefficient production processes shut down, are exports of industrial products likely to increase in the area.

Unequal Development

It is important to note that Ivory Coast plays the same role in CEAO as Nigeria in ECOWAS. In CEAO, Ivory Coast and Senegal have the highest gross domestic product per capita; the landlocked countries have the lowest. Per capita income in the monetized sector was estimated to average $505 in the sub region as a whole, but it was estimated at $1150 in Ivory Coast, $450 in Senegal, and only $250 and $190, respectively, in Mali and Upper Volta. When the next ten countries are added, the average per capita income for ECOWAs rises to $731; Nigeria was estimated at $1010 in 1980. At the sectoral level, Nigeria accounted for 55 percent of the agricultural production within ECOWAS compared to 8 percent to Ivory Coast. Its industrial output was estimated at 81 percent and accounted for 81 percent of the gross investment of the region, which compared unfavorably with 7 and 10 percent, respectively, for Ivory Coast. In CEAO, Ivory Coast has the dominant role as it processes 50 percent of total agricultural output, 65 percent of industrial output and accounted for 65 percent of CEAO gross investment. The two countries together accounted for 81 percent of the total foreign trade in the ECOWAS countries in 1979 and 84 percent in 1980. Their relative shares compared unfavorably. Nigeria alone accounting for 70 percent in 1979 and 73 percent in 1980. Ivory Coast on the other hand, accounted for 69 percent of the total foreign trade in CEAO countries in 1979 and 57 percent in 1980.

The coexistence of more and less developed economies within a regionally integrated market is likely to seriously challenge integration in CEAO and ECOWAS regions. As industrialization expands, more and more plants may be concentrated in a few centers for reasons of both external and internal economies. It is believed that within a single market area the growth of manufacturing industry and its dependent economic activities tend to become highly concentrated. Some EEC consultants project that 70 percent of the planned plants are likely to be located in Senegal and Ivory Coast, as the CEAO countries become more integrated. This process is thought to operate cumulatively, so that increasing inequality would be generated. The process of polarization may be avoided only if CEAO or ECOWAS countries industrialize in a more concerted and coordinated fashion. Despite the polarization effects, if CEAO or ECOWAS can produce substantial potential producitivity gains to the region as a whole, it should be possible to redistribute these in such a way that all members of the region are better off over the long run, if not necessarily in each short time period, assuming that the costs of redistribution are not too high. This aspect is one of the most crucial problems that the CEAO countries face today and there is not a clear indication that the trend will be reversed.

Table 6 shows that 33 percent and 35 percent of the gross inflow of external capital went to Ivory Coast and Nigeria, respectively, in 1980. These two countries alone accounted for 84.5 percent of the net foreign direct investment that went to ECOWAS countries in 1980. If this is to be interpreted as a sign of industrial potential and industrial health, it appears that as their economies expand faster than the rest of the ECOWAS region, Ivory Coast and Nigeria will attract more investments, further increasing the gap.

Trade diversion in the meantime may become substantial and detrimental to the balance of benefits among partner countries. That means that coexistence can lead to subsidization of the more advanced economies by the less advanced ones. Subsidization of the more advanced by the less advanced will be aggravated the faster the polarization effect operates. Furthermore the less advanced countries will find themselves foregoing a part of their revenue from customs and fiscal duties, which are by far the most important sources of budget receipts.

Another important obstacle to integration is to be found in the pattern and direction of the area's foreign trade. This trade is not diversified enough to allow for an increased mutual exchange of goods and is outwardly oriented, as shown in Table 7 through Table 11. The predominance of subsistence farming coupled with rapid expansion of cash crops, the outlets of which are traditionally assured in overseas markets, have resulted in the concentration of exports on a few primary commodities and a heavy reliance on imports of foodstuffs and consumer durables. Moreover CEAO and ECOWAS trade with EEC still accounts for 75 percent of total external trade of the region. On the other hand intracommunity trade is still weak, even declining. In 1972, intra-CEAO trade accounted for 11 percent of total trade; this rose to 12 percent in 1975 and started to decline after 1976 to reach 8.5 percent in 1977. In other words, intra-CEAO trade seems to have

TABLE 6 Flow of External Capital to West Africa (millions of U.S. $)

| | Public and publicly guaranteed medium- and long-term loans | | | | | | Net direct private investment | |
| | Gross inflow | | Repayment of principal | | Net inflow | | | |
	1970	1980	1970	1980	1970	1980	1970	1980
Benin	2	84	1	4	1	80	7	..
Cape Verde								
Gambia								
Ghana	40	129	12	48	28	81	8	10
Guinea								
Guinea Bissau								
Ivory Coast	77	1,426	27	534	50	892	31	109
Liberia	7	90	12	16	−5	74		4
Mali	21	85	—	7	21	78		84
Mauritania	4	153	3	17	1	136	1	
Niger	12	177	1	23	11	154	1	—
Nigeria	62	1,526	36	84	26	1,442	205	595
Senegal	15	283	5	123	10	160	5	..
Sierra Leone	8	88	10	34	−2	54	8	12
Togo	5	222	2	97	3	125	1	—
Upper Volta	2	79	2	9	—	70	1	—

Source: World Bank, 1982.

TABLE 7 Intracommunity Exports as a Share of Total Exports and Direction of Intra-Community Trade 1972–1978 (in thousands U.S. $)

	Ivory Coast	Upper Volta	Mali	Mauri-tania	Niger	Senegal	Total CEAO	CEAO as Percent of World	World
Ivory Coast									
1972	—	9,343	9,011		4,512	13,190	36,056	6.5	522,913
1973	—	16,330	14,340		3,718	14,852	49,240	5.7	880,577
1974	—	26,201	31,324	226	5,885	21,250	84,560	7.0	1,214,313
	—	10,192	15,809		3,157	14,947			
1975	—	32,455	51,566+		12,440	22,181	118,642	10.0	1,181,569
	—	12,547	30,400		3,177	15,547			
1976	—	32,904	34,433		12,185	27,147	106,669	6.5	1,630,790
	—	29,694	21,473		3,963	24,535			
1977	—	41,951	48,330		14,807	23,965	129,053	6.0	2,154,786
	—	23,493	9,491		10,542	21,659			
1978	—	40,547	45,363		17,773	29,716	133,399	5.7	2,322,853
	—	27,665				26,557			
Upper Volta									
1972	9,495	—	1,066	—	170	18[a]	10,749	52.8	20,349
1973	10,274	—	575	—	188	50	11,087	43.7	25,382
					553				
1974	12,272	—	1,578	—	238	39	14,127	39.2	36048
			1,514		1,566				
1975	20,845	—	15	—	401	13	21,374	49.1	43,531
			59		2,815				
1976	8,266	—	55	—	1,500	21	9,842	18.3	53,768

(continued)

TABLE 7 (continued)

	Year	Ivory Coast	Upper Volta	Mali	Mauritania	Niger	Senegal	Total CEAO	CEAO as Percent of World	World
	1977	17,405	—	187	—	1,164	24	18,780	34.0	55,232
	1978		—							
Mali	1972	10,012	733	—	26	335	4,857	15,963	43.5	36,718
	1973	(9,878)	(696)	—	(81)	(315)	(5,809)	16,779	32.4	51,850
			2,353			591	3,534			
	1974	9,740	659		155	295	6,761	17,610	27.5	64,147
		740	3,703			731	1,465			
	1975	12,407	45		190	162	3,853	16,657	45.6	36,538
		2,206	960			637	816			
	1976	10,666	782		12	2,258	4,667	18,385	21.7	64,537
		5,090	758			85	1,035			
	1977	17,947	1,488		(12)[b]	(2,258)[b]	958	22,663	18.2	124,542
		5,834	2,187				69			
	1978	8,052								
Mauritania[d]	1969	0	0	0	—		1,827	1,827	2.3	77,798
	1970	0			—		2,515	2,515	2.8	88,849
	1971	0			—		874	874	0.9	93,895
	1972	60			—	—	742	802	0.7	119,205
	1973				—	—	130			155,318
	1974				—					
	1972	1,204	424	696	—	—	39	2,363	4.3	55,049
	1973	694	703	739	—	—	204	2,340	3.7	62,773

Niger	1974	560	97 / 669	900 / 1,378	—	—	2	2,131	4.1	52,566
	1975	1,071	113 / 1,877	114 / 190	—	—	546	3,608	4.0	91,233
	1976	1,402	173 / 1,144	61 / 37	—	—	24	2,631	2.0	133,870
	1977		63 / 81		—	—		(2,631)c	2.0	(133,870)c
Senegal	1972	10,923	(600) / 1,588	8,596	10,286	230	—	30,635	14.2	215,880
	1973	16,125	549 / 1,256	7,386	13,883 / 7,131	305 / 781	—	38,248	19.6	194,658
	1974	18,280 / 17,728	423 / 1,261	8,009 / 8,816	17,505	2,458 / 1,080	—	46,675	11.9	390,718
	1975	20,859 / 18,186	883 / 1,720	13,104 / 15,951	24,358	1,146 / 10,399	—	60,350	13.1	462,403
	1976	15,226 / 18,360	876 / 1,599	10,314 / 14,605	17,254	3,349 / 1,899	—	47,019	9.6	490,741
	1977	23,162 / 18,393	4,430 / 1,436	21,891 / 13,282	28,068	8,159	—	85,710	13.8	622,690
	1978	31,126								

aEstimation based on Upper Volta imports from Senegal.
bMali's exports to Mauritania and Niger are not available for 1977 and have been replaced with 1976 figures.
cNiger's total exports and exports to CEAO are not available for 1977 and have been replaced with 1976 figures.
dExports of Ivory Coast, Upper Volta and Niger to Mauritania are not available for the period covered here. As they are very small, they have been omitted as well as Mauritania's exports to other CEAO countries except Senegal. The resulting error should be negligeable.
Source: The United Nations.

TABLE 8 Structure of Ivorian Exports to CEAO and ECOWAS (1975)
Relative weight of main export products (million CFAF and percent)

	Mauritania	Mali	Upper Volta	Niger	Senegal	Total CEAO
Raw agricultural	—	509	290	107	1317	2223
products		4	7	4	27	8.4
(of which cola nut)	—	(505)	(272)	(105)	(115)	(997)
		(4)	(7)	(4)	(2)	(3.7)
Coffee extract	14	97	55	95	576	837
	5	1	1	3	11	3.1
Refined palm oil	—	—	—	—	—	—
Cotton fabrics	—	2251	104	284	510	3149
and yarn		20	1	10	10	11.8
Sawn wood and	51	19	111	24	369	571
plywood	18		2	1	8	2.1
Insecticides	—	162	304	130	59	655
		1	4	4	1	2.5
Petroleum	10	3370	2746	99	36	6261
products	3	30	38	3	1	23.5
Maggi cubes, Sugar confectionery	—	—	—	—	—	—
Other locally	70	569	902	519	326	2390
manufactured goods	24	5	12	18	7	9.0
Goods in transit	143	4358	2730	1569	1697	10497
	50	38	38	55	35	39.5
TOTAL	288	11339	7242	2830	4893	26592
	100	100	100	100	100	100

*The grand total is the raw total. There is a small difference with the column total because of rounding errors.
Source: Ivory Coast, *Ministerè de l'Economie et des Finances.*

declined over the last ten years, in spite of the incentives provided by the treaty and common monetary arrangements.

The same trend is also observed at the country trade level. As shown in Table 12, Ivory Coast, the most advanced country in the area, experienced a decline in its trade with its partners from 10.4 percent in 1975 to 7.1 percent in 1979. As to industrial exports, the CEAO market absorbed 57.4 percent of the Ivorian manufactured exports in 1978, compared to 60.7 percent in 1976 and 75 percent in 1975. Likewise, it appears that Ivorian industrial exports have a definite outlet and that Ivory Coast may be able to increase its share as per capita income in these countries increases, too. Given the

Benin	Togo	Ghana	Nigeria	Liberia	Other ECOWAS	Total ECOWAS
—	1	20	134	18		2396
	2		10	2		7.4
—	—	—	(134)	—		(1131)
			(10)			(3.5)
8	2	8	365	11	7	1238
		1	28	1	4	3.8
—	—	—	—	—	—	—
471	10	18	66	72	17	3803
30	1	2	5	9	10	11.8
35	12		49	21	5	693
2	1		4	3	3	2.1
416	299	159	38	—	7	1574
26	33	20	3		4	4.9
—	1	2	26	213	—	6503
			2	26		20.1
—	—	—	—	—	—	—
69	72	2	31	11	40	2615
4	8		2	1	24	8.1
585	520	591	613	476	87	13369
37	57	74	46	58	53	38.7
1596	919	802	1321	825	164	32219*
100	100	100	100	100	100	100

common background and the similarities of the institutions, Ivory Coast has a definitive advantage over potential Nigerian competition in CEAO. In fact, it is believed that as trade barriers are eliminiated, or if CEAO extends the most favored nation regime to all ECOWAS members, Ivorian manufacturers will face stiff competition from Nigeria and eventually lose some part of their CEAO market to the benefit of Nigerian industrial exporters. This situation may not arise in the short-run. Over the long-run, when industries in the two countries are mature, it is not evident enough that Ivorian exports will be less competitive. The reasons for this are examined further on in this section.

TABLE 9 Structure of Ivorian Exports to CEAO and ECOWAS (1979)
(million CFAF and percent)

	Mauritania	Mali	Upper Volta	Niger	Senegal	Total CEAO
Raw agricultural	1	363	583	134	1030	2111
products		3	5	2	18	5.5
(of which cola nut)		(260)	(199)	(64)	(172)	(695)
		(2)	(2)	(1)	(3)	(2)
Coffee extract		296	430	185	1305	2216
		2	3	3	23	5.8
Refined palm oil	152	95	269	360	425	1301
	52	1	2	6	7	3.4
Cotton fabrics	36	3416	300	1167	277	5195
and yarn	12	25	2	21	5	13.6
Sawn wood and	36	144	155	29	725	1089
plywood	12	1	1	1	13	2.9
Insecticides		143	374	252	252	1021
		1	3	4	4	2.7
Petroleum products		6267	5680	32	—	11979
		46	45	1		31.4
Maggi cubes, Sugar	15	257	421	87	188	968
confectionery	6	2	3	2	3	2.5
Other locally	20	900	1245	1389	297	3851
manufactured	7	7	10	23	17	10.7
goods						
Not elsewhere	35	1800	3300	2000	1250	8385
specified	12	13	26	37	20	22.0
TOTAL	295	13681	12757	5635	5749	38117

Source: Ivory Coast, *Ministère de l'Economie et des Finances.*

Another difficulty that constitutes a barrier to trade within the West Africa area is the lack of adequate transport facilities. In the ECOWAS area, lack of transportation facilities and particularly high transport costs make it difficult for exports of the landlocked countries to compete with those of the coastal countries. The former are compelled to reduce producer prices below those prevailing in the costal countries and thus lower rural incomes. The removal of tariffs between Ivory Coast and Niger, for instance, may not add significantly to the market for industrial goods established in either country, nor would it add substantial incentives to investors. Tariff concessions will be irrelevant until the Abidjan-Niger railroad is completed. Even within each country the lack of communication networks and

Benin	Togo	Ghana	Nigeria	Liberia	Other ECOWAS	Total ECOWAS
11		67	31	322	5	2547
		4		30		5.1
—	—	—	(31)			(726)
						(1.5)
219	35	50	1607			4217
8.7	3	3	36			8.5
		337	253			1805
		21	5			3.8
960	425			172	60	6813
38.3	32			16	28	13.8
551	14		105			1759
22	1		2			3.6
276	31		111			1439
11	3		2			2.9
75	127	446	231	420		13278
3	10	28	5	41		26.8
35	41	275				1319
1	3	17				2.7
80	161	101	257	36	47	4533
3	13	6	5	3	22	8.7
300	500	300	2000	100	100	(11685)
12	37	19	43	10	47	24
2507	1334	1576	4685	1050	212	49481

infrastructure is seen as the main cause of unbalanced development and growth. In the ECOWAS area, an integrated transport system is the prerequisite to a rapid and comprehensive expansion of intraunion trade and industry. In this regard, the transport and communications program adopted, for which the Executive Secretariat has been instructed to seek funding, which constitutes a positive step in the right direction. Reversing the transport system that these countries have inherited from the colonial powers are designed to move goods from the interior to the port cities for overseas shipment, will add significantly to tariff and customs effects, and enhance trade within the community. It would also tend to eliminate unfair competition to the benefit of all member states.

TABLE 10 Ivorian Imports from CEAO and ECOWAS (1975) (million CFAF)

	Mauritania	Mali	Upper Volta	Niger	Senegal	Total CEAO	Benin	Togo	Ghana	Nigeria	Liberia	Other ECOWAS	Total ECOWAS
Fresh and smoked fish	11	143			1166	1400						5	1405
Animals for breeding		130	16			146							146
Other live animals		7	100	128		235							235
Vegetables		95	26	28	12	161							161
Fruit		6		3	16	25							25
Cereals (including maize)		6				6							6
Groundnuts		3	35		37	75							75
Other raw agricultural products		17				17			15				32

Cotton linters	51													51
Groundnut oil		24				52	52							76
Salt			7			530	530							537
Cigarettes						589	589							589
Calcium phosphates						47	47		128					175
Paper and paper-board						44	44							44
Cotton fabrics and yarn						355	355			21			12	388
Apparel						272	272			2				274
Shoes						125	125			69				194
Petroleum products											11,898			11,808
Miscellaneous products	5	36	182	20	20	944	944	20	13	55	23	39	3	961
Total Imports	96	494	359	210	701	3946	5105	20	141	163	11,921	39	20	14,409

Source: Ivory Coast, Ministere de l'Economie et des Finances.

TABLE 11 Structure of Ivorian Imports from CEAO and ECOWAS (1979) in percent

(million CFAF)		*Mauritania*	*Mali*	*Upper Volta*	*Niger*	*Senegal*	*Total CEAO*
Fresh and smoked fish	14.9	84	24	—	—	3463	3571
Animals for breeding	6.1	—	1470	—	—	—	1470
Other live animals	0.4	—	80	13	—	—	93
Vegetables	0.5		117	—	—	—	117
Other raw agricultural products	22.0	—	—	—	—	16	16
Cotton linters	—	—	—	—	—	—	—
Groundnut oil	0.4	—	—	—	99	—	99
Salt	5.7	—	—	—	—	1353	1353
Cigarettes	0.2	—	—	—	—	57	57
Calcium phosphates	0.3	—	—	—	—	80	80
Paper and paper-board	0.3	—	—	—	—	79	79
Cotton fabrics and yarn	3.1	—	—	—	—	732	732
Apparel	0.1	—	—	—	—	26	26
Shoes	0.2	—	—	—	—	52	52
Petroleum products	59.9	—	—	—	—	—	—
Miscellaneous products	7.7	17	675	21	34	800	1547
Total Imports	100	101	2366	44	34	6757	9302

Source: Ivory Coast, *Ministere de l'Economie et des Finances.*

While the economic barriers present some danger to economic cooperation, they may be dealt with adequately, however, it is not certain how countries will react to noneconomic factors that may not be as easily masterable.

Non-Economic Barriers to Integration

The foregoing analysis showed that the elimination of discrimination may not significantly add to integration in West Africa unless it is

Benin	Togo	Ghana	Nigeria	Liberia	Other ECOWAS	Total ECOWAS
—	—	—	—	—	—	3571
—	—	—	—	—	—	1470
—	—	—	—	—	—	93
—	—	—	—	—	—	117
—	—	—	—	—	—	16
—	—	—	—	—	—	—
—	—	—	—	—	—	99
—	—	—	—	—	—	1353
—	—	—	—	—	—	57
—	—	—	—	—	—	80
—	—	—	—	—	—	79
—	—	—	—	—	—	732
—	—	—	—	—	—	26
—	—	—	—	—	—	52
—	—	—	14115	304	—	14319
16	38	42	44	159	3	1851
16	38	42	14159	364	3	23914

accompanied by other measures to correct present disequilibrium. The elimination of imbalances depends as much on realistic economic policies as it depends on the political climate in every country and between countries, and finally on the relationships that ECOWAS will develop with the industrial nations of Europe, America, and Asia.

Nigeria, by virtue of its economic potential and demographic advantage, will play a key role in fostering economic integration in West Africa, the success or failure of which depends upon its attitude towards its partners. The fear that Nigeria dominates the community was echoed from the start

TABLE 12 Ivorian Exports to CEAO and ECOWAS (million CFAF)

	1975	1976	1977	1978	1979
Upper Volta	7,242	8,148	11,016	9,899	12,758
	(2.8)*	(2.1)	(2.1)	(1.9)	(2.4)
Mali	11,329	8,451	12,464	10,836	13,681
	(4.4)	(2.2)	(2.3)	(2.1)	(2.5)
Mauritania	288		986	398	295
	(0.1)	(0.1)	(0.2)	(0.1)	(0.1)
Niger	2,830	3,065	4,202	4,550	5,635
	(1.1)	(0.8)	(0.8)	(0.9)	(1.0)
Senegal	4,893	6,640	6,370	7,137	5,749
	(1.9)	(1.7)	(1.2)	(1.4)	(1.1)
Total CEAO	26,582		35,038	32,820	38,118
	(10.4)		(6.6)	(6.3)	(7.1)
Benin	1,596		1,472	1,032	2,507

Gambia	8		16	6	18
Ghana	802		1,570	1,772	1,575
Guinea	14		134	50	113
Guinea Bissau	—		2	0	2
Liberia	825		1,741	1,229	1,049
Nigeria	1,321		1,398	3,194	4,685
Sierra Leone	142		95	57	79
Togo	919		1,294	1,382	1,334
Total ECOWAS without CEAO	5,627 (2.2)		7,722 (1.5)	8,722 (1.6)	11,362 (2.1)
Total ECOWAS	32,209 (12.7)		42,760 (8.1)	41,542 (7.9)	49,480 (9.3)
Total Exports	254,572	393,501	529,760	524,382	534,847

*The percentages in brackets refer to total Ivorian exports.
Source: Ivory Coast, *Ministere de l'Economie et des Finances.*

and is still real in the area. To counter the Nigerian influence and counter Anglophone domination, Senegal sought to extend ECOWAS to include Cameroon and Zaire, two French-speaking countries. This proposal never received popular support and the subject is assumed to be closed. This cautious attitude towards Nigeria was justified as she attempted to introduce the notion of votes based on a system of proportionality according to each country's contribution to ECOWAS. This would have given Nigeria a clear advantage and, implicitly, a veto power on any decision.

The role of Nigeria as a financer and referee is well accepted by its trading partners. But this attitude would change if Nigeria tried to extend this role to all West Africa. The Nigeria decision in February 1983 to expel all illegal immigrants is hardly compatible with the spirit of the Lagos treaty for which she has fought so much over the past ten years. Fears of a Nigerian take-over with ECOWAS would only escalate the long acknowledged friction between Nigeria and Ghana, the most advanced countries in the Anglophone West Africa. How this friction will actually influence relationships between the two countries depends on the assessment of the political as well as economic costs to Ghana over the next two years.

It is obvious that ECOWAS means a lot to Nigeria. ECOWAS provides a potential market for its still nascent industries, which will compete easily with the manufactured exports of developed countries in ECOWAS, since Nigerian exports will be produced behind the tariff walls, giving them an unfair comparative advantage over the long-run. Per capita income in ECOWAS is still low but steadily increasing, providing further incentives for intracommunity trade growth. Nigeria needs to keep these options open. The success of her long-term strategy will depend on whether Nigeria will be able to create a competitive industry within the next 20 to 25 years, during that time it could still rely on its petroleum export revenues.

As in the case of Nigeria, CEAO countries reproach Ivory Coast with interference and a desire for hegemony, even of imperialism. However, contrary to Nigeria, Ivory Coast has always sought better and closer relationships with its neighbors since their markets present definitive outlets to her expanding light industries and her agricultural exports. As shown in Table 13, Ivory Coast's trade balance is positive with every country in West Africa, with the exception of petroleum imports from Nigeria. This explains why Ivory Coast has demonstrated a genuine interest in regional economic cooperation instituted by a treaty which extends beyond the traditional Francophone framework to include the Anglophone states. It also seeks to avoid conflict with its neighbours. Thus, Abidjan has turned down proposals to become headquarters of both CEAO and BCEAO. As far as export competition with Nigeria is concerned, Ivory Coast has a comparative advantage at the present moment. Should this situation develop in a way unfavorable to Ivory Coast, there is always the possibility of confining initiatives to CEAO where she plays the lead role.

At the international level it is worth stressing the importance of West Africa as an outlet for industrial countries exports. The West African market is essential to the EEC, the United States, and Japan. The import substitution strategy, which goes along with the regional cooperation, limits the outlet possibilities of traditional suppliers. However, when goods are produced within the regional market through the intermediary of a multinational, production benefits from the common external tariff while the competitors are forced to retreat from the market. The formation of a free trade area or customs union may force foreign suppliers to export capital to preserve outlets or open new ones. The response of foreign powers to economic cooperation in West Africa will result from their position in these markets and from the structure of their exports to this region. Thus, when trade barriers are dismantled, it can be expected that Europeans, Americans and Japanese will compete in the same market on an equal basis, forcing less efficient competitors to retreat from the market.

The danger is that some countries will tend to avoid competition by seeking preferential trade concessions through bilateral arrangements. Over the past years France has been active in fostering closer relationships with Nigeria, which constitutes a potential market for French exports. On the other hand, the United States has succeeded in displacing part of French influence and economic interests in Ivory Coast. This development will add further stimuli to economic cooperation in West Africa, as foreign powers export more capital to take advantage of reduced costs of production, to the benefits of the West African consumers. But the economic competition may present some risk to West African countries if former colonial powers consistently lose traditional partners to the benefit of newcomers. This will result in political pressures and tensions that may eventually endanger the precarious political state in which most of the West African countries live.

Finally, it can be argued that the success of failure of ECOWAS and CEAO will ultimately depend on the political climate that will prevail in the West African states. Out of the sixteen countries forming the economic community of the West African states only four have not changed their heads of state over the past twenty years, and only one changed heads in a peaceful manner. Political stability will play a major role in the success of integration in West Africa. Historical evidence has shown that countries in which the armed forces came to power through a coup experience economic disruption, stagnation and eventually disintegrate completely. The reason was that these regimes came to power ill-prepared, without a definite plan to stimulate growth; most of the time they have eliminated democratic institutions. The concern of these regions has always been changes in economic and political

TABLE 13 Trade Balance of Ivory Coast with CEAO and ECOWAS Countries (million CFAF)

	Mauritania	Mali	Upper Volta	Niger	Senegal	Total CEAO
Exports 1975	288	11,339	7,242	2,830	4,893	26,592
Imports 1975	96	494	359	210	3,946	5,105
Trade Balance (X-M) 1975	192	10,845	6,883	2,620	947	21,487
Exports excl. oil 1975	278	7,969	4,496	2,731	4,857	20,331
Imports excl. oil 1975	96	494	359	210	3,946	5,105
Trade balance excl. oil 1975	182	7,475	4,137	2,521	911	15,226
Exports 1979	295	13,681	12,758	5,635	5,749	38,118
Imports 1979	101	2,366	44	34	6,757	9,302
Trade Balance 1979	194	11,315	12,714	5,601	-1,008	28,816
Exports excl. oil 1979	295	7,414	7,077	5,603	5,749	26,138
Imports excl. oil 1979	107	2,366	44	34	6,757	9,302
Trade Balance excl. oil 1979	194	5,048	7,033	5,569	-1,008	16,836

Source: Ivory Coast, *Ministere de l'Economie et des Finances.*

orientation that distort resource allocation and alienate consumers and producers. In this respect it is important to note that CEAO and ECOWAS must seek to establish and reinforce political links in order to move smoothly towards complete economic integration in the area.

CONCLUSION

In this study we sought to assess the contribution of CEAO and ECOWAS to economic integration and cooperation in West Africa. It was seen that given the new emerging international economic relationships between developed and developing nations, the countries of the West Africa area cannot rely on traditional economic development theory to stimulate growth of their economies. This is because these strategies are no longer suitable to the social and economic conditions in these countries. Nor is

Benin	Togo	Ghana	Nigeria	Liberia	Other ECOWAS	Total ECOWAS
1,596	919	802	1,321	825	164	32,219
20	141	163	11,921	39	20	14,409
1,576	778	639	−10,600	786	144	17,810
1,596	918	800	1,295	612	164	25,716
20	141	163	23	39	20	5,511
1,576	777	637	1,272	573	144	20,205
2,507	1,334	1,576	4,685	1,050	212	49,482
16	38	42	14,159	364	3	23,924
2,491	1,296	1,534	−9,474	686	199	25,548
2,432	1,207	1,130	4,454	630	212	36,203
16	38	42	44	159	3	9,604
2,416	1,169	1,088	4,410	479	199	26,509

traditional economic integration theory, based on static assumptions, preoccupied by gains and losses from trade, more relevant. We also showed that past attempts at economic integration did not survive because the conceptual framework was inspired by the traditional economic thinking and little account was made of the social, cultural and economic realities of the area.

By extending traditional integration theory to cover dynamic aspects and location theory, it appeared that widening the market beyond national boundaries provides opportunities to domestic as well as foreign investors. The economies of scale expected, along with the elimination of trade barriers, will enhance economic growth, lead to an increase in per capita income and will improve living standards. Thus, it was argued that CEAO has made a limited but tangible contribution to economic cooperation in Francophone West Africa through its specialized institutions, particularly the Regional Cooperation Tax, the Community Development Fund, and the

Fund of Solidarity and Intervention for Community Development. These institutions, which operate quite efficiently, made it possible to channel investment in sectors where it was needed the most, in particular in the agricultural sector, cattle breeding and infrastructure. However, it was understood that the Regional Cooperation Tax needs to be phased out over the long term. As the ECOWAS, it has shown that decisions reached in political enthusiasm were never implemented, and thus ECOWAS appears as a political forum, without a real commitment from the member states to implement the Lagos treaty. On the other hand it was argued that the success or failure of any integration scheme that envisages including all countries in West Africa will depend to a large extent upon the attitude of Nigeria towards its neighbours. The fear that Nigeria will dominate the community cannot be underestimated, given its economic potential and demographic advantage. As to Ivory Coast, it is believed that should ECOWAS fail, it still has CEAO to turn to, where it enjoys significant advantages. Even in a wider framework of integration, competition from Nigeria is not expected to create any serious unbalance at the expense of Ivory Coast in its trading relationships with the rest of ECOWAS countries.

Furthermore, a customs union in West Africa will induce the industrial nations to Europe, North America, and Japan to export more capital, through the intermediary of multinational firms, to take advantage of the common tariff. That competition among foreign powers to supply the regional market will lead to cost reduction benefits for the West African countries. However, full economic integration will ultimately depend on the political climate that will prevail within each country and among countries in the area. Constant changes of political power through coups in West Africa will not foster closer economic relationships among countries that seek to harmonize economic development policies.

NOTES

1. Bela Belassa sets forth five categories of economic integration ranging from a free trade area to total economic integration. R.E. Caves and R.W. Jones also set forth five categories ranging from a preferential trading club to economic union. In this study we retain the Caves and Jones categorization.

2. The main factors which accounted for the poor performance of the African economies were discussed in World Bank, 1981. The report also suggests ways to deal with this economic situation.

3. A brief historical survey of past attempts at economic integration in Anglophone West Africa can be found in Asante, 1978.

4. A survey of past economic integration in Francophone West Africa could be also found in an earlier paper by the author (Atsain, 1975, pp. 5–9, in particular).

5. Wording from the ECOWAS Treaty document, Chapter 1, Article 2 (Manu, 1982).

BIBLIOGRAPHY FOR THE POLITICAL ECONOMY OF IVORY COAST

Compiled by Howard Sugar

POLITICAL DEVELOPMENT

Acker, V. 1971. *La Cheferie en Cote d'Ivoire* (Paris: (Memoire) Institut d'Etudes Politiques).

Alalade, Fo. 1975. "President Felix Houphouet-Boigny, the Ivory Coast and France." *Journal of African Studies*, Vol. 6(3):122–31 (Autumn).

American University. 1973. *Area Handbook for Ivory Coast* (Washington, D.C.: American University, Foreign Area Studies Division).

Chapters on social, political, and economic backgrounds; and on national security.

Amin, Samir. 1971. *L'Afrique de l'Ouest Bloquee* (Paris: Minuit).

Aron, R. 1950. "Social Structure and the Ruling Class." *British Journal of Sociology,* Vol. I(1):1–6 (March); Vol. I(2):126–143 (June).

_____. 1960. "Classe sociale, classe politique, classe dirigeante." *Archives Europeennes de Sociologie*, Vol. I(2):260–281.

Antoni, P.J.C. 1976. *Les ministres de la Ve Republique* (Paris: Presses Universitaires du France).

Asso, Bernard. 1976. *Le chef d'etat africaine.* (Paris: Albatros).

Baulin, Jacques F. 1982. *La politique interieure d'Houphouet-Boigny* (Paris: EuraforPress).

Covers to period 1950 and 1968 in great detail with much documentation on the 1963 plot, seen as a struggle between the planters and the new Ivorian bourgeoisie.

Berrady, L. et al. 1973. *La formation des elites politiques maghrebines* (Paris: LGDJ).

Biarnes, Pierre. 1981. "La Cote d'Ivoire au Creux de la Vague." *Le Monde* (25 March), 23–25.

Blanchet, G. 1977. *Elites et changements dans une perspective africaine et dans le cas du Senegal*, These 3ᵉ Cycle de Sociologie X. Paris: Nanterre.

Bocoum, M.T.A. 1972–1973. *La naissance d'une elte nouvelle en Cote d'Ivoire*. Premier quart du XXᵉ siecle: *Memoire de maitrise d'histoire* (2 Volumes. Aix en Provence).

Bottomore, T.B. 1967. *Elites et societe* (Paris: Stock).

Campbell, B. 1978a. "The Ivory Coast," In J. Dunn, ed., *West African States: Failures and Promises* (Cambridge: Cambridge University Press).

_____. 1978b. "Social Change and Class Formation in a French-West African State." *Canadian Journal of African Studies*, Vol. 8(2):285–306.

Charbonneaux, Rene. 1971. "Planning in the Ivory Coast," *Marches Tropiceaux et Mediterrenees* No. 1361 (11 December), 18 pp.

Traces the various steps that went into the formulation of the 1971–75 planning including planning ministry, public investment, programming, regional planning and private investments.

Chazan, Naomi. 1976. "The Manifestation of Youth Politics in Ghana and the Ivory Coast," *Geneve Afriques*, Vol. 15(2):38–63.

Cherif, M. 1978. "Le Rassemblement democratique africain et les questions fondamentales de l'apparentement et du disapparentement." *Memoire DEA de Science Politques X* (Paris: Nanterre).

Clignet, Remy, and Foster, Philip. 1964. "Potential Elites in Ghana and The Ivory Coast: A Preliminary Comparison." *American Journal of Sociology*, Vol. LXX(3):349–362 (November).

_____. 1966. *The Fortunate Few: A Study of Secondary Schools and Students in the Ivory Coast* (Chicago: Northwestern University).

Cohen, Michael, 1974. *Urban Policy and Political Conflict in Africa* (Chicago: University of Chicago Press).

A study of the Ivory Coast describing overcentralization producing wastes in allocation of funds because of political favoritism, aggravating cleavages between cities and rural areas and creating resentment in general.

Collier, Ruth. 1982. *Regimes in Tropical Africa* (Berkeley: University of California Press).

d'Aby, F.H. Amon. 1951. *La Cote d'Ivoire dans la cite Africaine* (Paris: Larose), 47–50.

History of French colonization of the Ivory Coast.

Decraene, P. 1982. *Vielle Afrique et jeunes nations. Le continent noir au seuil de la troisiene decendie de l'independance* (Paris: Presses Universitaires du France).

A study of the institutions and judicial system of the ivory Coast and their effects on development.

Diabate, H. 1975a. *La marche des femmes sur Grand Bassam* (Abidjan & Dakar: N.E.A.).

_____. 1975b. "Le role des femmes dans l'histoire du R.D.A." In Fondation Houphouet-Boigny, *Revue de l'Institut Africain de Recherches historiques et politiques*, Vol. 2:88–102.

Dje Bi Dje, C., and Thirot, A. 1980. *Introduction a l'etude des Institutions politiques ivoiriennes* (Abidjan: Faculte de Droit), 65 pp.

Duprey, Pierre. 1962. *Naissance d'une Nation*. (Presse de l'Imprimerie de la Cote d'Ivoire).

A thorough study of Ivory Coast history from the middle ages to 1961, from an Ivoirian point of view.

Encyclopedie General de la Cote d'Ivoire 1978. (Abidjan: Les Nouvelles Editions Africains, Editions Franco Impressions), (Three vols.).

The only encyclopedia ever published by an African country. Vol., I Le Milieu et L'Histoire; Vol. II, L'Etat et l'economie; Vol. III, La Vie et la Nation.

Fadika, L. 1978. "Strategie Ivioirenne et nouvel ordre maritime international." *Revue Francaise d'Etudes Politiques Africaines* 150/151 (June/July):29–56.

Faure, Y-A. and Medard, J-F. 1982a. *Etat et Bourgoisie en Cote D'Ivoire* (Paris: Editions Karthala), 251 pp.

The most comprehensive and up to date book on the political dimension in Ivory Coast with chapters on international relations, class structure, Ivorian entrepreneurs, and peasant and functionaries in the state culture and state policy.

_____. 1982b. *Hommage a Houphouet-Boigny, homme de la terre*. (Paris: Presence Africaine), 269 pp.

_____. 1982c. "Le pouvoir d'etre riches" *Politique Africaine*, Vol. II:6 (May).

Foltz, William J. 1965. *From French West Africa to the Mali Federation* (New Haven: Yale University Press).

Foster, P., and Zolberg, Aristide. 1971. *Ghana and the Ivory Coast: Perspectives on Modernization*, (Chicago: University of Chicago Press).

Compares political, social and economic history of Ivory Coast and Ghana with emphasis on legitimacy, gradualism versus radical change and education.

Gbagbo, Laurent, 1983. *La Cote d'Ivoire: Pour une alternative democratique.* (Paris: Harmattan).

Halberstam, D. 1972. *The Best and the Brightest.* (New York: Random House).

Hermet, G., Rouquie, A., Linz, J.J. 1978. *Des elections pas comme les autres* (Paris: Presses de la Fondation nationale des Sciences politiques).

Houphouet-Boigny, Felix. 1978. *Anthologie des Discours* 1946–78. (Adidjan: CEDA), (Four volumes) 2247 pp.

Ivory Coast. 1965. "Population" (Abidjan: Cote d'Ivoire, Ministere du Plan).

A detailed demography of the Ivory Coast.

Johns, Sheridan. 1982. "Reform of State Enterprises in Ivory Coast," presented to African Studies Association, Washington, D.C.

Keita, M. 1966. "Les origines sociales des elites politiques". *Memoire DES de Droit.*

LaPorte, Mireille. 1970. *Le Pensee Sociale de Felix Houphouet-Boigny, lePresident de la Republique de Cote d'Ivoire* (Bordeaux: Centres d'etude d'Afrique Noir), 100 pp.

Traces the effect that Houphouet-Boigny has had in determining the policy of Ivory Coast.

Lasswell, H.D., Lerner, D., Rothwell, C.E. 1952. *The Comparative Study of Elites* (Stanford: Stanford University Press).

Lawson, George H. 1975. "La Cote d'Ivoire: 1960–70. Croissance et diversification sans Africanisation," in D. Esseks, (ed.), *L'Afrique de l'independance politique a l'independance economique* (Paris: Maspero).

LeVine, V.T. 1966. "Political Recruitment and political structure in French-speaking Africa." *Cahiers d'etudes africaines* VIII Vol. (31):373–388.

———. 1980. "African Patrimonial Regimes in Comparative Perspective." *XVIII Journal of Modern African Studies*, Vol. 4:657–673 (December).

Lloyd, P.C. 1966. *New Elites of Tropical Africa.* London.

Loucou, J.N. 1976. "Les premieres elections de 1945 en Cote d'Ivoire." *Annales de l'Universite d'Abidjan*, Vol. I(IV) (Historie):5–33.

_____. 1976. *La vie politique en Cote d'Ivoire de 1932 a 1952*. Aix en Provence. Doctoral Thesis (de 3ᵉ Cycle-History), in two volumes.

_____. 1977. "Aux Origines du Parti Democratique de la Cote d'Ivoire." *Annales de Universite d'Abidjan Histoire*, Serie I, Vol. V:81–105.

Masquet, B. 1981. "Cote d'Ivoire pouvoir presidential, palabre et democratie." *Afrique Contemporaine* No. 114 (March–April), 10–22.

Memel-Fote, H. 1980. *Le systeme politique de Lodjoukrou*. (Paris: Presence Africaine).

Mescteriekoff, Alain G. 1982. *Le Droit Administratif Ivoirien*. (Paris: Economia), 247 pp.

Miller, R.A. 1974. "Elite Formation in Africa: Class, Culture and Coherence." *The Journal of Modern African Studies*, Vol. 12(4):521–542.

Monnet, B. 1976. "Role des femmes dans la politique en Cote d'Ivoire". *Memoire de maitrise Sciences Sociales*. Abidjan.

Morgenthau, R.S. 1964. *Political Parties in French-speaking Africa*. (Oxford: Oxford University Press).

Mosca, G. 1939. *The Ruling Class*. (New York: McGraw Hill).

Nadel, S.F. 1956. "La notion d'elite sociale." *Bulletin International des Sciences Sociales*, Vol. VIII(3):419–431.

Newsweek. 1981. "Ivory Coast: African Success Story," (October 26).

N'gatta, E. 1970. "Le phenomene ethnique dans la vie politique en Cote d'Ivoire." *Memoire DES Science politique* (Strasbourg).

Nunes, Luis C. 1972. *La Participation d'Syndicalism a la Construction Nationale en Afrique: Exemples du Senegal, Mali et Cote d'Ivoire*. Universite de Geneve: Editions Medecine et Hygine. Doctoral Thesis no. 211.

Compares trades unions and comments on the role of a sole organized labor movement in face of a single party system in Ivory Coast.

Paulme, D. 1971. *Classes et associations d'age en Afrique de l'ouest* (Paris: Plon).

Pareto, V. 1966. *Sociological Writings* (New York: Praeger).

PDCI. 1975. *VIᵉ Congres du Parti Democratique de Cote d'Ivoire* (Abidjan: Fraternite-Hebdo).

Penouil, M. 1971. "Le Miracle Ivoirien ou l'application realiste de theories irrealistes." *Annee Africaine*, 321–348.

Person, Yves. 1981. "Colonisation et Decolonisation en Cote d'Ivoire." *Le Mois d'Afrique* 188–89 (August/September):15–30.

Examines the extent that Ivorian decolonization has perpetuated and added to the contradictions inherent in French colonialism.

Piat, C. 1981. *La Republique de Mysogines* (Paris: Laffout).

Pomonti, J-C. 1980. "La Cote d'Ivoire, une Afrique Parvenue." *Le Monde*, 29, 30, 31 (Parts I, II, III) January.

Potholm, Christien P. 1970. *Four African Political Systems*. Englewood Cliffs: Prentice Hall.

Compares South African, Tanzanian, Somali and Ivorian political systems pointing out the reliance of Ivory Coast on French support for its regime that might not continue after Houphouet-Boigny.

Putnam, R.D. 1976. *The Comparative Study of Political Elites* (Englewood Cliffs: Prentice-Hall).

de la Rochere, Jacqueline D. 1976. *L'Etat et le Developpement Economique de la Cote d'Ivoire* (Paris: Editions Pedone).

Semi Bi, Zan. 1973 "Le PDCI." *Revue Francaise d'etudes politiques africaines*, Vol. 94:61–75 (October).

Seurin, J.L. 1958. "Elites sociales et partis politiques d'AOF". *Annales africaines* (1958):126–130.

Sklar, R.L. 1967. "Political Science and National Integration. A Radical Approach." *The Journal of Modern African Studies*, Vol. 17(4):531–552.

Siriex, Paul Henri. 1975. *Felix Houphouet-Boigny, l'homme de la Paix* (Abidjan: Seghers Nouvelles Editions Africaines).

Staniland, Martin. 1965. "Single Party Regimes and Political Change: The PDCI and Ivory Coast Politics," 135–175. In Colin Leys (ed.), *Political Change in Developing Countries* (London: Cambridge University Press).

———. 1968. "Local Administration in the Ivory Coast." *West Africa* Numbers 2649–2650 (6 March–9 March).

Stirn, Gerard. 1967. *Aspects juridiques du secteur public industriel et commercial en Cote d'Ivoire*. (Rennes: Universite de Rennes Faculte de Droit.

Stryker, Richard. 1971. "A Local Perspective on Development Strategy in the Ivory Coast," In Michael Lofchie, (ed.), *The State of the Nations* (Berkeley: University of California Press).

Suret-Canale, Jean. 1972. *Afrique Noire: de la colonisation aux independances 1945-60* (Paris: Editions Sociales).

Sy, Seydou Madani. 1965. *Recherches sur l'Exercise du Pouvoir Politique en Afrique Noire (Côte d'Ivoire, Guinee, Mali)* (Paris: Editions A. Pedone).

Examines the personalization of power of the President Houphouet-Boigny which by-passes the intermediary institutions and the influence of French political institutions.

Sylla, L. 1977. *Tribalisme et parti unique on Afrique noire* (Paris: Presses de la Fondation Nationale des Sciences Politiques).

Taÿ, Hugues. 1974. *L'Administration Ivoirienne* (Paris: Institut International d'Administration Publique, Editions Berger-Levrault).

A study of the institutions and structures of the Ivorian state with a strong legal point of view.

Thompson, Virginia. 1962. "Ivory Coast," 237–324. In Gwendon M. Carter, ed., *African One-Party States* (Ithaca: Cornell University Press).

Tice, R.O. 1974. "Administrative Structure, Ethnicity and Nation Building in Ivory Coast." *The Journal of Modern African Studies* June, Vol. 12(2):211–229.

Traxler, Elizabeth. 1982. *French Relations with Francophone Africa* (Columbia: University of South Carolina doctoral dissertation).

Vignaud, M. 1956. "Les elections du 2 Janvier 1956 en Cote d'Ivoire". *Revue francaise de Science politique* VI, Vol. (3):570–582 (June–September).

Wallerstein, I. 1965. "Elites in French Speaking West Africa: The Social Basis of Ideas." *The Journal of Modern African Studies,* Vol. 3(1):1–83.

Wodie, F. 1969. "La vie politique en Côte d'Ivoire de 1945 à 1969." *Revue algérienne de Sciences juridiques politiques et économiques* VI, Vol. (3):822–842 (September).

Wodie, Francis, and Bléon, D. Martin. 1981. *La Chamber Administrative de la Court Supreme et a jurisprudence (Commentaires d'arrets).* Vol. 6. (Abidjan: Universite (Series A) Faculté de Droit), 174 pp.

Woronoff, Jon. 1972. *West African Wager, Houphouet versus Nkrumah* (New Jersey: Scarecrow Press), 335 pp.

Compares the economic and political balance sheets of Ghana and the Ivory Coast between 1957 and 1972.

Zartman, I. William. 1966. *International Relations in the New Africa* (Englewood Cliffs: Prentice Hall).

_____. 1974. "The Study of Elite Circulation. Who's on First and What's He Doing There?" *Comparative Politics* 6, 3:465–488 (April).

_____. 1983. "Europe and Africa: The French Connection," In Bruce Arlinghaus (ed.), *African Security Issues* (Boulder: Westview Press).

Zolberg, Aristide. 1966. *Creating Political Order* (New York: Rand McNally).

_____. 1964(1969). *One Party Government in the Ivory Coast* (Princeton: Princeton University Press).

Studies the transfer of power from French rule to independent Ivory Coast in which the Parti Democratique de Cote d'Ivoire effectively gains a monopoly of political power.

_____. 1971. "Political Development in the Ivory Coast since Independence." In P. Foster and A. Zolberg (eds.), *Ghana and Ivory Coast: Perspectives on Modernization* (Chicago and London: The University of Chicago Press).

_____. 1975. "Political Generations in Conflict: The Ivory Coast Case," In W.J. Hanna (ed.), *University Students and African Politics* (New York and London: Africana), 103–133.

SOCIETY AND SOCIAL CONDITIONS

"Abidjan, Cote d'Ivoire." 1969. *Urbanisme: Revue Francaise* No. 111–112.

Bonnet, Philippe. "La Minorite Francaise en Cote d'Ivoire." *L'Afrique et l'Asie modernes* No. 118:29–40 (Third trimester).

Bolibaugh, J. 1977. *Educational Development in Guinea, Mali, Senegal and Ivory Coast* (Washington, D.C.: U.S. Department of Health, Education and Welfare, Office of Education, 141 pp.

Criticizes Ivory Coast for poor returns on investment in education with high drop-out rates at all levels, poor quality graduates and poor attitudes in face of a demand for skilled labor.

Boutillier, B. 1960. *Bougouanou, Cote d'Ivoire* (Paris: Edition Berger-Levrault).

A detailed study of the Agni in the Bougouanou which examines how prosperity in the region has attracted immigration, and as well the tendency for people in the region to give up crafts and town occupations to farm on plantations.

Bozon, S. 1967. "Les Dahomeens en Afrique de l'Ouest." *Revue Francaise de Science Politique*, 718–726 (August).

Cerych, Ladislav. 1967. *L'Aide exterieure et la plannification de l'education en Cote d'Ivoire* (UNESCO: Institut International de Plannification de l'Education).

States the dominance of French aid and educational system and the central role of the government in orienting education.

Cohen, Michael A. 1980. "Francophone Africa," In Donald Rowat, ed., *International Handbook on Local Government Reorganization*. Connecticut: Westport Press.

Debarrin, J. 1968. *De la Savone a La Ville, Essa: sur la Migration des Mossi ver Abidjan et sa region*. (Paris: Aubier Montaigne), 415–424.

Traces the immigration of the Mossi from Upper Volta to the Ivory Coast in search of a higher standard of living and the effect of this immigration on the Voltan and Ivorian economies.

Deniel, R. *Une Societe paysanne de Cote d'Ivoire* (Abidjan: I.N.A.D.E.S.), 225 pp.

Dje Assane, Ajeto. "Essai d'explication de la main-d'oeuvre etrangere dans le Moronou." *Cahiers Ivoriens de la Recherche Economique et Sociale* No. 23:97–107.

DuBois, Victor. 1971. "The Economic, Social and Political Implications of Voltaic Immigration to the Ivory Coast." West African Series XIV, No. 1, *American Universities Field Staff Reports*.

Gibbal, Jean-Marie. 1968. "Societes urbaines de l'Ouest Africain: l'Exemple d'Abidjan." *Le Mois en Afrique*, No. 29 (May).

_____. 1974. *Citadins et Paysans dans la Ville Africaine: l'Exemple d'Abidjan* (Presses Universitaires de Grenoble: Francois Maspero).

Analyses the unequal insertion of various groups into large cities as well as the disolution of traditional ethnic and family values by cosmopolitan pressures.

Haeringer, Philippe. 1969. "Quitte ou Double: Les Chances de l'Agglomeration Abidjanaise." (*ORSTOM*).

————. 1973. "Cheminements migratoires, Maliens, Voltaiques et Nigeriens en Cote d'Ivoire." *Cahiers ORSTOM Serie Sciences humaines* Vol. X, No. 2/3:195–202.

Hallak, J., and Poignet, R. 1967. *Les Aspects Financiers de l'Education en Cote d'Ivoire* (Paris: UNESCO Institut International de Plannification de l'Education).

Traces costs and financing of education in the Ivory Coast.

Hinderink, J., and Templeman, G.J. 1978. "Rural Change and Types of Migration in Northern Ivory Coast." *Ivory Coast in African Perspectives* (Leiden).

Holas, B. 1961. *Changements Sociaux en Cote d'Ivoire* (Paris: Presses Universitaires de France).

Traces the impact of modern plantation farming on the traditional values of the Ivory Coast, concentrating on the Oubi.

————. 1965. *Le Separatisme Religieux en Afrique Noire, L'Exemple de la Cote d'Ivoire* (Presses Universitaires de France).

Studies regional differences as distinguished by religions as well as new sects created by mixtures of domestic and imported religions (Islam, Christianism).

Institut Universitaires d'Etudes du Developpement. 1975. *Le Village Piege. Urbanisation et Agro-Industrie Sucriere en Cote d'Ivoire* (Geneve: Institut Universitaires d'Etudes du Developpement (and Paris: Presse Universitaires de France, 1978)), 366 pp.

An uneven account of architects attempting to create a local city to house workers for the sugar plant in Zuenoulu incorporating the village social values of the local in their planning. Seven writers contributed to the study.

Josh, M., Lubel, H., and Moncy, J. 1976. *Abidjan, Urban Development and Employment in the Ivory Coast* (Geneva: Bureau International du Travail), 115 pp.

Kacou Aoulou, Jerome, 1962. "M. Kacou Aoulou presente le programme gouvernmental en matiere d'habitat." *Fraternite Hebdomadaire* (2 March), p. 6.

Launay, R. 1978. "Transactional Spheres and Inter-Societal Exchange in Ivory Coast." *Cahiers d'Etudes Africaines* 72 (XVIII 4):561–573.

Marshall, T.H. 1965. *Class, Citizenship, and Social Development* (New York: Anchor Books).

Meillassoux, Claude. 1964. *Anthropologie Economique des Gouro de Cote d'Ivoire* (Paris: Mouton & Co).

Traces the transformation of the traditional subsistence economy to commercial agriculture among the Gouro.

Monson, Terry D. 1979. "Educational returns in the Ivory Coast." *Journal of Developing Areas* Vol. 13 (July):415–430.

The focus of this study is on the manpower and educational policies that contributed to a configuration of estimated returns different from that commonly found in many LDCs. These policies promoted a peculiar composition of Ivory Coast's labor force.

Schurtz, A. 1979. "Colonisation agricole spontanee et emergence de nouveaux milieux sociaux dans le sud-ouest ivoriien: l'exemple du Conton Bakue de la sous-prefecture de Soubre." *Cahiers de l'O.R.S.T.O.M. Serie Sciences Humaines* (Vol. XVI) No. 1/2:83–102.

Stren, Richard. 1978. *Housing the Urban Poor in Africa: Policy, Politics and Bureaucracy in Mobasa* (Berkeley: University of California, Institute of International Studies).

Toure, Abdou. 1982. *La Civilisation Quotidienne en Cote d'Ivoire: Proces d'occidentalisation* (Paris: Karthala), 244 pp.

A criticism of the blind adoption of Ivorians of Western models of society and government that do not function well in Ivory Coast.

Walker, Sheila S. 1983. *The Religious Revolution in the Ivory Coast* (Chapel Hill: University of North Carolina Press).

Zachariah, K.C. and Conde, Julien (eds.). 1981. *Migration in West Africa* (New York/Oxford: World Bank and OECD).

AGRICULTURE

Ancey, Gerard. 1974. *L'Economie de l'espace rural de la Region de Bouake* (Paris: O.R.S.T.O.M.), 251 pp.

Benveniste, C. 1974. *La boucle du cacao, Cote d'Ivoire* (Paris: O.R.S.T.O.M.), 216 pp.

Berthelemy, J.C. 1977. *La Filiere cacao en Cote d'Ivoire* (I.N.S.E.E. Department de la Cooperation), 57 pp.

DelaPorte, G. 1970. "Le Role du Cafe dans l'economie de la Cote d'Ivoire." *Marches Tropicaux et Mediterraneens* (April).

Frelastre, G. 1980. "Les nouvelles orientations du developpement rural de la Cote d'Ivoire." *Revue d'Etudes politiques et economiques Africaines* 176/177:37–80. (August/September).

Food and Agricultural Organization of the United Nations (FAO). (Yearly) *Trade Yearbook* (Rome: FAO).

Gbetibouo, Mathurin. 1982. *Export Strategies for Ivory Coast Cocoa*. University of Illinois Department of Agricultural Economics.

Unpublished Ph.D. dissertation.

Gill and Duffus (occasional). *Cocoa Statistics* (London: Gill and Duffus PLC).

International Cocoa Organization (ICCO) (quarterly). *Quarterly Bulletin of Cocoa Statistics*. London: ICCO.

Kirschen, L. 1983. "Why the Ivory Coast Must Join the Agreement", *Coffee and Cocoa International*, Vol. 3:44.

Lee, E. 1983. "Export-led Rural Development: The Ivory Coast," In D. Ghai and S. Radwan (eds.), *Agrarian Policies and Rural Poverty in Africa* (Geneva: International Labor Organization).

Liabeuf, J. 1979. "Des Handicaps a Surmonter Mais de Belles Promesses". *Afrique Agriculture* Vol. 46:54–56 (June).

Ministere de l'Agriculture, Ivory Coast. 1974. *Recensement National de l'Agriculture*. (Abidjan).

_____. 1980. *Statistiques Agricoles 1980*. Abidjan.

_____. 1980. "Etude sur la Politique des Prix, Aides et Subventions Agricoles". (Abidjan: Agroespo. Ltd.) (Unpublished report).

Naigon, Christophe et al. 1978. "L'Agriculture Ivoirienne." *Afrique Agriculture* (October), 60–65.

A collection of interviews and articles.

Pelissier, P. 1974. "Agriculture et developpement: l'exemple de la Cote d'Ivoire." *Bulletin de l'Association des Georgraphes francais* (March/April).

Priovolus, Theophilos. 1981. *Coffee and the Ivory Coast, An Econometric Study* (Lexington, Mass.: D.C. Heath and Company).

Explores the impact of export instability of coffee proceeds on Ivorian policymaking and economy with additional observations on timber and cocoa.

Rondos, Alexander. 1980. "Farmer and Foreigners." *West Africa* (28 April), 735–37.

Sawadogo, Aboulaye. 1977. *L'Agriculture en Cote d'Ivoire* (Paris: Presses Universitaires de France), 367 pp. (Published as doctoral thesis in 1975).

Stern, W. 1975. "A Method of Forecasting Cocoa Prices." *Forecasting Commodity Prices*. (New York: Commodity Research Bureau).

World Bank, Commodities and Export Projects Division. 1982. *Cocoa Handbook* (Washington, D.C.: World Bank).

ECONOMY

Achio, A. 1974. *Le secteur prive en Cote d'Ivoire*. (Abidjan: Ministere de l''ensei nement technique et de la formation professionnelle, Office national de formation professionelle).

Charts and matrices of the professions.

Akoi Ahizi, Paul. 1976. *Droit du Traivail et de la prevoyance Sociale en Cote d'Ivoire*. (Abidjan: C.E.D.A.), 301 pp.

Amagou, Victor, and Gleizes, Gerard-Louis. 1975. "Le groupe SODEPALM et l'agro-industrie du palmier a huile en Cote d'Ivoire." *Economies et Societes* Series AG No. 13. Cahiers de l'I.S.M.E.A.

Amin, Samir. 1967. *Le Developpment du Capitalism en Cote d'Ivoire* (Paris: Edition de Minuit), 307 pp.

A study of economic and social development of the Ivory Coast between 1950 and 1965 criticizing what the author calls "growth without development."

Anyang Nyougo, T. 1978. "Liberal Models of Capitalist Development in Africa: Ivory Coast," *Africa Development* 3, 3:5–20.

Atsain, A. 1975. "Financial Arrangements and Economic Integration in French-speaking West Africa." (Unpublished master's thesis) Department of Economics, State University of New York at Albany.

Aubertin, C. 1980. *L'industrialisation regionale volontariste, notes sur le programme sucrier ivoirien* (Abidjan: O.R.S.T.O.M.), 187 pp.

———. 1980. *Histoire et Creation d'une region sous developee: le nord ivoirien.* (Abidjan: O.R.S.T.O.M.), 97 pp.

Bach, D. 1972. "La Question de Main-d'oeuvre en Cote d'Ivoire." *Connaissance du l'Afrique*, Vol. 40:22–25 (October).

Balassa, B. 1965. *The Theory of Economic Integration* (New York: George Allen & Unwin).

Borgoin, H., and Guilhoume, P. 1979. *Cote d'Ivoire, economie et societe* (Paris: Editions Stock), 334 pp.

Bra Kanon, D. 1978. "Pour une nouvelle problematique de developpement agricole." *Revue francaise d'etudes politiques africaines* 150/151 (June/July):17–28.

Bresson, Y., and Ponson, B. 1978. "Repartition personnelle des revenues et croissance en Cote d'Ivoire." *Annee Africaine*, 13–34.

Caisse Centrale de Cooperation Economique and World Bank. 1982. "Rapport sur les Entreprises Publiques en Cote d'Ivoire" (World Bank, mimeo).

Calamanti, Andrea. 1975. "La Borsa valori di Abidjani uno strumento di mobilitazione del risparmio e di indigenizzazione dell'attivita economia." *Risparmio*, Vol. 7:885–937.

Camier, L.L. 1975. "Aspect economiques de la Constituton du reseau urbain de la Cote d'Ivoire." *Mondes en Developpement*, Vol. 9:89–105.

Campbell, Bonnie. 1976. "Neocolonialism, Economic Dependence and Political Change: Cotton Textile Production in the Ivory Coast." *Review of African Political Economy*, Vol. 2:36–53.

Caves, R.E., and Jones, R.W. 1974. *World Trade and Payments* (Boston: Little, Brown & Co).

Chauveau, Jean Pierre. 1972. *Notes sur l'histoire economique et Social de la Region de Kokumbo.* (Baule-Sud Cote d'Ivoire: O.R.S.T.O.M.).

Chevassu, J. and Valette, A. 1975a. *Donnees Statistiques sur l'Industrie de la Cote d'Ivoire* (Abidjan: O.R.S.T.O.M.).

_____. 1975b. *Les Revenues Distribues per les Activites Industrielles en Cote d'Ivoire* (Abidjan: O.R.S.T.O.M.).

_____. 1975c. "Les Industriels de la Cote d'Ivoire: ou, qui et pour-quoi?" *O.R.S.T.O.M.* Centre de Petit Bassam, reneote, 36–38.

Comte, G. 1972. "Un Rapport du F.M.I. remet en question le miracle ivoirien." *Le Monde Diplomatique* (March).

La Cote d'Ivoire en Chiffre (CIC). 1976 (Dakar: Ste Africaine d'Editions).

Le Courier. 1982. No. 74 (July-August): 10–25.

Special section on the Ivory Coast prepared by Amadou Traore.

Dervis, K., de Melo, J. and Robinson, S. 1982. *General Equilibrium Models for Development Policy* (Cambridge; Cambridge University Press).

Dervis, K., and Robinson, S. 1982. "A General Equilibrium Analysis of the Causes of a Foreign Exchange Crisis: The Case of Turkey." *Weltwirtschaftliches Archiv*, Vol. 118(2):259–280.

Diabate, M. 1977. "Examen de quelques grands problemes theoriques et pratiques des societes et Entreprises d'Etat en Afrique de l'Ouest (Cote d'Ivoire, Mali, Senegal)." *Annales de l'Universite d'Abidjan* Serie F(VI) Ethno-sociologie, 5–38.

Dozon, J-P. 1979. "Impasses et contradiction d'une societe de developpement: l'exemple de l'operation 'riziculture irriguee' en Cote d'Ivoire." *Cahiers de l'ORSTOM* Serie Science Humaines Vol XVI, Nos. 1/2:37–58.

Ediafric. 1982. *L'Industrie africaine en 1982.* (8e Edition, Tome 2 "Cote d'Ivoire") (Paris: Ediafric).

Fargues, Philippe. 1981. "Les Migrations en Cote d'Ivoire." *Cahiers du CIRES* (December; March 1982).

France, Service de Presse, Edition Information. 1975. *Structures et Actions Socio-Economiques de la Republique de Cote d'Ivoire* (Paris, Service de Presse, Edition Information), 683 pp.

Galbraith, V.L. 1972. "Trade as an Engine of Growth: The Ivory Coast," In S.P. Schatz, ed., *South of the Sahara: Development in African Economics.* (London: Macmillian Press), 300–316.

Garrity, Monique P. 1972. "The 1969 Franc devaluation and the Ivory Coast Economy." *Journal of Modern African Studies* 10(4):627–633 (December).

Gastellu, J.M., and Affou Yapi, S. 1982. "Un Mythe a Decomposer: La Bourgeoisie de Planteurs, pp. 149–180. In Y.A. Faure and J-F. Medard, eds., *Etat et Bourgeoisie en Cote d'Ivoire* (Paris: Karthala).

Glasman, Monique, 1981. "La Cote d'Ivoire dan l'attente de la Manne petroliere." *Presence Africaine* (Third Quarter).

Goreux, G.M. 1977. *Interdependence in Planning Multilevel Programming Studies of the Ivory Coast* (Baltimore: Johns Hopkins University Press for the World Bank).

Essentially a book on planning in 3rd World countries, which uses the Ivory Coast as the country in which its models are applied.

Guerrini, M-C. 1975. "Le Role du tertiaire superieur dans la domination de l'economie ivoirienne." *Revue Tiers Monde* (XVI), Vol. 61:113–134 (January-March).

Hayter, Teresa. 1966. *French Aid* (United Kingdom: Overseas Development Institute).

Hecht, Robert 1983. "The Ivory Coast Economic 'Miracle': What Benefits for Peasant Farmers?" *The Journal of Modern African Studies*, Vol. 21(1):25–53 (March).

Hinderick, J., and Templeman. 1979. "Development Policy and Practice in Ivory Coast: A Miracle or Mirage." Utrecht: Geografish Instituut, Rijk Universiteit (July).

A paper presented at Polish-Dutch Seminar, on regional planning which provides good overview on Ivory Coast planning and its effects on development: criticizing overdependence on foreign capital markets.

IBRD. 1980. *World Bank Development Report* (Washington, D.C.: IBRD).

Ikonicoff, M. and Sigal, S. 1978. "L'Etat Relais, un modale de developpement des Societes peripheriques? Le Cas de la Cote d'Ivoire." *Revue Tiers Monde* XIX 76:683–706 (October-December).

International Monetary Fund. 1982. *International Financial Statistics Yearbook, 1982* (Washington, D.C.: International Monetary Fund).

Ivory Coast, Strategic Base for Developing West Africa. 1977 (Geneva: Business International S.A. Research Report).

A business oriented view of the Ivory Coast, which looks at the problems of foreigners doing business in the Ivory Coast: tax laws, policies toward foreign business. As well, as attempts at economic integration in West Africa.

"Ivory Coast 21 Years On." 1981. *African Business* (June), 57–77.

Survey of the Ivorian economy.

Johansen, L. 1960. *A Multi-Sectoral Study of Economic Growth*. Amsterdam: North-Holland.

Koffi, Eao, and Kreuzgieser, Elke. 1981. *L'Internationalisation des Activites bancaires et les marches financiers dans les pays en developpement: Le case de la Cote d'Ivoire* (Paris: OCDE, Centre de developpement) (March).

Kouadia, Konan. 1979. "Situation et objectif de plan quinquennal ivoirien (1976–1980)." *Revue francaise d'etudes politiques africaines,* Vol. 159 (March):14–27.

Kouame, L.K. 1977. "Regional Statistics and the Structure of Regional Planning in the Ivory Coast," pp. 222–26. In A.L. Mabogunje and A. Faniri (eds.), *Regional Planning and National Development in Tropical Africa* (Ibadan: Ibadan University Press).

Lassailly, Veronique. 1979. "Une Operation de Developpement Integre en Cote d'Ivoire Central: l'operation Koussou." *L'Espace Geographique* (January/March), 57–63.

The description of a dam building project.

La Tremoliere, Jayne. 1982. "La Cote d'Ivoire en 1982." *Marches Tropicaux et Mediterraneans* 38 (April 23): 1065 ff.

LeCaillon, J., and Germidis, D. 1977. *Inegalite des Revenues et developpement economic* (Paris: PUF), 236 pp.

Covers Cameroon, Ivory Coast, Madagascar and Senegal.

Lewis, (Sir Arthur. 1980. "The Slowing Down of the Engine of Growth." *American Economic Review*, Vol. 70(4):555–564 (September).

Lysy, F. 1982. "The Character of General Equilibrium Models under Alternative Closure Rules" (World Bank, mimeo).

Manu, A.L. 1982. "ECOWAS in the Context of the Lagos Plan of Action," paper delivered at the Conference of Directors of Social Science Research Institutes and Policy Planners. (Addis Ababa, mimeo).

Marches Tropicaux. 1971. "Cote d'Ivoire 1960–1970: Dix ans de developpement economique et social" (October).

————. 1971. "Etude sur la plannification Ivoirienne." (December 11).

Masini, Jean, and Ikonicoff, Jedliki and Lanzarotti. 1979. *Multinational and Development in Black Africa: A Case Study in the Ivory Coast.* (United Kingdom: Farnborough, Saxon House), 181 pp.

Case studies of three multinational firms (Air Liquide, Carnund and Nestle) in

Ivory Coast and the links between Ivory Coast governmental policy, the MNCs and Ivory Coast development.

Mazoyer, M.L. 1976. "Developpement de la Production et transformation agricole marchande: d'une formation agraire en Cote d'Ivoire," 143–166, In S. Amin, ed., *L'Agriculture Africaine et le Capitalism* (Paris: Eds. Anthropos).

_____. 1981. "Cote d'Ivoire," 50–73, In Rene Dumont, Claude Reboul, Marcel Mazoyer, eds., *Pauvrete et inegalites rurales en Afrique de l'Ouest francophone* (Geneva: BIT).

Michel, G., and Noel, M. 1983a. "A Social Accounting Matrix for the Ivory Coast: A Technical Note" (World Bank, mimeo).

_____. 1983b. "Short-Run Responses to Trade and Incentive Policies in the Ivory Coast" (World Bank, mimeo).

Ministere de l'Agriculture. 1981. *Recensement National de l'Agriculture* (Abidjan).

Ministere de l'Economie et des Finances, Direction Generale des Douanes. 1982. *Commerce Special Exportations-Importations* (Abidjan).

Ministere de l'Economie et des Finances. 1983. *Budgets Economiques, 1980–82* (Abidjan).

Miracle, Marvin P. 1969. "The Economy of the Ivory Coast," 194–235, In P. Robson and D.A. Lury (eds.), *The Economies of Africa* (London: Allen and Unwin).

de Miras, Claude. 1980. "Essai de definition du Secteur de subsistance dans les branches de production a Abidjan." *Revue Tiers Monde* XXI, Vol. 82:353–372 (April-June).

_____. 1980b. *L'Entrepreneur ivoirien ou une Bourgeoisie privee de son etat.* (Abidjan: ORSTOM, Centre de Petit-Bassam), 93 pages.

_____. 1981 "L'entrepreneur Ivoirien ou une Bourgeoise Privee de son Etat," 181–230, In Y. Faure and J-F. Medard, *Etat et bourgeoisie en Cote d'Ivoire,* (Paris: Karthala/ORSTOM).

M'Lan, O. 1978. "Le Role des entreprises publiques dans le developpement de la Cote d'Ivoire." *Revue Juridique et Politique, Independance et Cooperation,* Vol. 1 (March):69–83.

Monson, T., and Pursell, G. 1976. "An Evaluation of Expatriate Labor Replacement in the Ivory Coast." Discussion Paper no. 4 (April) (Ann Arbor: University of Michigan Center for Research and Development).

An economic paper on replacement cost for foreign labor which finds that the accent should be put on secondary education and not on a university education.

Mytelka, Lynn K., and Dolan, M. 1980. "The Political Economy of EEC–ACP Relations in a changing International Division of Labour," C. Vaitsos and D. Seers (eds.), *European Integration and Unequal Development* (United Kingdom: Macmillan).

Mytelka, Lynn K. 1981. "Direct Foreign Investment and Technological Choice in the Ivorian Textile and Wood Industries." *Vierteljahresberichte*, Vol. 83:61–79.

_____. 1982. "In Search of a Partner: The State and the Textile Industry in France," 132–150. In Stephen Cohen and Peter A. Gourevitch (eds.), *France in a Troubled World Economy* (United Kingdom: Butterworth).

Noel, M. 1982. "The Evolution of the System of Industrial Incentives in the Ivory Coast from 1970 to Present" (World Bank, mimeo).

Paillet, M. 1975. *Desequilibres regionaux et administration en Afrique Noire: le cas de la Cote d'Ivoire et du Senegal* (Bordeaux: C.E.A.N.), 60 pages.

Paillet, M., and Maxim, B., Schandel, S. 1976. *Etudes sur de developpement regional en Cote d'Ivoire* (Bordeaux: I.E.P.–C.E.A.N.), 265 pages.

Penouil, Marc. 1973. "Reformer la zone Franc entre le neo-colonialisme et la balkanisation. *Le Monde Diplomatique* (January).

Republique de Cote d'Ivoire, Ministere du Plan. *Les Grandes Orientations du Developement Economique, Social et Culturel 1970–80* D'une economie de croissance a une societe de promotion (Abidjan).

Republique de Cote d'Ivoire, Ministere du Plan. 1971. *Plan Quinquennal de developpement economique, social et culturel 1971–1975*, edition resumed (Abidjan).

Revue Economique et Financiere Ivoirienne. 1981. "L'Industrialisation de Regions en Cote d'Ivoire." *Revue Economique et Financiere Ivoirienne* (November), 4–9.

Rolfo, J. 1980. "Optimal Heading under Price and Quantity Uncertainty". *Journal of Political Economy,* Vol. 88(1):100–116.

Sawadogo, Patrice. 1980. *Impact de la Croissance Demographique sur le développment economique et Social en Republique de Cote d'Ivoire, Population et Economie de Cote d'Ivoire*. (Nations Unies: Commission economique des Nations Unies pour l'Afrique), 78 pp.

An excellent compact study of current Ivorian economy, including government planning, changes in consumption trends, growth, etc., which are being undermined by continual immigration from Upper Volta and Mali.

Smith, Adam (pseud.). 1976. *The Money Game* (New York: Random House).

Stolper, Wolfgang F. 1980. *Income Distribution and Income Policies*. (Tubingen: Mohr.), 45 pp.

den Tuinder, Bastiann A. 1978. *Ivory Coast: The Challenge of Success* (Baltimore: Johns Hopkins University Press for the World Bank).

Uhleman, Ingrid. 1971. "Aspects of economic growth in the Ivory Coast," 47–68, In Jozef Bognor (ed.), *Proceedings of the Conference on the Implementation problems of Economic Development Plans* (Budapest).

Valette, A. 1980. "Resultats et reflexions sur une etude emperique d'industrialisation de la Cote d'Ivoire." *Cahiers de l'ORSTOM. Sciences Humaines* Vol. XVII, 1/2:45–66.

World Bank. 1981. *Accelerated Development in Sub-Saharan Africa: An Agenda for Action*, (Washington, D.C.: World Bank).

———. 1982a. *World Development Report*, (Washington, D.C.: World Bank).

———. 1982b. "Yugoslavia: Adjustment Policies and Development Perspectives." Washington, D.C. (Report No. 3954-YU).

———. 1983. *Commodity Trade and Price Trends* (Baltimore: Johns Hopkins University Press).

FOREIGN POLICY AND REGIONAL INTEGRATION

Adedeji, A. 1972. West African Economic Integration in West Africa to ECOWAS. See *Bank of Sierra Leone*, Research Department, West African Economic Cooperation. Problems and Possibilities, Occasional Paper, No. 1 (April).

———. 1970. "Prospects of Regional Cooperation in West Africa." *Journal of Modern African Studies*, Vol. 8, no. 2:213–231.

Afana, Osende. 1977. *L'Economie de l'Ouest Africain: Perspectives de developpement* (Paris: Maspero), 203 pp.

Afrique de l'Ouest. 1980. Communate Economique des Etats de Afrique de l'Ouest. Deuxieme Colloque sur 'Integration Economique de l'Afrique de l'Ouest, Conakry, 15–20 April; Conakry, Imprimerie de l'Education et de la Culture. 1982. 2 Volumes. 807 pp.

Alalade, F.O. 1976/1977. "French-Speaking Africa-France Relations: A Critical Bibliographical Survey with Particular Reference to Ivory Coast." *Current Bibliography on African Affairs* IX, Vol. (1):84–93 and Vol. (4):325–324.

Aluko, S.A. 1963. "Problems of Financial and Monetary Integration." *The Nigerian Journal of Economic and Social Studies* (March).

Anyatonwu, G.N. 1982. "ECOWAS: An approach to Sub-Region economic Integration." *Journal of African Studies* No. 9:30–38 (Spring).

Asante, S.K.A. 1978. "Polities of Regional Economic Integration: The Case of the Economic Community of West African States (ECOWAS)." *Vierteljahresberichte* Vol. 74:283–301.

Atsain, A. 1975. "Financial Arrangements and Economic Integration in the French-speaking West Africa." M.A. Essays. Albany: State University of New York (Summer).

Bach, D. "The Politics of West African Integration in the 1970s: A Comparison between CEAO and ECOWAS." *The Journal of Modern African Studies.*

Baker, K. 1970. "The Role of the Ivory Coast in the Nigerian-Biafra War." *The African Scholar* I: Volumes 4, 5, 8.

Barbour, K.M. 1972. "Industrialization in West Africa: The need for Subregional Groupings within an Integrated Economic Community." *Journal of Modern African Studies* 3 (October).

Baulin, Jacques F. 1980. *La Politique Africaine d'Houphouet-Boigny* (Paris: Editions Europa Press), 215 pp.

Benoist, J.R. de. 1979. *La Balkanisation de Afrique Occidental Francaise* (Abidjan: Les Nouvells Editions Africaines).

Berg, Elliot et al. 1981. *Accelerated Development in Sub-Saharan Africa* (Washington, D.C.: World Bank).

C.E.A.O. 1972 (June); 1973 (April). *Traite et Protocoles.*

C.D.E.A.O. 1975 (May); 1976 (November). *Traite et Protocoles*.

"Colloque sur Integration Economique en Afrique de l'Ouest, Conakry 1980." *Integration Africain* (Ouagadougou) 10:33–47 (aout).

"Communaute Economique de l'Afrique de l'Ouest." 1979. Revue Economique et Financiere *Ivoirienne* 6 (May).

Judicial framework of the community, industrial development and tarif harmonization.

Constantin, F. 1970. "Les Etats Africains face a la guerre du Nigeria." *Annee Africaine 1969*, 114–139.

Cooper, C.A. and Massell, B.F. 1965. "A New Look at Customs Union Theory." *Economic Journal.*.

Dalloz, J.P., and Cisse, D.A. 1979. "Office de la Monnaie et Proceccus d'Integration Economique en Afrique de l'Ouest." *Annales de l'Universite d'Abidjan* Serie K(2):5–27.

Delorme, N. 1977. "The Foreign Policy of the Ivory Coast," pp. 118–135. In Aluko, ed., *Foreign Policy of African States*. London: Hodder and Stoughton.

De L'UDEAO a la CEAO. 1975. *Banque Centrale des Etats d'Afrique de l'Ouest*, Notes d'Information et de Statistiques No. 175 (July).

Desneuf, Paul. 1978. "La Chambre de Compensation de l'Afrique de l'Ouest." *ECOWAS Magazine* No. 3: 39–43.

Studies the means of action by the Chamber and its impact on the West African region.

DuBois, Victor. 1967. "Rise of Opposition to Toure: The Formation of a Common Front Against Guinea by the Ivory Coast and Ghana." *West Africa Series* X Vol. (1): American Universities Field Staff Reports.

Economist Intelligence Unit. 1970. *Possibilities of Economic Cooperation between Ghana, Ivory Coast, Upper Volta, Niger, Dahomey and Togo* (London: Africa Development Bank, 4006 pp.

Essienne, D. 1974. *Le Ministere des Affaires etrangeres de Cote d'Ivoire* (Paris: Libraries Techniques 89 pp.

Faugas, A. 1971. "M. Houphouet-Boigny et la Diplomatie Ivorienne." *Revue Francaise d'Etudes Politques Africaines* (aout), 23–36.

Gabriel, J.M. 1974. "Regionale Integration in Afrika: Ein Neues Modell." *Annaire Swisse de Science Politique* 14:43–56.

Develops idea of core-periphery relations rather than functional relations in East-West Africa.

Goudian, Ousmane. 1980. "La Liberte de Circulation en Afrque Francophone." *Revue Juridique et Politique* 1 (January-March).

Grellet, G. 1982. Les Structures Economiques de l'Afrique Noire. E.E.D.E.S. Collection Tiers-Monde: Presses Universites du France.

Gueyo, Mouhamadou Mourtada. 1979. "Industrialisation et Development des echanges en Afrique de l'Ouest." *Integration Africaine* (Ougdougou) 6 (March).

Hazelwood, A. (ed.) 1967. *African Integration and Disintegration* (London: Royal Institute of International Affairs).

Houphouet-Boigny, Felix. 1974. "On Dialogue with South Africa," In Joan Roland (ed.), *Africa: The Heritage and the Challenge* (Greenwich: Greenwood).

The message to the 1971 OAU Summit.

International Monetary Fund, 1970. *Surveys of African Economies* Vol. 3.

Jalloh, A.A. 1973. *Political Integration in French-Speaking Africa* (Berkeley: Institute of International Studies), 208 pp.

Launay, Robert, 1982. *Traders Without Trade*. (Cambridge/New York: Cambridge University Press).

"Le Fonds de Solidarite et d'Intervention pour le developement de la Communaute Economique de l'Afrique de l'Ouest." *Jeune Afrique* 1026:54–57 (September).

Legvold, Robert. 1970. *Soviet Policy in West Africa* (Cambridge and Harvard).

Cooperative analysis of five states including Ivory Coast.

Martin, Guy. 1982. "Africa and the Ideology of Euro-Africa: Neocolonialism or Pan-Africanism? *The Journal of Modern African Studies*, Vol. 20(2):221–238 (June).

Meade, J.E. 1956. *The Theory of Customs Union* (Amsterdam: North-AL Holland Publishing Company).

Meite, V. 1980. *La Politique Africaine de la Cote d'Ivoire*. (Doctoral Dissertation) (Paris: Universite de Paris), 434 pp.

Mixon, F.I. 1973. *Economic Integration and Industrial Location* (Longman Group Limited).

Mutharika, B.W.T. 1972. *Toward Multinational Economic Cooperation in Africa* (New York: Praeger).

Mytelka, L.K. 1974. "A Genealogy of Francophone West and Equatorial African Organizations." *Journal of Modern African Studies*, Vol. 12(2):297–320.

Nowzad, B. 1969. "Economic Integration in Central and West Africa." *IMF, Staff Papers* XVI (1) March.

Pearson, Scott R., and Ingram, William D. 1980. "Economies of Scale, Domestic Divergences and Potential Gains from Economic Integration in Ghana and the Ivory Coast." *Journal of Political Economy*, Vol. 5:994–1008 (October).

Robson, Peter. 1968. *Economic Integration in Africa* (London: George Allen & Unwin).

Sako, Souleman. 1973. *Les Relations exterieurs de la Cote d'Ivoire* (Doctoral Dissertation). (Paris: Universite de Paris).

Shepherd, George W. 1970. *Nonaligned Black Africa: An International Subsystem* (Lexington: Heath-Lexington Books).

Simmons, A. 1972. "Economic Integration in West Africa." *Western Political Quarterly* XXV, Vol. (2), June.

Skurnick, W.A.E. 1979. "Ivoirian student perceptions of U.S. Africa Policy." *Journal of Modern African Studies* Vol. 17: 409–432 (September).

An attempt "to draw a map of the perceptions of Ivoirien students about aspects of U.S. policy towards Africa."

_____. 1981. "A new look at foreign news coverage: External dependence or national interests?" *African Studies Review* Vol. 24:99–112 (March).

"This study addresses the notions (a) that the dependence of African newspapers upon Western agencies determines what gets published, and (b) that the American press tends to ignore the third world. Specifically, it compares the foregoing news coverage, in March 1976, of two African newspapers (the Ivory Coast's *Fraternite-Matin* and Kenya's *Daily Nation* and *The New York Times*."

Tamboura, A. 1972. "La Communaute Economique de l'Afrique de l'Ouest." *Journal of African Law* (Autumn).

Thomson, V. 1972. *West Africa's Council of Entente* (Ithaca: Cornell University Press), 314 pp.

Toube, Clement Dekio. 1982. "La Cooperation monetaire et le developement economique et sociale en Afrique." *Revue Economique et Sociale Voltaique* (Ouagadougou) VIII(16): 27–37.

A good description of the basic principles underlying the West African monetary union which allows a favorable climate for development.

U.M.O.A. 1981. "Les Echanges commerciaux entre les pays de l'Union 1969–1978." *B.C.E.A.O. Notes d'information* No. 292 (March), 22 pages.

Veit, Winfried. 1978. *Nationale Emanzipation Entwicklungsstrategie und Auszenpolitik in Tropish Africa-Die Beispiele Elfenbeinkuste und Guinea.* (Munich: Ifo. Institut fur Wirtschaftsforschung Welfforum Verlug). (Strategy of Development and Foreign Policy in Tropical Africa, the examples of Guinea and Ivory Coast) Resumed in French.

This book compares the development of Guinea and Ivory Coat in terms of achieving goals of real independence, crediting the Ivory Coast with higher economic growth, but growth which depends on foreign capital which is diminishing.

Vellas, Francois. 1981. "La Fonction de Pays relais dans les echanges Nord-Sud: le cas de la Cote d'Ivoire." *Tiers Monde,* Vol. 22:121–39 (January-March).

Yannopoulos, T., and Martin, D. 1972. "Domination et Composition en Afrique: le Conseil de l'Entene et la Communaute est-africaine face a eux-memes et face aux 'grands.'" *Revue Algerienne des Sciences juridiques, politiques et economiques* IX, Vol. (1):129–151 (March).

INDEX

ABOUT THE CONTRIBUTORS

I. WILLIAM ZARTMAN is Professor of International Politics and Director of the African Studies Program at the Johns Hopkins School of Advanced International Studies in Washington, D.C. He is the author of *International Relations in the New Africa, The Politics of Trade Negotiations between Africa and the European Communities, Ripe for Resolution: Conflict and Intervention in Africa* (for the Africa Project of the Council on Foreign Relations), and co-author of *Africa in the 1980s* (for the Council on Foreign Relations), *Africa and the United States: Vital Interests, African Diplomacy*, and *Soldier and State in Africa*. Dr. Zartman is also editor of the SAIS African Studies series, including *The Political Economy of Nigeria* and *The OAU after 20 Years.* He received his M.A. from the Johns Hopkins University and his Ph.D. from Yale University.

CHRISTOPHER L. DELGADO received his B.A. from Tufts University and a Ph.D in economics from Cornell University. He is a veteran of the Peace Corp (Chad) and formerly an assistant research scientist at the Center for Research on Economic Development of the University of Michigan (at the University of Ouagadougou). He is currently a Research Fellow with the International Food Policy Research Institute in Washington, D.C. where he coordinates an international research program investigating the implications for food policies of the substitution of imported wheat and rice in West African diets to the detriment of locally produced coarse grains, and part-time faculty of The School of International Studies of Johns Hopkins University. Dr. Delgado has published several monographs and articles on agricultural development and food policy in West Africa including, *Livestock versus Foodgrain Production in Southeast Upper Volta: A Resource Allocation Analysis* (for Africa Rural Program, Michigan State University), *The Southern Fulani Farming System in Upper Volta,* "Constraints on Oxen Cultivation in the Sahel," with John McIntire in the *American Journal of Agricultural Economics*, "Livestock and Meat Production, Consumption and Exports in Mali" for the Center for Research on Economic Development, University of Michigan.

ACHI ATSAIN is director of the Ivorian Center of Economic and Social Research (CIRES) of the University of Abidjan and maitre de conference in Economics at the University. He is the editor of the *CIRES Review* in which he has published articles on the Ivorian economy. He received his doctorate from the State University of New York at Albany.

TESSILIMI BAKARY is lecturer in law at the University of Abidjan and at the Institute for Political Studies at the University of Bordeaux. He is author of *The Political Elites in Ivory Coast*. His doctorate is from the University of Paris X at Nanterre.

MICHAEL A. COHEN is the Chief of the Operations Review and Support Unit in the Urban Projects Department of the World Bank (IBRD). He is the author of *Urban Policy and Political Conflict in Africa: A Study of the Ivory Coast*, as well as articles in *The Journal of Modern African Studies, The Journal of Developing Areas, World Development, Finance and Development*, and other journals on urban development in the Third World, and is also author of World Bank reports on the subject. He has taught at the University of Abidjan. His A.B. degree is from Cornell University and his Ph.D from the University of Chicago.

MATHURIN GBETIBOUO is charge de recherches at the Ivorian Center for Economic and Social Research (CIRES) of the University of Abidjan and consultant for the World Bank (IBRD). His doctorate is from the University of Illinois.

GILLES MICHEL is an industrial economist with the World Bank, on leave from INSEE, Paris. He has taught in Ecole Nationale de la Statistique et de l'Administration Economique (ENSAE), is author of *L'Economie Française* and co-author of "Short-Run Rigidities and Long-Run Adjustments in a Computable General Equilibrium Model of Income Distribution and Development" (with F. Bourguignon and D. Miqueu in Journal of Development Economics, 1983) and "Estimation of a Quarterly Macroeconomic Model with Quantity Rationing" (with P. Artus and G. Laroque in Econometrica, 1984). He graduated from Ecole Polytechnique, Paris, ENSAE, Paris, and Institut d'Etudes Politiques de Paris.

LYNN KRIEGER MYTELKA is Professor of Political Science at Carleton University. She is author of *Regional Development in a Global Economy: The Multinational Corporation, Technology and Andean Integration*, co-author of *Africa in the 1980s* for the Council on Foreign Relations, and author of articles on France and Africa, among other subjects, in *International Organization, Journal of European Integration, Journal of Common Market Studies, World Politics, The Journal of Modern African Studies*, and others. She has been a consultant for the ECA, UNCTAD, OECD, AID, and Canadian Government. Her doctorate is from the Johns Hopkins School of Advanced International Studies and her A.B. from Douglass College.

MICHEL NOEL is a Country Economist with The World Bank, and postdoctoral candidate in Economics at The Johns Hopkins University. He holds the M.A. degree in Economics from the University of Namur, Belgium. In 1977 his Master's thesis "Project Appraisal in Developing Countries: A Multilevel Approach" was published by the Faculty of Science, Economiques et Sociales, University of Namur.